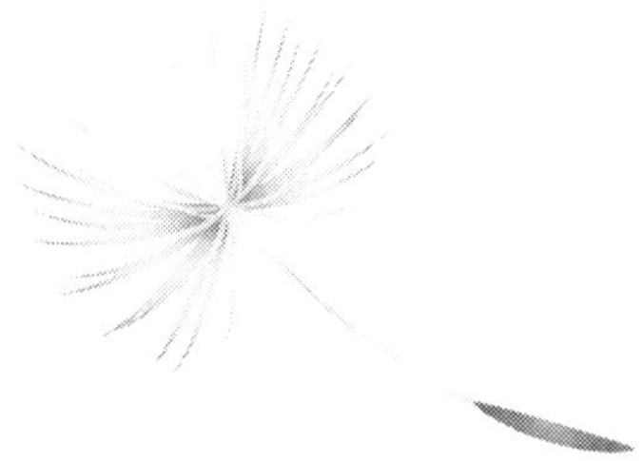

Points of Perception

Prophecies and Teachings of Saint Germain

THE GOLDEN CITY SERIES
BOOK ONE

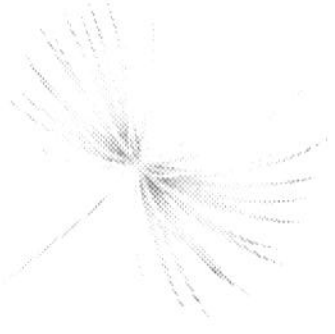

Received and written by
LORI TOYE

Host and questions by
Lenard Toye

Foreword by
Barbara Hockabout

to Saint Germain

*"The lesser mysteries are rituals of self-control and purification.
The greater mysteries are rituals of creation."*
~ Manly P. Hall

THANKS FROM THE AUTHOR AND PUBLISHER:

To my partner and husband Len—without his support and love throughout the years, this work would not be available. I express deep appreciation to my editor Felicia whose consummate craft inspired a re-calibration that honed the appendices, bibliography, index, and almost every page of this book. I also acknowledge Barbara who took precious time from her busy life to write the foreword for this book. I cherish her friendship and wisdom alongside her continued contribution to this work. Many thanks to Mark whose insights during the creative process were helpful, especially with the first chapters. Eternal gratitude to the many students who have crossed my path, and courageously asked the questions so we could all learn: Sherry, Lynne, Julie, Jan, Susan, Elsa, and many others. A special thank-you to Elise for her expert transcription; Kirby and Jan, for proofreading the manuscript; Pat, who wrote my bio (just when I needed it); my dear friend Denise who generously shared information for Appendix N; my talented daughter Bryn who helped with suggestions, design, and graphics; and to my Mom who was always just a call away with an encyclopedia of experience to help dot the "i's" and cross the "t's." Also, big hugs to Jean—everyday she devotedly sends our books and maps out the door. Above all, thank-you Treson, Emma, Chloe, Mackenzy, Katelyn, Ethan, Hailey, Grayson, Elias, Mitchell, and Zachary, and all the other New Children who've bravely arrived at this important and amazing time; you give us hope. This book is for you, and your children.

OM MANAYA PITAYA HITAKA

I AM America Maps and Books have been marketed since 1989 by I AM America Seventh Ray Publishing and Distributing, through workshops, conferences, and numerous bookstores in the United States and internationally. If you are interested in obtaining information on available releases please write or call: I AM America, P.O. Box 2511, Payson, Arizona, 85547, USA. (800) 930-1341 or (928) 474-1341, or visit:
www.iamamerica.com

Graphic Design and Typography by Lori Toye
Host and Questions by Lenard Toye
Editing by Felicia Megdal

Love, in service, breathes the breath for all!

I AM AMERICA

Print On Demand Version

10 9 8 7 6 5 4 3 2 1

Contents

LIST OF ILLUSTRATIONS vi

FOREWORD *by Barbara Hockabout* ix

PREFACE xiii

CHAPTERS:

1. *Earth Healing* 17
2. *Love's Service* 23
3. *Changing of the Guard* 31
4. *The Fourth Dimension* 43
5. *The Work of a Master* 53
6. *No Need for Change?* 59
7. *Weaving the New Web* 69
8. *Golden City Classes* 77
9. *Vibrational Shifting* 91
10. *Closing the Circle* 99
11. *Dooms Day—Peace Day* 107
12. *The Fountain of Life* 115
13. *The First Golden City* 121
14. *The Ever-Present Perfection* 125
15. *The Point of Perception* 133

SPIRITUAL LINEAGE OF THE VIOLET FLAME 149

GLOSSARY 151

APPENDICES 165

BIBLIOGRAPHY 277

DISCOGRAPHY 281

INDEX 283

ABOUT LORI TOYE 297

ABOUT I AM AMERICA 298

Appendices

Appendix A

TOPICS AND TERMS FOR EARTH HEALING 165

Appendix B

TOPICS AND TERMS FOR LOVE'S SERVICE 171

Appendix C

TOPICS AND TERMS FOR CHANGING THE GUARD 179

Appendix D

TOPICS AND TERMS FOR THE FOURTH DIMENSION 187

Appendix E

TOPICS AND TERMS FOR THE WORK OF A MASTER 191

Appendix F

TOPICS AND TERMS FOR NO NEED FOR CHANGE? 199

Appendix G

TOPICS AND TERMS FOR WEAVING THE NEW WEB 205

Appendix H

TOPICS AND TERMS FOR GOLDEN CITY CLASSES 219

Appendix I

TOPICS AND TERMS FOR VIBRATIONAL SHIFTING 229

Appendix J

TOPICS AND TERMS FOR CLOSING THE CIRCLE 233

Appendix K

TOPICS AND TERMS FOR DOOMSDAY—PEACE DAY 237

Appendix L

TOPICS AND TERMS FOR THE FOUNTAIN OF LIFE 241

Appendix M

TOPICS AND TERMS FOR THE FIRST GOLDEN CITY 247

APPENDICES *(continued)*

Appendix N

TOPICS AND TERMS FOR THE EVER-PRESENT PERFECTION 253

Appendix O

TOPICS AND TERMS FOR THE POINT OF PERCEPTION 271

List of Illustrations

FIGURE I-A

Jesus xv

FIGURE 1-A

Doors of the Golden Cities 210

FIGURE 1-B

Northern Door Golden City 211

FIGURE 1-C

Eastern Door Golden City 212

FIGURE 1-D

Southern Door Golden City 213

FIGURE 1-E

Western Door Golden City 214

FIGURE 1-F

Star, Golden City 215

FIGURE 2-A

Golden City Structure, Perspective 216

FIGURE 2-B

Golden City Structure, Plan View 216

FIGURE 3-A

Adjutant Points, Gobean Northern Door 217

FIGURE 4-A

Sananda 225

FIGURE 5-A

Great Central Sun and the Seven Rays 227

FIGURE 5-B

Golden City Disburses Ray Forces 227

FIGURE 6-A

Eight-Sided Cell of Perfection Energy Map 254

ILLUSTRATIONS *(continued)*

FIGURE 7-A

Vedic Square (Yantra) Energy Map: The Nine Planets with Corresponding Directions 257

FIGURE 7-B

Vedic Square: 81 Portions 257

FIGURE 7-C

Vedic Square: The Five Elements 257

FIGURE 7-D

Vedic Square (Yantra) Energy Map: The Nine Directions and Vedic Deities 257

FIGURE 8-A

Earth's Wobble and Pole Stars 258

FIGURE 9-A

The 27 Nakshatras (Moon Signs) are the Basis of the Vedic Science of Ayadi 260

FIGURE 10-A

Chinese Pak'ua or Ba Gua Energy Map Early Heaven Devised by Fu Hsi 263

FIGURE 10-B

Chinese Pak'ua or Ba Gua Energy Map Later Heaven Devised by Yü 264

FIGURE 11-A

Energy Movement through the Nine Palaces of Classical Chinese Feng Shui 265

FIGURE 11-B

The Nine Movements of Consciousness through the Eight-Sided Cell of Perfection 266

FIGURE 11-C

World Map of the Nine Perfected Movements of Consciousness 267

FIGURES 12-A, 12-B

Source, New Experience, and The Web of Creation 273

FIGURES 12-C, 12-D

Projection of Light Bodies 274

Foreword

Reader,

By purchasing this book and opening these pages, you have invoked an inspiring journey, whatever degree your acquaintance has been with the Saint Germain teachings up to this point. If you are new to the concepts, you will revel in possibilities as thoughts clarify and doors in your mind fly open; if you are familiar with the material, you will appreciate the power a mature perception can bring to the written word. I say this with confidence as I have been a student of metaphysical teachings for the past 25 years, and I share your appetite for larger vision. I say this as a teacher of literature, a lover of words, for the past three decades. Yes, I am confident you will find your own stash of intellectual and spiritual treasure in the Golden Cities series.

You can read an excellent distillation of Lori Toye's life in the biography found at the end of this work, but I would like to add to this introduction my own down-to-earth, first-hand perception of this gentle and amazing prophet. I have known her since 1994. I have taken workshops from her, edited her books, hiked breath-taking landscapes with her, attended her children's weddings and she and Len were witnesses at our wedding, sat in medicine lodges with her, shared with her the experience of being a grandmother for the first time, watched her struggle as a private person in the public eye, shared recipes, helplessly witnessed the impact made on her by those who judged her and betrayed her trust, as well as rejoiced with those whose lives were deeply enriched by knowing her and hearing her message, listened to many hours of her channeled transmissions on audio tapes, observed her body's physical challenges and her triumphant self-healings. In other words, I am her friend—a celebrity, of sorts, only to the college students I teach, to my family, and to the wonderful friends I met on my life's journey. While Lori easily could have found someone with far greater name recognition to write a foreword to her culminating series, she preferred it be written by a person like me—someone who has shared the path with her for the past 15 years.

What distinguishes prophets from the rest of us is that at some turning point, at a designated cross road, prophets because of their understanding and commitment, are willing to take on a greater degree of risk. Lori's larger biography, a book for another day, will outline the details and specific trials of her life as a visionary, a prophet, and clairaudient trance channel. For our present purposes, perhaps it is best to remember what we have in common, what each came here to experience and learn—who I AM.

Lori and I share similar experiences of deep change—and as you have been drawn to this book, no doubt you have too. Consciously or unconsciously all of us initiate our transformative journeys, most of us from humble and ordinary beginnings. The debunked relationships, the divorces, the expulsion from groups to which we were attached, the lost job, the lost loved ones, the financial ruin, the great divide in friendships, rifts between family members—all these things have the potential to catapult us into the next level of consciousness. Lori calls this metamorphosis in consciousness "belief exploding." The term implies the violence of change, but it's actually a necessary shedding of the status quo; the skin that confines us must be shed in order to grow. In Lori's words:

> *Over time we have found that if we just believe what we are told, the teachings remain very one-dimensional—flat, limited and uninspired. The educational process of the Ascended Masters moves an individual beyond belief, into valuable personal experience and 'into the laboratory of the self.'*

The courage this takes can't be underestimated. So how did we get through it? How will we get through the next great skin-shedding cycle?

Indulge me here. Reflect. Think back on an awakening you had, a moment that served as an agent to change your life—the right book found its way into your hands, the perfect person timely dropped into your life, the divine phrase or lyric overheard unexpectedly, the film spoke to you at the right moment, the scene in nature you happened to witness, an economic downturn revised your priorities over night. Can you recall the feeling, the adrenaline pumping through your heart radiating out from every cell of your body and being, the thrill of breaking through the veil, catching the first whiff of freedom—electrifying and energizing, the skin of your cocoon splitting right down the middle? At those moments we understood what the chick feels when it first becomes aware of its ability to break through the egg shell.

In the School of the Four Pillars Len and Lori teach that thought, feeling, and action are the cornerstones for our human experience. When I finally grasped the power of this simple formula, life made a bit more sense. I realized my power to generate and direct my thoughts and feelings and in doing so, better understand what action to take. I finally understood the missing link to Renee Descartes' philosophical ideology, "I think, therefore I am." The missing link is feeling. Thoughts and feelings define my action and shape my experience. Feelings are truly divine gifts. So, what would happen if we flood our beings with the memory of those feelings of excitement and liberation I mentioned earlier, when we woke up each day? These feelings are the deserved fruits of our experiences. We own them and we have access to them. Why not use the energy they can ignite to fuel us through our lessons of the future? When we read books such as *Points of Perception* we are reminded of our internal power and magnificence. The vibration of the words fills up the tank of limitlessness for our future journeys.

We know now that every message we need is available or within our grasp, if only we recalibrate our PERCEPTION into a mode of reception and gratitude. We shed the confining skin of status quo, (or circumstance conveniently rips it off for us) and we reach out to others, to books, to authorities, to prophets in order to better understand our changes and validate them as human experiences in a much larger plan. But after all the reading, speaking and listening, we return to the deep sacred silence of our souls, the voice of I AM. Here we hear our truth; here we feel; here we know. This book is merely a guide post or a mile marker for our own precious PERCEPTION.

This book is also an incredible compilation of metaphysical information. As a member of the human race, I have a ravenous appetite for understanding the evolution of epochs as well as the consciousness that drives them. Not only is it one of the most accessible distillations of the Saint Germain teachings, having been culled and refined for our current perceptions, but *Points of Perception* is also accompanied by one of the most helpful and thoroughly researched appendices I have ever read. It is an intellectual as well as a spiritual treasure trove.

Yours in a perpetual state of shedding and recalibrating perception,

Barbara Hockabout
Show Low, Arizona
April, 2009

***Barbara Hockabout** is an editor and teaches English and Humanities at Northland Pioneer College in east central Arizona. An Agnihotra practitioner, she and her husband Clark, work together in their naturally grown produce business Lodestar Gardens, hosting gatherings and networking in the Gobean Golden City Vortex community. She frequently practices the Violet Flame Ceremony, is deeply appreciative of Saint Germain's teachings and most grateful for his devotion to our planet.*

Preface

The words you will read on the pages of this book and in the ensuing Golden City Series are teachings, not essays, dissertations, or for that matter, literary prose. Keep this in mind as you study the text; it will help your intellect absorb and process the material. The messages of the Masters can be heady at times, filled with nuances, layers, and undertones, so be patient if you don't comprehend it at first glance. After all, understanding the process of how these spiritual ideas make it to the printed page in the first place is half the battle: the challenge is imparting meaning to the nonverbal white space of language.

The art of storytelling, also known as the oral tradition, was once the preferred medium through which spiritual information and knowledge was passed from mentor to student. In fact, even before consciousness fell to the darker states we are now experiencing, the Master Teachers worried about the memory's ability to retain information, so these wise souls gave humanity the gift of the alphabet. Through written symbols and characters, they thought important knowledge could still impress consciousness and the sacred traditions could be preserved. *Points of Perception* and its other four companions in the Golden City Series represent the spirit of bridging this dimensional gap.

The difference between the spoken word and the written word is immense. We have been acquainted with these nuances for many years because all of the *I AM America* material given by the Master Teachers is through the oral tradition. The subtleties and differences are not only in words, but often in the delivery and dramatization of phrases, which most written material simply cannot convey. Often it is the quiet space between each spoken word that transmits vital, consciousness-triggering energies.

Undoubtedly this work is a translation. It is received clairaudiently—a form of extrasensory hearing that perceives the Fourth-Dimensional conversations. It is then orally repeated and simultaneously recorded. After each session, the recordings are transcribed. Through the years we have worked with more than twenty different transcribers, each with varying skill levels. Again, we have discovered that the material in its final form depends on how the transcriber *hears* each word. Many of the transcripts are screened yet again, comparing printed words to the recorded version. Finally, the transcript is punctuated. Through this process we try to capture the nuance and subtlety of each spoken phrase. This is perhaps the most difficult and tricky aspect of my work. Since some of the words are delivered in a form of Elizabethan English, I modernize the language to enhance reader understanding. More often than not, however, I leave it. You will see throughout these teachings where a few words have been added to assist comprehension.

I have heard newcomers to channeled material complain, "You have to listen to a gallon of information to retrieve one pint!" The connoisseurs, those whose *ears are trained,* know differently. This channeled material is artfully layered with hidden meaning and numerous secrets, and your evolving consciousness is the key that unlocks its knowledge. It has always amazed me how I can read a lesson, think that I have absorbed its content, then return to it several years later and discover a whole new meaning. I'm still extracting new insights and understanding from this work on several different levels. To help the reader who may not be familiar with the language of the Fifth Dimension or the structure of the Master Teachings, I have added extensive appendices in the back of this book. Use these alongside the glossary to navigate definition questions. Just to keep your spiritual reading interesting, you won't find everything there. In fact, after rereading many of the lessons, I have discovered more information I could have included, however I intentionally restrained myself. Not all of this knowledge can be spoon-fed to you. There is a mystery and wonder in discovery, and I would never take that remarkable journey from you! Make sure you read the channeling aloud; it takes on a much more powerful energy. The most exciting information is hidden in plain sight.

The material here is presented in the simple form in which it was received—questions and answers between students and their teacher. Ironically, our greatest discoveries do not come from patented answers; instead they are often revealed *from the questions* we ask. As Saint Germain says, "Don't believe anything I tell you. Take it unto the laboratory of self!"

"The Christ breaks all barriers and perfects the bodies."
~ Divine Mother

FIGURE I-A: JESUS *See caption and notes next page.*

(From page xv) FIGURE I-A: JESUS

Derived from "Jesus in the Temple" by Heinrich Hofmann, 1824-1911. This is a depiction of Jesus as a youth by the renowned German painter of Christ, and an antique copy hung for years in my grandparents' kitchen. I cherish this family heirloom, and I've included it in these pages as I have always felt tremendous love radiating from it—I hope you do, too. During my research for this book, I came across an interesting link between Paramahansa Yogananda (founder of the Self-Realization Foundation) and Hofmann. The German's religious depictions captivated Yogananda so much, the guru described his experiences with Hofmann's artwork in detail: "Of all the pictures I have seen of him in the West, the rendering by Hofmann comes closest to showing the accurate features of the incarnate Jesus." Once Hofmann was asked whether he used living models for the remarkable continuity, which spanned from his youth into adult years, he achieved with his depictions of Jesus he responded, "I have never used a model for the face of the Savior—where on Earth should I find one? When I read about Christ in the Bible there arises quite spontaneously in my mind's eye a picture of his countenance—that is what I try to retain and reproduce." [1]

[1] Rosemarie Müller, *Heinrich Hofmann Painter of Christ*, http://www.yogananda-srf.org/writings/srm_w2004_pv.html (2008).

1

Earth Healing

Saint Germain in Bend, Oregon

GREETINGS IN THAT MIGHTY CHRIST LIGHT, I AM SAINT GERMAIN.

I stream forth on the Mighty Ray of Mercy and Forgiveness. As usual, Dear hearts, chelas, and students, I must ask permission to come forth.

"Please come forth, Dear one."

The work upon the Earth Plane and Planet is one where we shall say, tarry not. For this Time of Transition that comes is indeed, as we have said, a time when that Lady shall open her legs and you would perceive, in essence, a birth scream or a howl. But yet, we see this as that Time of Awakening, a Time of Transition, and a time for the opening of the Prophecies of Peace and Grace. May peace stream forth into your hearts, Dear ones, and be forever your infinite and eternal decree. Peace and grace, that which is, shall we say, that Law of the Best and Highest Good, that which streams forth from that Ray of Divine Will and that Ray of Divine Love.

We ask for you, Dear ones, dear Brothers and Sisters, chelas and students. Those who are gathered here for the ushering in that Mighty Law of Grace. To hold within their hearts, that Mighty Light of God that never fails. We ask for you at all times to see yourself as that transmitter, that generator, that mighty servant of light, who allows these energies to come and bring forth an enactment of the Divine Will upon the Earth Plane and Planet.

Dear hearts, the Time of Peace now comes to the planet. And, you as forerunners, as lovers of this peace, we ask you to play them as a grand symphony, one string harmonizing one with the next. Or have we not taught that the first law that streams forth, is the Law of Harmony? And now, we as members and as servants of lovers of peace and grace, ask that each of you consider that not only is this a Time of Change and Earth Change for that matter, but also a time which will be a Time of Peace and Prophecies of Peace.

The Spiritual Hierarchy of this Lodge has, for some time, decided that Earth Changes Prophecy will no longer be given for a short time. However, we will now allocate this time to bring forth what are known as those Prophecies of Peace.

For more information and study topics on *Earth Healing,* see Appendix A, page 165.

For Dear ones, as you have known, your attention is where energy flows! Have you not noticed this in all co-creation and manifestation? And, have you not noticed this in the work-about world in which you live?

Each and every one of you asks daily, "How is it that I can apply these teachings and utilize them for my life? How can I serve this spiritual awakening? How can I best serve my Brothers and Sisters?" I say to you, each and every one of you, that it is as simple as living in that Law of Harmony.

But first, that Law of Harmony is built upon agreement. That is, again, that harmonious response to thought—for it is the thought that is the premise of all creation. And we would ask that each and every one of you consider to align your thoughts to that plan of the best and the highest good. Allow a frequency and a vibration to come forth that serves that mighty plan of the Divine Will!

In the days to come, yes, there will be the shaking and the rattling of the earth forces. Not only shall we see eruptions in that Cascade Range, but also into the Sierra Madres, and in a counter-clockwise positing of that Pacific Rim. These were all the prophecies that we have dispensed in the I AM America material and we will continue to give brief updates on.

However Dear chelas and students, we ask for you to place your attention not only on the element of change, but to look deep within the heart of your own being and recognize the change that is happening within your heart. Are we not now in the middle of a spiritual transition? Are we not now in the middle of a spiritual awakening? I ask you Dear stalwart students of the Mighty Flame of Truth, to come forward in that breath of the Mighty ONE; come forward in that breath of that Mighty ONE Peace.

The Time of Transition is a time we are transiting not only from the Third Dimension, but onward into the Fourth and the Fifth dimension. For it is, shall we say, in the harmony of the spheres, where peace is gained; and the bitter Cup is taken from your lips. You have sought the sensation of this elusive reality and have found so contained within that duad, that form of clay, your body; and now we move into that Time of ONE, that Time of Monad, that Time of ALL Interconnectiveness of All Life!

Your emotions, your feelings, even your thoughts, Dear ones, run rampant at this time. And we would ask that you discipline them through enacting that first Mighty Law of Harmony. Call forth harmony in all your agreements; call forth harmony in all your transactions. Remember, you are a Oneship as beloved Kuan Yin has stated, "Each and every one of you shares this life." This ONE life that is contained upon the planet is ONE that is contained in your own being. You have studied, the energetics of change and also the energetics related to not only the human or electromagnetic field, but also study Dear chelas and students, that electromagnetic force that is of the planet itself.

Understand that each of the fifty-one Vortices, which have been brought forth in service to the awakening of humanity, are also those mighty focuses of energy contained upon the planet—and for her transit into what we would call, a quantum leap in Collective Consciousness.

The positing of your location at this moment is the location of one of those older Vortices of the planet. And yes, while you carry forward a readjustment and re-alignment of, shall we say that electromagnetic body, the impulse body, a natural feeling body of the planet, you are also assisting in anchoring in the energies which align to the Golden City Vortex known as Klehma. And we would ask that in your heart and in your thought today, that you hold forth that thought of Continuity, Cooperation, and Balance.

As members of this Lodge, Dear hearts, remember at all times we hold within our hearts, first, that Mighty Law of Cooperation. And we would ask each and every one of you become not only a symbol of this cooperation, but also to carry it forward in your daily demonstration. Choose and you shall act; act and you shall choose.

As we have stated before, Dear ones, as above so below. We ask for this Divine Will to stream forth in you—this day. And with these Prophecies of Peace, carry them forward not only in your heart, but also in that active hand.

In the times to come, after that time where that polarization of energy is balanced, we shall see not only changes in government, but also within the social structures, these, first Starting with the family unit. The Time of Equity now comes to the planet, and that inner marriage or marriage of the Kundulini energies will now be woven, not only as male and female, but the activation of the Christ.

In the family units, even conception as you have understood it, will come forward in a different manner. You have worries of the clay vessel and the carrying forth of energies in the human duad. We ask for you to consider forms of sponsorship of energy that are carried forward in consciousness and in thought.

Beloved Mother Mary brought forward, that first idea of divine conception. Held first immaculately in her inner eye, in her inner vision. We ask you now, Dear students, to hold that forward, to hold that perfect thought.

To assist the accelerations of energies upon the Earth Plane and Planet, we will encounter what is known as holo-leaping or the movement between the Third and Fourth Dimensions. How do we do this, Dear ones? Through what are known as our energy fields. How do we direct our energy fields? Through creative thought.

Many lifestreams from other planets now seek entry into the Earth Plane and Planet. However, at this time, we are seeing the ending [lifting] of the Mighty Law of Cause and Effect. This, you have known through many lifestreams, and through some, shall I say, even limited teachings as Karma. But we ask you to consider this as Dharma. For is it not joyful now to be ending this portion of the path, Dear hearts, this portion of the journey?

Now we have climbed to this new positing. And we look over the valley and we say, "It is good." Is it good for you, Dear ones? Is this, in that Law of the Best and the Highest Good? These are the choices that lay in front of you in this Time of Transition.

During these times that await us, as I have stated, many lifestreams are preparing themselves now to come upon the planet known as the Seventh Manu. I have spoken of them in previous discourse. Not only do they await entry through your conscious thought, but also through those Mighty Vortices on the planet.

They come to bring their service, Dear ones, and to bring their service not only to humanity, but to those other kingdoms of creation: Devas, Elementals, and Elohim. They come, in essence, to raise the vibrational frequencies of the planet, for these are the Times of Peace that await us!

Will a time come when humanity will again live in harmony with its environment? This I say—so! [yes] In this illusion, there is always an element of chaos! You are blessed, Dear ones, as Co-creators, inheritors that possess, that mighty spark, the Monad, the ONE.

As all life contains within it that One Mighty Breath, we ask for you to consider, Dear chelas, stalwart students of truth, that it is held within the frequency and the Vibration of your thought, the development of your consciousness.

These small exercises, the gathering of a group to hold collective thought, to hold collective consciousness, are those first steps that allow that involution of consciousness to become an evolution of humanity.

And then those higher frequencies are allowed, conceptualized and *To Be*. We fear so often, as when taking the human form, that the extent of all reality is contained [only] within that vessel of clay. Yet, Dear ones, your true life, your true inner spark, is made of neither. It is the pure consciousness from that which we have known as Helios and Vesta—that which is known as the Source—planted eons ago upon your planet by those Mighty Lords of Venus, those who have brought forth their sponsorship for your evolution.

A time now comes where you will assume these new positions as members of this Lodge, a Brotherhood and a Sisterhood of light and love. I ask for you to consider, Dear students, that you too shall become as the elders have become. And in this time that awaits us—a Prophecy of Peace—you shall become [as] those Elohims of Tranquility, Elohims of Peace. Holding the spark, the Jiva, the Monad of Consciousness for those residing in kingdoms of lesser consciousness and for those who await us, those beloved dear children of the Seventh Manu, who hold within their heart that spark and consciousness for your own evolution.

I shall take my leave from your frequency and ask you to carry the prayer of the ONE throughout the day. Understand that even though we enter into a time of limited turmoil and chaos, that this is also a Time of Peace and a Time of Awakening.

"Thank you."

2

Love's Service

Saint Germain's Message for a Small Group

GREETINGS AND SALUTATIONS; GOOD MORNING, STUDENTS AND CHELAS.

The work upon the Earth Plane and Planet is yet to be realized—that is, achieved or actualized through the being. We shall address that heart of intent, for the time that comes forth is a time of the opening of the heart of humanity. How shall this happen, Dear ones? So many of you ask this in your prayers and in your thoughts and in your meditations.

It is still through the use of the Violet Flame, that Mighty Flame of Mercy and Forgiveness. Dear ones, as you have understood, Forgiveness is not an energy that is meted out or granted; yet, it is an energy that allows and sustains all of creation—it is that portal of Oneness, that place where two shall meet and become as ONE. This is where the understanding of the heart begins and where we open to that Mighty Energy of the Christ.

There have been, throughout history, many misinterpretations of *the Christ*. But as we have practiced in this Lodge and in this tradition, the Christ is union achieved through Forgiveness. It is also that energy where an at-one-ment, a vibrational frequency occurs. That Oneship, as beloved Kuan Yin has stated "steps forward to grant a measure of grace."

The opening of this vibrational frequency of Love upon the Earth Plane and Planet has always been the concern of this Lodge of the Spiritual Hierarchy. And it has been the development of this vibrational frequency of love which has been entrusted to us through our traditions and is the focus of our intent in service to and with humanity. It is this Vibration of Love that was brought to us eons ago by those Mighty Lords of Venus and is now entrusted to you, Dear ones, and brought to you to bring about an evolutionary rise—to raise your vibrational frequency from the animal to the HU-man. It was planted, and it was known as the Monad, or Jiva. Of course, these are ancient words; and we now call it simply, *the Unfed Flame of activated Love, Wisdom, and Power.*

We have explained in previous discourse about those epochs of races from the Lemurian to the Atlantean. Now, this race known as the Aryan is, simply stated, meant to activate this intelligence. That is the definition of *Aryan*—to open the Heart of Love. We begin to activate this intelligence by the use of the Laws of Forgiveness.

For more information and study topics on *Love's Service,* see Appendix B, page 171.

As you all share in one life upon this Earth Plane and Planet, we would ask you to consider at all times, Dear ones, that even that spark, the mighty Monad is as ONE, which you all share.

The time now upon the Earth Plane and Planet is not only a Time of Transition but a Time of Prophecy. These prophecies have come to awaken that flame, to foster and engender it, to bring it forward into active use. War and pestilence are in your streets; and you ask, "What is it that I may bring forth in perfect service?" And [so] I would ask, Dear students and chelas, that each day you anchor yourself as a pillar of that Law of Forgiveness, and demonstrate it.

If you are having trouble forgiving, the utilization of this law is as simple as taking a few seconds and visualizing the Violet Flame streaming forth from your feet and extending to the top of your head. You will feel it as an electric shock throughout your system as it stimulates each of the centers of light upon and within the physical body. This is a gift from the Lords of Venus so that you would understand the ONE that is contained within each and every one of you. We understand that it is almost impossible for you to comprehend all languages [genetic codes] in your separated state of being, but we ask you to hold the Violet Flame throughout your being throughout the day. Visualize that flame in, through, and around those for whom you harbor thoughts of disharmony and discord. Use it for the healing of your physical vehicle. Use it in all situations that you feel might hinder or hamper your movement within this Lodge of Service. We ask you, Dear hearts, to utilize the Flame not only in your business practices but also in your bank accounts—for it is that Flame that allows a movement toward the ONE.

The ONE is contained in all things. It is that flame which is the bridge to the Universal Mind.

As we have stated before, the Prophecies of Earth Changes have been closed for a short time. However, with close attention to that Divine Plan and Mighty Will of the Light of God that never fails, we shall dispense again a series of Earth Changes Prophecies designed to awaken the hearts and minds of all those who slumber. [Editor's Note: This is in reference to the Six-Map Scenario.]

However, in this period of time, we ask you, Dear hearts, to place the emphasis upon the Prophecies of Peace. For not only do geophysical changes come to the planet; but as you have understood the dynamic of energetic reasoning, you know that first come the changes within the heart, reflected afterward in societies and communities—and only comes the true change, in the creations of your worlds of experience.

We shall see these changes occur first in each of the Vortices; in the order they have been assigned in the activation. You have all been called to that mighty Gobean energy, and you will first see the Prophecies of Peace anchored in that Vortex. You will also see the transformational changes occurring, first in the hearts of those who attend to them.

Second in the activation, as we have stated before, will be Malton; third in the activation will be Wahanee; fourth, Shalahah; and fifth, Klehma.

What is it that happens during the Times of Activation and the anchoring of the Prophecies of Peace? Transmutation occurs first with the purging of the body. There have been those who have experienced this as physical fire, within the system affected first, such as the lymphatic system, and then onward, into the joints. It is my advice, Dear ones, that as you experience this process, known as *Vibrational Toning*, you should increase your water intake. The fragrances of violets, jasmine, and cinnamon can also relieve these stresses.

I ask you to spend no less than ten minutes per day in thought and prayer upon the Violet Flame. Perfect this energy within the system, for you are as transmitters of light; you are vehicles of peace. Of course, first the physical body suffers as the soul purges that which is no longer needed; but then comes that time when you will outstretch your hand, and say, "Flame, you and I are ONE!"

There will be changes, as noted before, in the electrical field of the body. These Start at the end of this year and then extend onward for the next four years. Brilliant Gold light will begin to be seen, activated within the outer layers of the body's electromagnetic sphere, the ovoid of the aura. These sparks of light are flames emitted from the activation, both from the third layer of the Human Auric field and also from the opening of that Heart of Love. As the dove lands in the heart of humanity, you will notice an electromagnetic shock to metal and to inert substances such as wood and glass.

Will a Time of Good come amongst humanity? This I assure you, Dear hearts—yes! For it is the plan that love shall serve all, as love is the Original Intent. Send this message to the earth with love: a Time of Change has come! Open your eyes and open your ears, Dear ones.

Now we shall continue with more changes in the physiology. We have repeatedly asked for dietary changes, not only for the vibrational frequency but also out of concern for the toxicity contained in many of the food substances on the planet. We would ask you to consider that all food contains within it elements of light. We also ask you to breathe light into your light centers so that, when you do partake of food, you can assimilate and absorb the light contained therein. I have given the dietary requirements, and I would ask that you adhere to them strictly during these years of peace and transition. Why should this be so? That which is brought into the being thus attracts. It is simply a matter of magnetics. We would also suggest that you consider taking in those foods that have obtained the maturation process through light, such as fruits and vegetables. Do you understand, Dear ones?

"Yes."

We would suggest that you limit or eliminate all substances of flesh, as it is the vibration, Dear ones, that we are concerned with. It is the Vibration of Fear that is now leaving the planet, and that quantitative mass of consciousness shifting to love can also be held through what you choose to partake [eat, drink] within your being.

Let us continue now, and I will outline for you some suggestions for this time; not only is it a Time of Choice and Change, this is a time for your commitment. Gather together frequently into your groups of comradery. Hold your focus and intent through prayer, song, and meditation. As dear Morya has taught, "It is the focus that creates." During this time we suggest that you see around yourself a family unit as a structure held intact. You worry about structures you should build to house your bodies during this Time of Change; first build a structure that will house your spirit. Join together in the Oneship you share and let this be a celebration of joy and of life!

If only you could open your eyes beyond the judgment the ego calls forth, you would see Paradise revealed to open the Prophecies of Peace. There will be many manifestations of this during this five-year period, and it is important, Dear ones, that you are committed to a discipline as your demonstration of spiritual service.

The activation of Gobean has now been in effect for at least fifteen years. But now we shall see an acceleration, not only of the gathering of energy forces within the Vortex itself, but many will be drawn electromagnetically, and you will be called to impart this service. Share the teachings of the great I AM. Share the teaching of that great true self, the divinity, the spark, the Monad. Share the teachings of the activation through intelligence and choice. Move them to the Heart of Love. Take them into your family. For are you not all as ONE?

These are the Prophecies of Peace that come forward for your choice and demonstration.

I shall close now and open myself for your questions.

Question: "It appears that I have been working with many of the Spiritual Kingdoms integrating energy, in particular Shalahah. Is there anything that I can do that will assist my vibratory change and assist my attunement?"

Let me scan.

Lori: *Saint Germain scans the student's aura for diagnostic information.*

Physically, your body is lacking Vitamin C; and I would suggest using that variety known as rose hips. This will bring an assimilation of the Vegetable Kingdom into your system. We would also ask that you serve as that aforementioned Pillar of the Violet Flame, offering the assistance of Forgiveness and Mercy through choice. We would also ask for the current merging of the Kingdoms of Mineral, Vegetable, Animal, and HU-man. Send your thought, your prayer, and your meditation for the collective unity of these Kingdoms and for their collective healing.

It is important at all times, in your working space, to keep the Vibration of Mineral and Vegetable around you, for they work as transmitters of energy. In keeping live plants and flowers, do you not feel their consciousness?

Answer: "Yes, I do."

I would choose for you those colors of violet and green, for they best serve your vibrational fields. And from the Mineral Kingdom, rose quartz would assist you in the building of the physical body.

Question: "So should I wear more rose quartz, have it on me?"

Place it throughout the room to transmit its energy. Place it in a dish—four of them, to the four directions: one to the north, one to the south, one to the east, and one to the west. They will polarize one another and set up an energy field, which will be most conducive for your energy assimilation.

Answer: "Thank you. Would my body of work now be in sending energy as the Violet Flame to the Mineral Kingdom; is that my primary focus at this time?"

If you choose this service, Dear one, we would like to extend our thank-you for your loving service to this body of work known as Prophecy.

Answer: "Thank you."

Question: "Saint Germain, I would like some assistance concerning the alimony my ex-husband is sending me. I feel that there is a big element of control on my part, and I do not desire to control him in any way, and I know that he does not desire to be controlled by me. I need some assistance."

Dear one, in the teachings of the Brotherhood, the Violet Flame is used at sunrise and at sunset. I would suggest that you use it in regard to your question. The symbol of sunrise and sunset means a *New Day*. Can we have a day of just twenty-four hours crammed with twelve years? Today, Dear one, let each day be as that day.

I would suggest that you use the Violet Flame at sunrise and at sunset with the proper invocation. And use it energetically with all chakras. This will help eliminate the energy pattern you have created between you and this other individual.

I will also give you instruction on the dissolution of holographic patterns which no longer serve the path you choose to walk. This is assisted through the Vibration of Sandalwood, which is one of the highest vibrations of the Vegetable Kingdom. This will not only transmute, but bring into alignment all energies for the best and highest good.

Serve, too, as a Pillar of Forgiveness, regarding your question. This, too, is the service you bring.

In the case of the dissolution of patterns that no longer serve: Purify your Cup, in this instance, for three days in continuous light. And in the case of the sandalwood within that Cup: smudging, with its smoke between you and the other individual. As I have taught in past discourse, it is best to obtain that person's agreement. If this is not achievable, then a picture where the eyes are visible will work, for this carries within the energy, the pattern of that being. Call forth the Violet Flame for the best and highest good, and you will then receive the best course of action. [Editor's Note: Saint Germain is referring to the removal of Subjective Energy Bodies. For more information on this subject, see *Three Teachers*, New World Atlas Volume Three.]

Same Questioner: "I also need some clarification. You mention the elimination of all flesh from the diet. Were you talking about fish, too?"

Yes, in regard to flesh, we would ask you to eliminate even fish from your diet at this time as the pollutant activity upon the planet is consolidating within that Kingdom. If you wish to eat fish, or flesh from fish, eat that which comes from fresh water. The saltwater of the planet is no longer advisable to be utilized by the HU-man.

However, I would also like to state that there is a rise in the vibrational frequency, and that is also of the highest consideration.

Question: "Saint Germain, I did not understand your last sentence, about the waters. There is a rise in the saltwater's vibrational frequency or mine?"

In yours, Dear one. For humanity, this is the Time of the Evolution of Consciousness, a Time of the Return, a Time of the In-breath. It is a time when consciousness is leaping to that next dimension of creation.

You must remove the guilt from your life, Dear one, for it moves on you like a heavy stone. Transmute this through the Violet Flame; it has been given to you as a gift. Take repeat baths of saltwater with rosemary thrown into the bathwater. Focus upon the Violet Flame of Forgiveness, for, Dear heart, this time is your time of service; this guilt no longer serves you. Drop the heavy stone, and you may walk a bit farther. Do you have questions?

Answer: "No. Thank you."

Unless you have further questions, I shall take my leave from your realm and will be glad to return with further Prophecies of Peace.

Hitaka!

3

Changing of the Guard

Saint Germain and Kuan Yin Give a Teaching for a Group of Students

GREETINGS IN THAT MIGHTY CHRIST.

I AM Saint Germain, and I stream forth on that Violet Ray of Mercy and Forgiveness. As usual, Dear hearts, I request permission to come forth.

"Please, Dear one, come forth."

Salutations and greetings, Dear ones. You have arrived at this time known as the *Changing of the Guard.* A time comes to the Earth Plane and Planet when the earth will shake, shall we say, a rock, a rattle, and a roll. Or, perhaps a Time of Grace, a Time of Peace, a time when you shall face your immortal destiny.

I ask you, Dear ones, are you ready to face immortality? Are you ready to face the New Dimensional Shift? Over the past few weeks, you have felt a little uncomfortable... You have wondered, what is this new feeling around me? What is this new vibration that I am encountering?

Dear ones, each and every one of you has been prepared by the Spiritual Hierarchy, Brothers and Sisters all, for this day. Have you not sensed this? Have you not sensed that the energy is now shifting, pushing, and pulling, leaving each of you wondering, "Can I take this any more? Can I take much more of this?"

This is a time when dimensionally you are being shifted, along with that Cellular Memory encoded in each and every cell of your being. It is a time when you are going through tremendous changes. Even the DNA coding is shifting in, through, and around your being, each molecular structure changing, readying itself for the shift that is to come.

Dear hearts, I have been requested by those whom I love and serve to no longer dispense Prophecies of Earth Changes for a time; whereupon, we will begin anew. We will begin to dispense new prophecies, and in one year, many new things will have happened. A time will come when those who have eyes and ears open will be willing to see and hear, and then to act. Until that time, Dear ones, we, as your elder Brothers and Sisters, will be adjusting the

---

For more information and study topics on *Changing of the Guard,* see Appendix C, page 179.

energy fields of the Earth Plane, helping to adjust the collective consciousness to be ready for the times that are to come.

Tonight we shall discuss not only the Prophecies of Peace, but also those Prophecies of Change. Many of you have waited long for this time, for a field of neutrality arching through the dual forces of light and dark. That time, long needed, has come—Grace, Neutrality, a new vibration that is also known as the Fourth Dimension.

We long for you, Dear ones, to access these planes, for we know the benefits and wish you to find that vibration. We are here at all times to assist you to reach that new plane, but it is you who must do the work. We cannot pull you through; however, we can show you how. We have spent our time recently adjusting the collective consciousness for the times that are coming, but we would like to remind you that we cannot, at any time, readjust the Karma of mankind. For what mankind has created, mankind must now receive. This is the Law—cause and effect. And we work with those causes, readjusting always within that great plan of the best and highest good.

Yes, it is true, Dear ones, we have been working to adjust the energy up and down your western coastline of North America and working with great effort to adjust the energies of the Pacific Rim, that which is known as the *Ring of Fire*. Beloved Brother Kuthumi has been sending his energy to Indonesia, and this energy is traveling south, and in a counterclockwise fashion. You have all known that there is an energy collecting itself in the Cascade Range, with Mount Saint Helens being the first in this decade to explode, demonstrating that even beloved Babajeran must assist in this dimensional shift. Many of you are worrying about Mount Rainier, and, again, I refuse to give dates, as I have been instructed to continue adjusting the energy, for, as we know, the end results lie in the choices that you yourselves make.

Dear ones, Dear hearts, this Time of Change is coming. And, yes, it is true that the Prophecies of Peace will reign supreme—for each one who is willing to make that choice.

Let us make that choice.

Let us make that change, within our hearts.

Let us make these changes now—before it is too late.

For a time will come when you will greet the Earth Changes with a smile and say, "This is good." What are the alternatives? Shall we discuss them in a brief history, so that you will understand?

This country that you live in, known as America, extending from Canada into Central America and on into South America, was, at one time, one land—one continuous land—before that Time of the Seventh Moon, which crashed into what you now know as the Gulf of

Mexico. It contained within itself a vibration, an energy of this Earth Planet. And the people who walked the face of this land *were* you. Welcome, members of that I AM! For when you look at America, you are the I AM Race returning again, in service, to the Mother—to this which is known as the Feminine Energy, which I will later discuss. This land has a destiny, and that destiny has a time. Understand that Prophecy has a time. Even as Moses, in *his* time, dispensed Prophecy to his people, these prophecies are for *you* and *your* time.

This I AM Race of people has come to give service to this planet. You have known many incarnations, all of you, upon these lands, for you are ONE with it; and you cannot be subtracted from your own cellular memory and your own genetic code.

My work upon the Earth Plane and Planet, as Sanctus Germanus, now known as the Holy Brother, began with my incarnation as Sir Francis Bacon. I was educated through the Rosicrucians—known as the Rosy Cross—in geometric languages, the ancient mystic ways, and the Alchemy of the soul. After my initiation, I offered myself in service to that mighty Brotherhood and Sisterhood of the Light that have held the destiny of this Earth Planet in its hands.

I traveled, not only to the North American continent, where I had the privilege to meet with the leaders of the I AM Race, but was dispensed again to Europe, where I was to continue working on a plan which had first been set in motion in the Western World, a great United States of Europe—a United European Brotherhood on the one hand and, on the other, the United States of America to represent the Sisterhood. A polarity and a balance would thus be achieved.

However, Dear ones, we know there are those who hold within themselves a systematic program of greed; and so, this goal was not achieved. It was at this time that the Councils of the Great Violet Flame decreed, through the edict of Sanat Kumara, that the energy of the Brother [masculine] would temporarily be moved from Europe to the United States. Thus the energies of both Brother and Sister would be held within this ONE I AM land.

During this time, what you know as the Civil War broke out in the United States with, again, the monsters of greed electing to stomp upon that Plan of Light, in that constant intrigue of the push and pull of Lightness and Darkness. I repeat this history for you so that you will understand that there are those whose plans work on behalf of the Dark. Is it not true that you, Dear ones, work for the Light of God that never fails? Why, then, would there not be that balance on the Plane of duality—a Brotherhood of Darkness that would also follow its path upon this Earth Plane and Planet? And where is the one pivotal point of difference? In the Consciousness of Choice!

You, Dear ones, are inheritors of the divine, given that gift of free will, the Monad in the heart, the Choice of that Inner Flame of Freedom. You see, Dear ones, it has always been a game of who is weaker and who is stronger. And, again, this game has been played at many levels. But it is a game, I assure you, whose time will end. I ask you now to search within your consciousness, to search within your hearts, and to hear the truth of the words that I speak. It is important to choose and to stay committed to that choice. It is important to love as beloved Sananda has stated over and over again. It is important to forgive and to use that Mighty Law of Forgiveness at all times. Master that Law and there is your freedom.

So, how did this continue—this game of weak and strong? It evolved into your governments. It was once as simple as monarchy versus Liberty and Freedom. But now, in this time, the most important right you have is your right to choose your leaders. Yes, it is your right to vote.

This is a right you have earned through the blood of your own children. And yet, so many of you today feel that your vote cannot and will not make a difference. I encourage each and every one of you, Dear hearts, to become educated because you believe the power lays within the leader. Not so, for the power lays within he who selects the leader, for the leader is educated by those who vote for him or her. This I assure you, Dear ones, when you no longer value your right to vote, you lose that one privilege for which you have died many deaths. Haven't you noticed that difference in vibration that has come into your being over the past twenty years? Why is this so? It is simple—you and those about you have forgotten to hold the focus on Liberty and Freedom. Become educated. Educate your children, and educate those about you. Know those who go into those political offices, for they will determine your future. How are they empowered? They are empowered by your vote. Yes, there have been times when the outcome of elections has been slanted in one direction or another by misconduct. But I promise you that eventually the destiny of this land to serve will come to full fruition, and the vibration and energies of the Spiritual Hierarchy of Light and Sound will surround this country when that time arrives.

Now crime and pestilence run through your streets. Your children carry guns. Your teachers are not fit to teach. Why is this so? You have given up the right and the ability to enact your choice. Take back that first gift you fought so dearly for—your gift of choice—and use it each day.

And now, the economy. It is very important, Dear ones, as I have instructed the chelas close to my heart, to invest most monies into natural resources. When I say a natural resource, I mean Gold and Silver. That which is land—those natural commodities that can be bartered, that can be traded. For a time will come when your paper money will be worthless. Its value will not hold the value you think it does now. I ask you, Dear ones, to consider all of these things as perpetrators of these times. Have I not stated before that when insanity becomes sane, the Times of Change will soon be coming?

Dear ones, it is important to stay centered within your being and to stay centered within the teachings and the Laws of Truth. As beloved Sister Kuan Yin has so adeptly stated, "You are a Oneship, and each and every one of you forms this life." I remind you, as you apply these laws, it is important for you, too, to understand that Oneship we all share.

Yes, a time comes to the Earth Plane and Planet—a time for you to choose. Do you wish to live in a world where crime reigns? Do you wish to live in a world where your rights are systematically taken away because you refuse to choose? Is this the world you would want for your future generations? Is this a world of choice? Is this a world of Freedom and Liberty?

Only you can be the benchmark, and only you can answer that question.

It was decided in the year 1952 that, should the earth undergo a period of cleansing, Nature would provide the backdrop to afford all incoming lifestreams the ability to achieve the lessons necessary to accelerate this planet to the Fourth Dimension. It is your choice, Dear ones. During these upcoming Earth Changes, strategic points upon the planet will be adjusted—not only lei-lines and energy Vortices, which are the chakras of the planet, areas known as Adjutant Points. These are places where dense material becomes enlightened or, shall we say, spun to a degree where it is able to take on a finer vibration. With a shifting of the poles, we shall then be able to see an entry not only into the Fourth Dimension but the possibility and potential to enjoy Fifth, Sixth, and even Seventh Dimension consciousness.

As we have always taught, the Fourth Dimension is a dimension of vibration and attraction. It is also the dimension where bi-location begins. It is also the dimension of immortality—physical immortality, that is. So I refer to it as a Dimension of Alchemy. Is it possible to achieve a balance on this planet, and a Fourth Dimensional consciousness? Again, Dear ones, the choice is in your heart and in your hand. However, at this particular moment, we still work for the upliftment of humanity so that more eyes and more ears can open. When these times do come, fear not—rather, rejoice, for the entry into the New Dimensions has begun.

At this time, I should like to open the floor for questions. Are there any questions?

Answer: "Yes, Master, I have a question. You said earlier that Mount Rainier... that you were not going to give any specific dates... and you also talked about the Ring of Fire and the volatility in that area. Are we still poised on the edge of major change in that part of the country? If so, if people ask us for direction for relocation when they ask us about time frames, what would be the best way to address their concerns?"

Are we not in a Time of Transition? Are we not in a Time of the Thinning of the Veil between the Third and Fourth Dimensions? At any time this happens upon a planet, there are bound to be many physical changes. Do you not experience the physical changes within your own being? You are ONE with this physical planet. She, too, is readying herself for her shift, her acceleration into another dimension and another way of being.

This Time of Change is pivotal and critical for evolution. We call this the *Emergent Evolution*. Evolution sometimes follows a path through pain and suffering; but it is through pain and suffering that we grow along this path and gain the understanding of the glory of a new day. I ask you, Dear ones, to face this new day with eyes open, no longer brimming with tears, but able to face the rising of the sun and the Light of God that Never Fails. I would also ask at this time that you relocate to those strategic locations known as Golden City Vortices. These Vortices are holding a collective consensus in consciousness for a Time of Peace, a Time of Grace. But let us not dilute that message of change, for the change must come first; and then peace will reign supreme.

Answer: "Thank you, Saint Germain. You also addressed the changing of our DNA. Would you give more information about that?"

We are speaking about consciousness, and consciousness that is held in a continuum of the Fourth Dimension. Those who sought embodiment here first, through that Time of the Lemurian, encased that Monad for the first time in flesh and, working continuously through the motions of Hatha Yoga, split the body into two. So we now have a body with both masculine and feminine energy contained within it. Then, during the Time of Atlantis, the emotional bodies were allowed to develop.

And now we face this Time of the Aryan, a Time of Active Intelligence, a time when the employing of intelligence leads into wisdom. During the Atlantean period, instinct led to intuition. Now wisdom, intelligence, and instinct function as one. And now you, Dear ones, carry the DNA coding of the Lemurian, the Atlantean, as well as, at this time, the Aryan.

The cradle of this coding lays physically in the spine and in the pineal gland. These are locations in the body where consciousness can be activated to access the Fourth Dimension. We speak of consciousness being held in a continuum inasmuch as you presently hold consciousness in a continuum in the First, Second, and Third Dimensions. Now you expand your *circle of the known*. Consciousness expands once again, allowing you to Master it and drive your expanding consciousness into the next dimension. In this state, you will be aware of consciousness existing just beyond your ken at the Fifth, Sixth, and Seventh Dimensions; but at that moment you will actually be embodying Dimensions One through Four. Do you understand?

Answer: "I do. Thank you."

Are there any more questions?

Question: "I have another question that relates to preparing. We know that we are in these great Times of Change. Some here are feeling the need to relocate from areas where they live to this area in particular, which is Gobean. There is a thought coming up from me about the storage of food. I know that spiritual preparedness is the ultimate answer; but we must also look at some of our basic, immediate needs. What kind of suggestions—and guidance—do you have for us?"

Yes, we have always taught that preparedness of the heart is the first place to Start; we will also remind you, Dear students and chelas, do not throw the baby out with the bathwater! As you have developed each of your senses, is not common sense the most important sense to utilize? It is important to live near land where you can grow your own food; the pesticides and the chemicals within your food come from that dark side of the government, that dark side of that Brotherhood that wishes to annihilate your future. And when I say your future, I speak of your children. For this reason, should you not have some storage of food? Would this not be practical and economical?

However, there are times coming when you will require less food. As the light—and when I say "light," I refer to *prana*—increases upon this planet, you will notice that your chakras or energy centers will be moving at a higher rate of spin; and you will be able to take in more prana. [Energy] Our greatest concern during the Time of Changes is that your air will lose its quality, and your water will not be drinkable. These are the two most important things. For when we see the simultaneous explosions of all the volcanoes in the Ring of Fire, ash will cover your planet for almost four years. Can you imagine, Dear one, the air you will be breathing?

So this is what I would recommend to begin to clear out the lungs, to ready the physical vehicle for the times to come: find whatever breathing technique can strengthen the lungs' capacity. I would also suggest that storage of water is imperative, for during these Times of Changes, many rivers and streams will change course. Even underground aquifers will be drained within seconds. In the Canadian Prophecies, you can read how this can happen. As for food, remember that spirit is truly your first food to be taken; season it with trust! Do not allow a shadow of a doubt to enter into your heart during this time.

You are gifted with that ONE source, One Eternal Flame. Know, too, Dear ones, that we are by your side, ready and willing to lend our hand. Proceed...

Question: "To store a sufficient amount of water for a very long period of time is a large undertaking. Is there a purification system, or a way we can purify water to address our needs?

There is, of course, the use of Free Energy. I have taught the techniques of charging the water through the hands, for, you know, your body itself is a battery that generates energy. As I have taught before, you can draw this energy up from the Planet Herself. However, during the Time of Changes, I would suggest that you be careful in areas filled with turbulent change, for the energy will be unstable, and it will be hard to energize the water with this technique. Usually, I would ask you to charge the water with your own energy. However, if you have a doubt, research filtering systems.

Answer: "Thank you."

Question: "Master. During the Times of Changes, when peoples all over earth will be looking to communicate as ONE mind and ONE life, what advice do you have for bringing that forth in harmony?"

I shall let my Sister address this.

(*Saint German steps back, and Kuan Yin comes forward*)

MY DEAR CHILDREN, HOW WONDERFUL IT IS TO ADDRESS YOU ALL. SUCH JOY I TAKE IN PHYSICALITY AGAIN! I AM KUAN YIN.

It is the ONE and Absolute Harmony that we seek. It is the ONE Feminine Energy that opens now across your planet that you must access to achieve this harmony. Brothers and Sisters of Light and Sound, open your hearts to compassion to achieve your unity with ONE. Open your hearth within your heart and share your love. It is as simple as the Law of Love.

(*Kuan Yin steps back, and Saint Germain comes forward again*)

Proceed.

Question: "Master, in teaching all peoples to live within their hearts in the inner world so that their outer world may change, so that they may perceive things from a balanced point of view—what would you suggest?"

It is as simple as I have taught before: the use of the Violet Flame is imperative at this time. When you decree unto yourself, "I AM a being of Violet Fire, I AM the purity that God desires," do you not feel the marriage of your energies and the Kundalini current arching up and down your spine? Do you not feel a heat within your throat and a heat within your ears?

I AM a being of Violet Fire!

I AM the Purity God desires!

Alchemy—this is Alchemy, Dear one. The harmony you seek is as simple as decreeing it to yourself. This is the *Law of the Divine Inheritor*. Decree a thing unto yourself and it comes forward in two manifestations! Consciousness creates! Seek perfection first in your intent and bring it forth through the spoken word. For the word is the action that moves it through your emotional bodies. Is not the word the action of your heart? Transmutation and Alchemy are the keys to accessing the Fourth Dimension.

As I have stated before, do you not feel, Dear ones, that you have been walking through the fires of initiation, each day another day of purification? Each day when you say, "Take this bitter Cup from me!" You can lighten your load through the use of the Violet Flame—this gift, brought forth from the Lords of Venus to soften the suffering and to lessen your load. Use it, Dear ones, and you will enjoy the results. Proceed...

Answer: "Thank you, Master."

Question: "Master, can you explain why so many children of this planet suffer and die at this time?"

These are the *Laws of Balance*. These are the *Laws of Cause and Effect*. How do we know that these children weren't at one time the warriors of previous generations, slaughtering other children, and raping and killing their mothers? This is the challenge of the Third-Dimensional experience, Dear ones—it is the challenge of duality. At one moment you perceive the dark and in the next moment the light. How rare it is that you perceive them both, in tandem. Open your hearts of compassion to those who are suffering. Send them your energy of Alchemy. Transmute to the higher planes. Transmute through the *Law of Vibration*. The *Law of Correspondence* rules all things, Dear ones: "As above, so below." Remember this, and you shall be wise. Proceed...

Question: "Will you explain the best way to communicate this new information to other people who are not yet aware?"

Each day we take another step closer to the Fourth Dimension and the thinning of this Veil. At one time I would have recommended that you speak only when inquired of. The time now, however, is short; and the Spiritual Awakening is at hand. Ask me to come and give you that closer energetic reasoning you require. I ask of you, dear Brother, to consider our equality—to consider that you and I are ONE. Did this not open your ear?—that you and I are of ONE Omni-essence, of ONE Omnipresence? I ask you to share this message. It is as Kuan Yin has stated: We are ONE.

Question: "Master, in the Omnipresence of life in the Third-Dimensional world, and upon leaving the physical body, how may we teach others to communicate with people that have dropped the body?"

Are you inquiring about those who no longer use physical bodies to express?

Answer: "Yes."

The teaching we bring forward is the teaching of communicating with those who have achieved Mastery over the body, a Mastery of the spiritual world. What would be the benefit of this communication?

Answer: "To let people know that the soul is immortal and that this Third-Dimensional life is truly an illusion."

Do you sense my presence about you now, Dear chela? Is this communication not in itself a teaching of how to achieve that contact?

Answer: "Yes."

Proceed each day in the application and disciplines of breath. Proceed each day in the application and the disciplines of Alchemy and Transmutation through the Violet Flame. As we proceed during this Time of Change and the thinning of the Veil, it will be more apparent who has crossed over and not taken this physical vehicle with them.

Down with death, I have always said! Down with death! Come alive in that one spirit, that one omni-essence, that Mighty I AM! Life is eternal and is not dictated by our use of the physical body, is it?

There is, however, one thing that physical life may accomplish—it may be of service. The Life that commands itself into the discipline of service is a blessed life, a Life that is of the Mother *and* of the Father. Upon the Earth Plane and Planet there are many who would now say: "Let me leave, for I cannot face this time. Let me leave and ascend now." Dear ones, where would you ascend to? Again, I can assure you, into another realm of service.

The incarnation process, as taught by beloved Master K.H., is a process that entails approximately two hundred years and sometimes as long as five hundred years. There are, of course, exceptions to this rule. Also, there are other planes and dimensions where manifestation has taken form. Even though you may not see them, there are many life forms in this room, life forms that also have physical manifestation. They are all carrying life, the one omni-essence, the one omnipresence. We must erase this death consciousness. We must erase it from our being! How else would you be able to hold your vehicle for this Time of Shifting into the Service of the New Dimensions? Questions?

Question: "Beloved old friend, I understand that with the collective consciousness—realizing that it can be affected by free will—this is a question that may not be answerable yet, but I wonder if you would address it. I feel the hot breath of the dragon, of the Grey Man, of the tyrants that control the government, very close to our backs. I have been told and taught that some time, unless the Earth Changes occur first, we will have to endure, as Americans, the military takeover of our government. If the Earth Changes don't happen, our government will enslave us; but that the Earth Changes might be part of our freeing. I wonder if you or one of the Brotherhood or Sisterhood might address this, because I feel its presence so close."

Greetings, my beloved Sister and acquaintance. You so astutely know these times because you have experienced them before. In 1990 we released the prophecies of the camps of orphans, which had been the plan of the dark government at the time. We released the prophecies of the underground explosions in the areas of Nevada and New Mexico, carried out by, shall we say, that alien-nature of our being. And now a time comes when this dark force barks at your back. It barks at your back so that you will have to choose!

Each day you choose to give away a *right*, you lose your liberty. And you complain that it is taken from you, when in fact, you have so readily given it! This is a time when people have become *sheeple* and know not the power vested in their hearts through choice. For this is a Time of Choice. And truly, yes, your consciousness creates all that is part of this grand illusion, this dream of the mind. I present these prophecies to you through dear Lord Sananda who stated, "Send this message to the earth with love."

A Time of Choice comes. How then shall we understand the Liberty that was gifted to you through the blood of your Brothers and Sisters? This Time of Change that comes, it is true, is a purification. And it is, too, an initiation. Are your eyes then incapable of tears? Does your voice still carry the power to wound? Before the soul can stand in the presence of the Masters, the feet must be washed in the blood of the heart! These are the words of my Brother, Hilarion. Understand them, and understand them well.

In World War II, upon your earth, the dark forces used a holocaust to lead a group of people through their Initiation. Their feet were washed in the blood of the heart. Must we experience this again? Or, is there a different way?

Cause and effect, Dear one, this is the Plane of Karma. This is a Plane of Light and Dark. This is also a plane you can Master. For are you not here asking this very question?—does not this flame of desire burn within your heart?

Consciousness can change all things. Have you not noted the difference when you awake in the morning "on the wrong side of the bed?" That negative energy entraps the day, sending a rippling current throughout your every action. Where did that energy come from? It comes from you, from your consciousness.

Yes, there is an alternative plan to that dark government. But there is also an alternative plan to that light government. You are entrusted with that choice. Proceed.

Answer: "I guess there are no further questions."

If there are no further questions for this evening I should like to end this discourse with one final address.

As I opened this evening, I announced a Changing of the Guard. This Changing of the Guard is held within your hearts. This Changing of the Guard is that time when you shall all become Masters—Brothers and Sisters in a New Plane and Dimension of Reality. I invite you all onto this Path—the Path of Adeptship. And I ask each and every one of you to honor that flame within the heart, that Monad of consciousness. For a time comes when you must move on; and you must assume your position, entrusted with the plan of holding the Cup.

The bearer of the Cup of Life is one who has traveled the path through the *Laws of Pain and Suffering,* and has Mastered all, to become voided—and yet, through this, has become filled! For is this not the joy within the service?

In that mighty Violet Ray, I call forth freedom!

I AM the Violet Flame,
An ember in the heart.
I AM the Violet Flame,
Peace and grace I impart...

Hitaka!

4

The Fourth Dimension

Saint Germain

GREETINGS, BELOVED CHELAS.

I AM Saint Germain, and I request permission to come forth.

"Dear one, come forth."

The Time of Transition is intense, is it not, Dear ones? This is a time when you gather unto yourselves, asking for that refreshing drink, that inner stillness, that Time of Peace. When shall it come in a sustained manner? When shall this grace be the law that reigns supreme?

I serve as Cohan of the Seventh Ray, the Seventh Ray that rules the Laws of Mercy and Compassion. I also serve the Laws of Ceremonial Order and Alchemy. They are as simple as Transmutation; for example, have you seen how the snow turns to water? Fire into ash? Wind into sunshine? These are all acts of Alchemy in nature. How do we achieve these?

Through the spirit, the soul, the mind, and the feelings. These principles are based on the Law of Rhythm. Beloved Kuan Yin has taught "it is Sattva," or a harmonious response to rhythm. You understand, Dear ones, the concept "as above, so below." The Law of Correspondence states, "as in heaven, so shall it be below."

When you hear higher frequency sounds, those that are inaudible to the ear but audible to the senses, you cannot null and void that sound. It exists in another, higher dimension, and it corresponds—it also has an effect on—a lower dimension. The Law of Correspondence, you see, dovetails with the Law of Cause and Effect. The causes are engendered in one dimension, have their effects in other dimensions. In this way, you could even perceive the past and the future as being dimensional—a cause beginning in the past and having its effect in the future. And it all happens through these laws; which rule this grand creation of mind, which rule all things and inform the nature and the quality of Omni-essence. And we still ask, how is it that this Law of Rhythm can bring peace out of turmoil, grace after siege, harmony where there has been chaos?

For more information and study topics on *The Fourth Dimension*, see Appendix D, page 187.

Picture, if you will, a pendulum swinging, even the pendulum of a grandfather clock, arching back and forth, to and fro—these are the rhythms of all things that you experience in a Third-Dimensional body. The rhythms of life always surround you—the rhythms of seasons, the rhythms of time. And do these things have an effect on you? Think back. Remember your rhythm when you were seven; the rhythm that contained you when you were fourteen; and the rhythm you expressed when you were twenty-one.

Did you not then have a particular rhythm that arched to and fro, connecting to that specific point of consciousness in time? Your whole life has a rhythm based on the Law of Cause and Effect—the causes coming from the past, the effects playing out in the future. The thoughts you had when you were seven, fourteen, and twenty-one affected every ensuing year. This intellectual energy became your future and led you through your path in life: a path predetermined by the choices you made and blessed with the breath of Co-creatorship. Subconsciously, you know that through the mighty cosmic law, Alchemy and Transmutation change all things.

Oh, how you look back now on those years of your youth! But, with seeing eyes and hearing ears, you're wiser now. Those are the times I ask you to draw upon, Dear ones. Using that vibration and knowledge, which are wisdom, I ask you to draw upon those times in your Times of Peace, Contemplation, and Meditation. For then you shall see how far you have traveled on this path; and you will understand, through your tears, the joy of this spiritual work.

Sattva is that harmonious response to vibration, and that Vibration often is not the cause but the effect. Right now, as I have lowered my vibrations dimensionally, do you not feel my energy and my radiance around you, Dear ones?

Answer: "Yes."

That is a response—that feeling within your being responding to vibration. How many more vibrations do you feel during the day? I ask you to become aware, for just one hour in a day, of the vibrations around you. Experience the vibrations of nature, of consciousness, of the physical world, of business, of sound, and of light. Your body responds to all of these, adjusting your body temperature and assuring your comfort. You neutralize some of them in your mind. Some vibrations you respond to with criticism or awareness, and some you have no awareness of at all even though they bathe your body and your lifestream. Vibration, Dear ones, is the key to understanding Ascension.

The time has come to increase your awareness of vibration.

Vibration is known as the *Fourth Dimension. It is a dimension where you are freed to another Plane of Cause, to another experience and another existence.* It is a dimension that does not require such cautious and often tedious tending of the body. However, it is still a physical experience—but an expanded physical experience on your journey home.

The Law of Sattva, or Rhythm, follows the ascent and descent of the spirit. The soul prepares and readies itself for the universal lessons during its experiences on its journey through life. It clothes itself with the garments of flesh, placing one body on and discarding another—embodiment after embodiment. The soul goes through cycles of infancy, adolescence, and young adult facing maturity, until it finally arrives, through evolution, at wisdom. This process, with its many repetitions, has been taught as re-embodiment, or reincarnation.

However each successive lifetime is propelled by that Law of Cause and Effect. The soul—in seeking bodies with which to garb itself in each lifetime—seeks one that will bring balance to the past lifetime, the lifetime before that, and so on. However, each successive embodiment follows that Law of Rhythm; and, just as that pendulum swings, so a Time of Descent turns into a Time of Ascent, and you notice a lightening of the body, a lightening of circumstance and a lightening of world affairs. It is as if the hand of God now grasps yours and says, "Come to me; return to your home. But come to me not tired and weary; come to me in joy and celebration."

For the ascent of spirit is as this, Dear ones: it is a celebration, as shown in the stories of the feast.

As the pendulum stops swinging, the point at which it stops is the center. That center is the position of neutrality; a position where electromagnetic currents come to a truce, a space created in the *Law of Polarities* for choice. And yet, is there a choice?

Of course there is, Dear ones. For some souls have come to that position before and have failed to ride that pendulum to the other side—which ensures their journey in Ascension. Do you not feel the cosmic clock now poised at that Time of Zero and Neutrality? For this is the time we have referred to as the *Time of Transition*. It is your Time of Choice.

During the Time of Planetary Transition, all past experiences are brought to the forefront, including the many embodiments the soul has shared with physical experience. This memory follows a rhythm, a pattern, and a harmony. For this is where the soul chooses: shall I return on the downswing, or shall I ride the upswing, which will allow me access to the joy and the celebration of the Fourth Dimension?

It is this dimension that we ride on the upswing, on the journey home, the journey to the ONE. And the journey to all Omni-essence. And while the soul will continue in its ascent through many other dimensions of cause and effect, and more of the dimensions based on the Law of Correspondence, it will be a joyful journey, filled with only the breath of the omnipotent ONE.

I ask you Dear chelas and students of this time—those who have chosen to ride the pendulum of transition and the path of Ascension—to consider the importance of choice, and how each choice you make can put you two steps forward or two steps backward. And now let us discuss the Fourth Dimension—the vibration—and your ability to walk two steps forward.

When I brought forward the Prophecies of Change, I discussed a time when some would seek cataclysm and disaster, while others would choose peace and grace. Throughout the eons, the Spiritual Hierarchy of the Great White Brotherhood and Sisterhood has prepared retreats. These havens carry finer dimensional energies, allowing souls to achieve that quantum ride and that quantum return to the journeys lying on the upswing of the pendulum.

These places are known as the Golden City Vortices. They have been charged from the beginning of their conception and arrival here. Beloved Babajeran [Mother Earth] has held them in the state of cause, always ready and willing to commune with you for the desired Effect.

Many Vortices have existed on the planet at other times; but now, at this Time of Transition, fifty-one have been prepared for you. These are places to visit; places to experience Fourth and Fifth Dimension energy; and places to understand the creation of these dimensions. They can help you in your journey to another world.

Many of you are of the opinion that you will be leaving this planet, leaving this world in a global ascent. Let me be specific: you are leaving a narrow consciousness, and expanding your consciousness in your journey and in your ride of the pendulum. Expanding into the Fourth Dimension requires discipline and service to that mighty ONE. It requires a broadening of the mind and an opening of the heart. It requires your awareness and understanding of the Law of Synchronicity, which states that "all things are effects of causes" therefore, "nothing is happenstance."

Each day, become aware of the vibration around you and the vibration you create within your being. I ask you to become aware of collective consciousness, or collective vibration. Have you ever entered a room and noticed that the people as a group emit a consciousness and a vibration through the blending of their thoughts, feelings, and actions. And then you enter another room and notice again the shifting energy and the changing vibrations. You grab your coat, go outside, and notice immediately yet another vibration.

To prepare for and allow yourself a new physical experience, you must become aware of the vibrations and the differences among each room, shall we say, the differences inside and outside the house. These are new experiences for you, Dear ones—new experiences in Co-creatorship and the Mastery of your energy.

I shall take a short break for questions.

Question: "Thank you, Holy Brother. It has been my observation that when you and other members of the Brotherhood and the Sisterhood come and speak to us from the Fourth Dimension that, individually and as a group, it appears as though you all have bodies, as we do in our Third-Dimensional experience. Will you please elaborate?"

At times we are required to lower our vibrational frequency to take on a holographic, illusive body to serve your need. When we are sent on a Mission to give a specific message or contact a certain person, we come attired in a garment of reciprocity. Otherwise, the recipient would not recognize us or affirm their contact with, or an awareness of, our vibration.

Dear ones, as you ready yourselves to spring into a New Dimension and awareness, you, as our students engendered in the same cause, will one day be asked to hold the positions we now occupy. We are asking you to become stewards of a greater plan, to serve your Brothers and Sisters who live now in lower worlds of consciousness. It is important that you understand these *rooms of consciousness* and how, when thought is projected into another realm or dimension, it forms a nucleus, a physical matter, to which it can adhere.

However, the Laws of Correspondence, of Cause and Effect, and of Rhythm and Sattva will determine the rate of Vibration of that matter, since each realm or dimension has its own vibration, its own ability to receive physical matter in a certain form, and its own ability to carry out the Divine Plan of Life and Omni-essence. Therefore when we say that we "bi-locate" we mean we've perfected the moving among these rooms of consciousness, the moving of a vibration without its affecting our response.

You all respond greatly to vibration, so Master your response to vibration. That is, learn how to meditate in the midst of noise; learn how to work with joy in the midst of sorrow; and learn how to rise to that *other dimension*—that other, ever-present, and contained quality "as above, so below." For as the Law of Correspondence would state, "even as the lower dimension is present, so is the higher."

At this moment you are responding only to the First, the Second, and the Third Dimensions. But remember, Fourth, Fifth, Sixth, and Seventh Dimensions exist, too. But, if you would attune your *response-ability* to those others, you would in turn experience and begin to understand their existence—or, better yet, their co-existence—in your world.

Have you not noticed, at times, flashes of light at the corners of your eyes? Have you not seen, at times, light haloed around the body of a friend? Have you not, at times, heard a voice—an audible voice—whispering, singing, or repeating a message in your ear? These are your Brothers, Sisters, and friends of an expanded experience who have learned to respond with their energies to those of other dimensions and other experiences.

A time will come when you will lay aside the physical body as we know it. Many have taught Ascension as the burning away of the grosser energies to respond to these energies of the finer dimensions. In some respects, how true this is. But, as above, so below—as all things come, so all things go.

Understand the Law of Rhythm; understand the Law of Correspondence. Begin to respond from the Plane of Neutrality of the Fourth Dimension. Open your awareness in times of meditation; open your awareness to your times of breath, and you will begin to experience and to understand a New World that has always existed *beside* the old.

To move gracefully through the dimensions, it is important to understand the Laws of Alchemy and how one substance can be turned into another. For example, I have always taught the Law of the Violet Flame. I have always taught how fires of hatred and anger can be tempered and transmuted into the fires of compassion and of grace. This is accomplished through the Law of Rhythm, which captures the attention of the mind and then expands its energy through an open heart.

When you work with these Laws of Alchemy and of Transmutation, you open the doorways to your response. You create a Plane of Neutrality—that positing of the pendulum where it almost stops—and you are allowed to glimpse and experience a corresponding world.

In the Golden City Vortices, which are now holding a consciousness of neutrality, the energies contained within those areas allow the chela and the disciple to access Fourth Dimension more readily. As we originally discussed in the *Prophecies of Change*, a Time of Global Ascension, a Time of Mass Ascension, and a Time of Response-ability will come. This is that Time of Global Ascent. It is a Time of Mass *Response-ability*. Do you see, Dear one, how this Ascension has begun? Many of you have decided to return, through the energy of your spirits, to that natural rhythm and harmony, which will return you to your home of origin. So this is the Time of Change. It is a Time of Celebration and it is a Time of Joy. This journey is an ascent filled with joy; it is an ascent filled with discovery.

Do you have questions?

Question: "Yes, I do. Even though, to our appearance, you take on this certain form when you come and speak to us, as you are doing now, it appears as though you do have a body existing in that resonance or vibrational frequency that we will call Fourth Dimension. In light of this appearance, it has been my experience that viewing the aura is not much different than viewing the other dimensions. Will you please elaborate?"

This vision of yours is an opening into the patterning of the dimensions layered one upon the other, existing side by side with one another. However, many of those in the physical experience have not yet opened an awareness to, and therefore cannot manifest, Fourth-or Fifth-Dimensional light. The aura, or light field, seen around the adept, the avatar, or the Master Teacher, is an energy of light that comes through as a manifestation of their response in that Fourth Dimensional experience. They understand their harmonious response and begin manifesting it upon that level of experience. But, they need another body to share the experience with, hence, their *light body* is born—a light body that will encase the spirit or the soul after the shedding of the physical.

I hope this gives you a further understanding of light and the qualities it contains. For light, in and of itself, is a manifestation of mind... Questions?

Question: "Yes—this is another question. Light, being the manifestation of mind... as we think something today, it becomes something else tomorrow. According to the Law of Cause and Effect, is it the mind that is the director and the refractor of light in the co-created world?—is it this mind, this attention that we give, this focus, this energy, that is the seed of creative activity on this plane and planet?"

Thought is the seed of all creation. And—as I have always taught, Dear one—thought can be transmuted and changed into another thought. Have you not heard the phrase, "change your mind?" Insofar as you are able to change your mind, you can change your existence and the very body that now clothes your spirit and soul.

Within the realm of mind exist both the cause and the effect—simultaneously. And when a thought is seated as an encapsulated thought, it is a seed of manifestation, able to bring about an appearance in that dimension where the focus resonates. That appearance is when you see the Law of Cause and Effect in action. Do you understand?

Question: "Yes. The next question I would ask is: Is the true Alchemy the transition, the Violet Flame activity, beginning always with our thoughts?"

The Law of Alchemy is based not only on the Law of Rhythm—that all things change—it is based on the *Mastery* of the Law of Change. It is based equally on the Mastery of the Law of Cause and Effect. For it understands the cause of all things.

When you bathe your thoughts with the words, "I AM Forgiveness," do you not notice a calming effect which comes over past thoughts of hatred and unforgiveness? Do you not notice how instantly all is changed, gathered unto itself, and given a sensation of peace and neutrality? This Law of Alchemy, which opens the doors to new experiences, uses your physical body as a laboratory of experience. Here you can learn those transmuting laws and those Laws of Decay and Death, which exist simultaneously with them.

And would this again not be the Law of Polarity, which also exists in all dimensional force fields? Simultaneous experience comes side by side and corresponds to the other. Have you not noticed that happiness and despair sit side by side? And to further understand, have you not noticed how male seeks female, or female seeks male, side by side? And so it is.

Question: "Then our consciousness moves from the polarities to the neutrality to seek the expansion into the other dimensional realms?"

The polarities provide an experience. And through that experience, or what we call the "opening of the heart" thought becomes neutrality. It is through that neutralization, brought about by the uniting of energies, that one then begins to understand Transmutation.

Questions?

Question: "As we move through this dimensional shift on this Plane of consciousness, would it be wise for all who seek to shift their consciousness to move to those Golden City areas?"

For those who wish to receive an initiation in vibration and those who wish to understand the opening of the Fourth Dimension in mass consciousness, it is advised. For these are areas that will experience the melding of polarized energies. As a result, an opening of the heart will help you understand the worlds that exist simultaneously.

It is with love that these teachings have been brought forward—love for life at all levels of experience. This teaching comes out of love: love for the Devas and the Elemental Kingdoms; love for the Mineral Kingdom; love for the Vegetable and Animal Kingdoms; and love for those Kingdoms of the Fourth and Fifth Dimensions. For are you all not filled with Omni-essence? Do you not all polarize, and contain the Laws of Rhythm and Correspondence within you? Are you not all ONE of the same source? The One Omni-essence?

Yes, you are all, in varying degrees, of that Rhythm and that Law of Descent and Ascent. But open your hearts, stewards of the plan! For this time comes to increase your awareness and allow your service to come forward. Questions?

Question: "As our service does come forward through the opening of our hearts, which seems as if it is on a path of neutrality and a path of love, who among us are brought into contact with this vibration?"

Even those who hear these words are made aware of that Kingdom of Vibration. Even those who read these words will be affected by the vibrations surrounding them. For these vibrations are words from another Kingdom. And, yet, is this not a familiar Kingdom? Another Kingdom—which has and always will exist side by side?

Question: "Yes, this is so. This next question may seem irrelevant, but it has been my observation that the beloved beings whom we call our pets, for whom we develop close attachments—do these beings, too, move on in consciousness and become our chelas in the future?"

Some of them are brought here to help adjust and open the energy of vibration, for they have chosen simple lives of service to help at this critical Time of Awakening and Choice. However, some—ready at their own particular time—continue on the path of evolution, riding the pendulum of Sattva.

Unless there are further questions, I shall take my leave.

"There are no further questions, Holy Brother. I thank you for your radiance and your guidance."

I thank you for your *response-ability*. Always carry within your hearts the Violet Flame.

Almighty I AM Violet Flame. Come forth, and heal and soothe the minds of men. Hitaka!

5

The Work of a Master

Personal Instruction from Saint Germain

BELOVED CHELAS, I AM SAINT GERMAIN; AND I REQUEST YOUR PERMISSION TO COME FORWARD.

"Dear Saint Germain, please come forward."

The work upon the Earth Plane and Planet, as we have seen through your dispensation of material, has reached a portion of completion. Some among the masses have heard parts of that message and are ready to receive that refreshing drink. The portion of this message known as Prophecy will open ears and eyes to that deeper water or river.

It is time for us to step forward, and to think and plot our course, for the coming time is critical. During the next six to eight years, which will complete the planetary time known as Transition, decisions and choices will be made that plot the course. And the hands of humanity will hold the end result.

We have known for some time that humanity has stood upon the precipice of nuclear war, and cataclysmic Earth Changes. Did you know that earlier in this century your planet was barely missed by an asteroid? The work of the Hierarchy prevented this impact from happening. Those of that realm have held back the events leading to the great purification by fire. They know this event is not in the plan of the best and highest good of humanity. It is better that humanity understands and is able to plot that course itself. Humanity, in the form of collective consciousness or collective consensus, is then able to make that choice.

Those who work in that inner circle have laid down many plans, for as you know—as I have stated before—your governments are held by a handful of powerful men, and these powerful men hold only money. Mankind—humanity at large—vests money with power. Do you understand what gives these men their ability to control and manipulate your world economies and your societies? Humanity must evolve to a place where it understands that money and greed can't control mankind any longer. The breath of the spirit—sparked within the heart through the divinity of men and women—shall accomplish this understanding.

For more information and study topics on *The Work of a Master*, see Appendix E, page 191.

And, when one decides to Master that force within the heart, ... will we see an awakening—a time when a new, ever-present vibration and energy come to the planet?

Now is the time to avert our focus and energy from the things that don't work, from the old and tired, and from what we cannot change. Instead, focus on what we can change: things we can control and Master.

And what would that be, Dear students and chelas? Our focus and attention is on that spark in the heart, that mighty Monad or Jiva. We have taught this concept, and you have learned it through the many teachings of the Mastery Courses. It's time for us to put our attention on this individualized energy of the soul, which can be developed.

For the gathering, that mass rapture, and that mass Ascension, a group of people have focused their attentions on the development of the individual, melding mankind and spirituality into the collective will. The forces—which can hold back the fire of purification, the winds of ceaseless change, and those earthquakes and sinking lands—are contained in this collective will. Only that collective force of the "intentional spirit of will" can save humanity.

We have spoken before of the choice that is now in the hands of those who are willing to see, who are willing to hear, and who are willing to act. Dear ones, make the choice to serve that desire, that spark in the heart.

Is it as simple as following the heart's desire? Yes, it is as simple as that. And that degree of awakening is as simple as making a choice.

But let us move one step further, beyond desire, into the causeless cause, where the eyes shed no more tears and the heart has sufficiently bled upon your feet. This is the chela or student who has emptied his vessel. But is the vessel weakened? No I say. The vessel—one that won't bend in the winds of change and will hold the waters through the tempest of a storm—is now strengthened and ready to serve.

I ask you now, Dear ones, to move this work forward, to work upon all the attributes, and to have courage. The times ahead will require many of you to make difficult choices. You may lose friendships and family members. Your Brother may confront you and say to you, "I do not understand," and yet, you do. You understand, and you carry this work forward with loving hands and loving hearts.

Dear Sananda has always instructed you to "send this message to the earth with love." Never engage in disharmony or discord as you carry this work forward. In regard to those who are not yet willing to hear, simply plant the seed, and then move forward. Should you become angry or emotional with those who slap you or spit in your face, you must simply love them and understand that to back away is an act of courage and strength. I would also encourage you, Dear chelas, not to tolerate this type of behavior repeatedly. However, if the other is not ready, or has not developed an understanding, it is important for you to back away. For, just as you couldn't feed a child's small body a rich feast, some people aren't ready to digest your ideas. As you carry this work forward, you'll encounter those who are like small children, babies, and infants. Give them what they can to assimilate.

Know, too, that the work of the Prophet is never congratulated. Know, too, that the Prophet himself is never loved in his or her homeland. But always remember. The work that you carry forward through these prophecies paves the pathway for a time to come, a Time of Peace and a Time of Grace.

You must hold that energetic pattern of peace and grace in all you carry forward. You are the servants of the devoted Christ; you are the servants of the ONE; you represent the New World, that New Time to come. Many Prophets have foretold the New Age. You are the embodiment of this message and must carry it forward.

Love one another, as your dear Brother has stated; and if you have trouble forgiving someone, I would instruct you to spend time away, in silence, until you come to a place of Forgiveness.

Understand that those who fear are not afraid of a world that is ending; rather, they fear the birth of the world to come—the Age of Cooperation, the Age of United Sisterhood and Brotherhood. For is this template something they haven't experienced?

We encourage you, Dear ones, to carry the torch for this dawning age. Lead through your demonstration. Forgive those who have injured you. Simply transmute. Turn your back, walk your path, carry your message forward, and do not engage.

Those who come forward, who choose to walk the path of peace with you, shall be gathered unto you, and they shall be as your Brothers and Sisters. This will be apparent by the lives they lead.

It is important to carry a Vibration of Harmony at all times, in your office environment, in your homes, and among your families. Reason with your children. Sit them down and honor that Divine Oneship within their own beings, honor the flame within their hearts, that Monad or Jiva you all share. Come to the understanding that you all live together as one family, and then seek resolution through the Laws of Cooperation.

As our beloved Brothers and Sisters have stated in the Twelve Jurisdictions, your harmonies [spiritual growth] cause troubles in the home. Therefore, find the rhythm of harmonies I discussed; find the rhythm of harmonies I taught to you as Sattva. This doctrine will allow the vibration to enter your business, your home, and your family. During this time, instruct all those who work with you to increase their harmony, and therefore, their abundance.

Dear ones, we have not been permitted yet to discuss the catastrophic prophecies that will commence their dispensation in several months. [Editor's Note: The Six-Map Scenario.] However, we have been encouraged to discuss the Prophecies of Peace and Grace in those times to come. I have relayed to you information about your own physiologies and your own bodies. At this time, many of you have been practicing the healing of the body and the release of energy through the adjustment of the Human Aura. It is important to disseminate this information at the local and the global levels to initiate Cellular Awakening. These spiritual practices then create energy fields around the human body. Energy fields open the third eye of the practitioners, allowing them to see this electrical force.

This is part of the dispensation, so that many people will begin to understand that one life force permeates all beings. They will see this life force around the human form and other life forms such as plants, animals, and even those of the Mineral Kingdom. This awakening is dispensed at this time to promote a greater sensitivity to and an understanding of all life forms. The majority of humanity doesn't comprehend that all life is connected as ONE—that this life force permeates all things and all beings.

Therefore, for the opening of the third eye, I would suggest the scents of sandalwood and jasmine, as they are both very soothing.

During this Time of Transition, many people will notice a high-pitched ringing in their ears, sometimes accompanied by a slight headache. This is a result of the following two things: the spiritual accelerations happening at this time, and the pollution that permeates the environment and your waters. The accelerations are somewhat hard on the body because they cause it to expel certain toxins.

I would instruct you, Dear ones, to use the vibration emanating from citrus fruit to purify your waters. Also, purify [cleanse] your air with the scents of honeysuckle, citrus, and orange blossom. It is important that you use the energies within the body to help bring about a purification of the environment. [Editor's Note: This is a reference to Free Energy Techniques and Energy Field Balancing.]

When you notice an area that needs a cleansing or a purification, simply gather your energies as you have been instructed: hold your hand over your heart, and direct the energies through the palm of your right hand to that area. It is always best to visualize Gold and green lights streaming from your body.

During this Time of Acceleration, many of your elder Brothers and Sisters will assist you in bringing this kind of healing to the planet. Just as you have learned to use certain energy work to assist in the healing of your Brothers and Sisters [See Appendix A], you can also use it in the air or on a group of trees. You can use it over a landfill to adjust the energy and bring forth balance. What greater acts of the heart, which serve all so selflessly, could come forward at this time?

In regard to the people you trained—those who can adjust the energy of others and those who have attained a balanced state of optimum health and Mastery—ask those persons to come forward and perform these same selfless acts of healing our planet. For the time is critical, particularly in those areas of the Golden City Vortices. It is important now to carry forward these energetic alignments by serving as purifiers of the environment, just as you have served each other through the path of the healer. As you know, the Prophet only paves the pathway for the priest.

I ask you, therefore, to gather in ceremony to gain strength. You must stay committed to your choice for the improvement of humanity. I ask for your involvement at the social levels. I ask for your involvement in health care and in your schools. Develop an organization that educates people about this type of healing. See to it that people are empowered at the grass-roots level to understand the healing power that lies latent within their own physiologies.

This is the work of a Master.

See that this work is accelerated in the schools so that the children to come, and the generations to follow, are educated from the heart. See that they are first taught the Laws of Honor and Intent. Get involved at that level, Dear ones.

This is the work of a Master.

In this Tme of Change, it is important to be involved—not only with those of, shall we say, the New Age, but with those who do not understand. Bring them this understanding in gentle ways. Bring them this understanding in ways they can accept and assimilate, as with that small child who drinks milk at the feast.

There is much work for you to do. I would ask you to dispense all materials at this time. As I have stated before, I will set up an electronic vibration to bring forward the money and the abundance that is necessary to fulfill this leg of your journey.

I AM America is to become a clearinghouse for the New Humanity. It is important to dispense material that opens the eyes and ears of humanity to alternative forms of healing and education. As I have stated, the work of those who toil tirelessly behind the scenes is usually the work that achieves the greatest result. So do not worry about gaining attention. Do not worry about achieving recognition. Instead, tend the seeds you plant: water, fertilize, and nurture them so they may grow, until a New Time and a new life spring forward.

These are perilous times indeed. It's important that you carry forward the plan—the plan that focuses energy on the highest and best use of humanity and the plan that best serves humanity. So be it.

6

No Need for Change?

A Shamballa Message from Saint Germain, Sananda, Kuan Yin, and Mother Mary

GREETINGS MY BELOVED CHELAS, I AM SAINT GERMAIN, AND I STREAM FORTH ON THAT MIGHTY VIOLET RAY OF MERCY AND FORGIVENESS.

As usual Dear hearts, I request permission to come forward.

"Please Dear one, come forward."

As you well know, Dear ones, this is the Time of Shamballa, a great Time of Feasting, and a Time of Celebrating the divinity of all life, all Omni-essence. During this time, we would like to bring a message for you to share with all of humanity. A message from the Great White Brotherhoods and the Sisterhoods of Light, which have a timing and an intent to inspire the many who have opened their eyes and their ears.

There is a Time of Change that is coming to the earth. There is also a Time of Change that is coming among humanity. You have studied that the human and the earth are related as ONE. You've studied this through electromagnetics, and now you are beginning to understand that even in the social structures and in the thinking of the individual all of these components fit together as one large body, which composes the Omni-essence, the universal life.

Not one of these is dissociated from the other. For all are connected in that Mighty One-ship. All are connected in that Mighty ONE that expresses all of life.

Dear ones, many among humanity ask the question, "What is the purpose of Prophecy?" And if these changes do not happen, "then what?" We feel it is important to relay this message to those who are ready to hear, those who are ready to see, and to those who are ready to take an action that serves the greater good, that greater ONE. It is our hope that those who are now ready will serve their Brothers and their Sisters, and will serve the planet in whatever form that may help at this time. However, a great change is coming. And it is important that you be prepared!

If these changes do not happen, what type of a world would we live in [the future]? Let me assure you, Dear ones, it would be a world that you would not recognize. However, let me

---

For more information and study topics on *No Need for Change?*, see Appendix F, page 199.

remind you of the world that you *would* live in if it were *not necessary* for these changes to happen.

Many Prophets have come before you and many Prophets will come after you. Each Prophet speaks in a [certain] tongue, and carries a vibration which is necessary to open the eyes and ears of those that they serve. Some of the prophecies that have been dispensed, shall we say, through other eyes and ears, by members of this spiritual hierarchy, are those who speak of the ending of this earth, or the beginning of a One-World Government.

Should this happen, let me assure you, Dear ones, that you would be much happier living in that Time of Change! [Earth Changes] For the alien governments, and their technologies, will take over the earth at large. And this planet becomes again, a slave planet! All life comes through genetic mutations which serve the consciousness of this government.

However, it has also been our intent and our service to bring forward material to inspire leadership among the masses, and to re-instill the spark of freedom so some will recognize the divinity within all. And through these [types of] choices, the leaders rise among all of you and take this message to the world and share it among all—divinity is celebrated first! Now, there are those who understand the true spiritual nature of humanity, and the true spiritual nature of this work.

If these changes [Earth Changes] were not necessary, let me tell you about the type of world you would live in. First, let us Start with the family structures. Within the family, breakdown between husband and wife never happens. And marriages are perfect unions—ones not touched or shattered by separation or conflict. Marriages foster the growth of children who are brought into this world. Marriages [parents] are productive and lead children into literature, the arts and, the understanding of foreign languages. Parents serve children to become world leaders and group servers. Parents understand their role as a contribution to the greater ONE, live with self-acceptance, and are employed at all times to ensure the necessary growth and stability of their families.

Let me explain. The economies that would exist if Earth Changes were *not necessary* would be balanced economies throughout the world. Those [economies] share openly with the fruits of one another, and do not trade through inflated coins or printed money, but trade with natural goods. This is known as a *true state economy*—one that never becomes inflated and one that is based on what it produces.

Few middle men would exist in these economies and an agrarian society—with a low impact on the environment—would flourish. No longer would we see the necessity for petrochemicals polluting your planet. Alternative energy supplies would be allowed, because greed would be wiped off your planet!

This is the type of economy that would exist, an economy that allows all humans to express their inborn divine stature to live without degradation. It is an economy without welfare. What would be the need? All would share so openly; all would give compassionately and from their hearts.

It would be an economy without useless taxation. It would be an economy of those who [voluntarily] pay the taxes needed to support municipalities to bring forward and flourish the arts, literature, music, and all else that would enhance the lifestyle of the citizens of the republic.

Let us talk about the social conditions of a society where the experience of Earth Changes is not necessary. This society is without crime or deviant behavior. All express according to the Oneness and the unity of the group, *and* the Oneness and the unity of their hearts. How can you separate the two when each and every one has been brought up with a sense of love and cooperation.

The spark of competitiveness is wiped forever from the face of this society. The spark and the ember of Brotherhood and Sisterhood are tended and fed. The measurement of men and women, families and societies, come not through the amount of money one holds in a bank account, but through the integrity and the principles that they uphold and represent. Governments are reflected through these principles; based on the Laws of Harmony and Cooperation, first. Special interests are no longer allowed, for what would be the point? All serve the harmony and the cooperation of that mighty greater good.

A police force would rarely be needed. Would there be criminals? Hardly not! And the prison system would not exist.

Open libraries and schools flourish, and are not limited [segregated] to one age group. All participate *freely* in this Open Society. For wiping away the ignorance of the masses is the total focus of a society that lives on the basis of cooperation and harmony.

Communication among many different peoples comes openly and freely, as foreign languages are encouraged among all. Although humanity will share a universal tongue that communicates with the ONE consciousness of all, most people will speak five to six different languages. And they [languages] would be understood and celebrated, for language is the key to the growth of the human. This society honors languages and understands that through sound each intonation and syllable carries forth the thrust of DNA.

Health systems will not be filled with the atrocities of greed. These health systems come forward in a holistic manner based first on reason, and second on common sense. Virtually all disease that would come to this society would be naturally wiped away. For *balance* is the first principle that all practice, not only in their dietary standard, but in their mind and in their thinking.

This is a society without a need for Earth Change.

And now, let us talk about the environment. This is an environment without pollution. This is an environment without the threat of nuclear destruction. This is an environment that sings sweetly and naturally to its inhabitants and a communication is occurring at all times between nature and humanity. The Elemental and Deva Kingdom is no longer threatened, and they come forward to give instruction for that which will serve the great crops of nuts, fruits, and grains. They will give of themselves naturally to feed humanity. Starvation is wiped away forever, and no longer will the famines of earth be allowed to exist.

These are civilizations without the need for Earth Change.

These are civilizations that have learned to live in balance and harmony. These are civilizations that live in grace on the back of the Earth Mother. Why would there be a need to remove even one? These are civilizations that realize their destiny is in the heart of divinity. This is the excellence that the Great White Brotherhood and Sisterhood [purposely] inspire humanity to become and offer. Live and breathe the Law of the Best and Highest Good and put each foot forward in that law!

This is a society without the need for catastrophic change; balance and harmony reign supreme.

And so Dear ones, if I need go further, please instruct me! But those of you with eyes and ears open may now measure through your own sense of reason.

Do your societies, do your governments, do your schools reflect the perfection that I have portrayed for you? Are they to this caliber? Are they [evolved] to a place that needs *no* change? If so, then their energy is open and flowing in balance. Look today at each of the structures in which you participate. Look today and ask yourself [these questions]. The answers are within your heart.

Today, most families live separated from one another. Children are raised by the Laws of the Streets! Today, the schools have lost the ability to educate; for most schools seek the Law of Money first.

Your medical and your political systems, need I say more? And your environment for the past thirty years has been in grave danger and you say, "Everything is fine...Why should we have a change?"

Perhaps the change should come first in the heart.

Awaken to the conditions that exist outside of your own home.

Understand the needless suffering that occurs on this planet because of the thirst for greed and power. When these two ignorances are wiped from the planet, then and only then, can this great New Age—a New Age of Utopia—be built. It is the plan of the [Spiritual] Hierarchy that serve the greater plan and the heart of humanity, that this Utopia comes forward! We remind you of the perfection you hold, the perfection of what you can be, and the perfection that the future holds. A Time of Grace, indeed, will come—a time that will be an Age of Peaceful Cooperation.

However, this Age of Peace is not just a Prophecy! It is an age that comes forward through your willing hands, and you must take it into your being; live it, breathe it, and then demonstrate it. That is why we have spent so much time with you, Dear ones. We strive to raise your vibrations, work with you daily through discourse, and help you understand another way of being. You call this a, "Revolution of Consciousness." We call this *the Divine Spark* of your being!

Let this perfection blaze forward in all that you do, and this New Year becomes a new day! Take this New Year to become a new day for a Time of Change. Do you see now, the necessity for change? Again, you have a choice: will these changes be cataclysmic or hold consciousness? Now is the time to go forward and be the World Servers that you truly say that you are.

Share the message of peace, and demonstrate the peace in your own hearts.

Share the peace with your families.

Share the peace with your neighbors, and extend it into your communities and into all of your daily affairs.

Let this peace be decreed, which you profess.

Let peace reign supreme. Questions?

"There are no questions."

(Now he is backing away from the lectern, and Sananda is coming forward.)

Dear Brothers and Sisters of the Golden Flame. I AM Sananda, and I request permission to come forward.

"Please Dear one, come forward."

This project of change, which is known as transition, is one where again you have wondered, "What is the purpose?" What would be the meaning of such a catastrophic change to herald in a day of peace? Let me assure you, Dear ones, of my heart; the intention of our service is at all times to foster the love within you and the love without.

The Time of Collective Cooperation and of Collective Peace will come only through hearts that truly wish to serve. Over and over again, we have spoken of service to humanity, and now it is time that each and every one of you looks within your own heart and asks of yourself, "Can I truly serve my Brother? Can I truly serve my Sister?" The service of the heart must be the first condition of moving into the Age of Cooperation. It is important that you begin to observe and understand that you are all ONE. There are very few differences among you.

Look at your Brother, look at your Sister, and recognize that he or she has traveled the path of many embodiments, that he or she, too, has had many incarnations and has traveled the path like you, lifetime after lifetime—the joys, the sorrows, the wins, the losses. All of these things your Brother has experienced too. How would he be any different from you? Hardly could he! And yet, why would you perceive such a difference among you, and your Brother and your Sister?

Humanity has worried much over the differences that they experience. But now it is time to come and celebrate unity for an Age of Cooperation to come forward. The unity and the Oneness of consciousness must be celebrated within the heart. Realize first the Divine Spark that *all* share and *all* are of.

I have come forward in sponsorship of this transition to allow a consciousness of the ONE, and to allow a consciousness of divinity to spark itself among humanity so that an Age of Cooperation will never again leave this planet. When I came forward in this sponsorship, first, I celebrated and realized the Oneness that I shared with my beloved Brother, El Morya; with my beloved Brother, Saint Germain; with my Sisters Portia and Mary; with my beloved Kuan Yin. How could there be a difference among us if we were to move forward and collectively serve that greater ONE?

Do you argue over your differences? Do not allow differences to stop you from your movement into *ONE consciousness*. This is a Time of Peace and Grace. Celebrate, sup, and feast with all. So be it.

(He is backing away, and now Mary and Kuan Yin come forward.)

GREETINGS AND SALUTATIONS, WE MERGE OUR ENERGIES AS ONE, FOR WE REPRESENT A QUALITY OF THE DIVINE MOTHER.

We ask permission to come forward.

"Please beloveds, come forward."

This is a celebration and a time of honoring all energies as ONE. We have held Soleteta—the Divine Feminine—to come forward. Yet we remind you, Dear ones, that it is the feminine within and *not* feminism. It is the feminine [energy] that comes forward in service to help and assist the masculine. The masculine energy protects and assists the feminine. Both of these energies, together within the individual, serve the Age of Cooperation. It is [through] the masculine and the feminine energies, which come forward in the totality of balance, that beat the heart with the perfection of cooperation.

Live with balance, Dear ones. Live with the balance of your masculine and feminine energies serving that greater ONE. Celebrate this Oneness you share—that is the balance of your energies. Honor your feminine, and honor your masculine. Let them come forward and merge as ONE in the glory of the Christ, for it is through the Christ that you can see one another in the Oneness that you share. It is the glory of the Christ that breaks all barriers and perfects the bodies [physical and light bodies] upon the Earth Plane and Planet. Through the marriage of your energies, you will become readied for a dimensional leap to a new understanding of cooperation and unity.

Come together, Dear ones, in the marriage of your energies; come together in the spirit of cooperation; come together in the spirit of the Christ, I AM.

(Saint Germain is now coming forward.)

Dear chelas, as usual, if there are any questions, I would be willing to address these now.

Question: "In conceiving of the perfect world, it would seem that the genetic qualities of cooperation and harmony also follow hand-in-hand with common sense. It would seem that our world goes through turmoil and discomfort through a lack of practicality. Will you please elaborate?"

It is time that we celebrate an Age of Reason. It is time that we allow consciousness to be consumed first by mighty common sense! It is time for each of the senses to become alive and aware, but *disciplined.* You are a society experiencing, shall we say, great birth pains! And with these birth pains the many fields of auras are experiencing explosions. Many are unable to grip expanded sensibility.

Let me assure you, Dear ones, it is also a Time of Discipline. First, find discipline within. For is discipline not another form of cooperation? Then check all words that cross your tongue. Check all words that cross your mind and all thoughts that will not serve your moving forward with the focus of Brotherly Love.

NO NEED FOR CHANGE?

The time that is coming is a Time of Perfection! This perfection will only be achieved through the weaving of Brothers and Sisters through the Vibration of Love. Beloved Mother Mary has often spoken of the Divine Cloak that covers all of you. It is a cloak woven in the spirit of cooperation, not in competition!

This, of course, is a difficult idea because so many humans have just recently risen out of the animal state. However, it is the choice of those who listen; it is the choice of those who see this message and rise out of their animal state, and take upon them that mantle of consciousness, a mighty common sense! Discipline is the only answer at this time. And the only hope for our perfected utopia will come when humanity embraces discipline.

The embracing of these concepts will allow humanity to experience the true freedom for which it was created. It is the embracing of discipline through which humanity will embrace freedom.

Question: "Is this discipline not a personal choice?"

At this moment, Dear ones, discipline is a necessity for the survival of the human race. The work we have brought forward has always been presented through the medium of choice. However, have you not noted the many changes now occurring on your planet: wars, famine, tremendous crime, and the breakdown of your families? And some of those still ask, "Why is such a change necessary? Why, would we even want to have the Earth Changes Prophecies to come to full fruition?"

Perhaps now's the time (humanity) addresses the fear it holds in its heart—not only the fear of change but the fear of the death of the physical body. I have known many before me who have gladly laid their lives down for the principle of freedom and the principle of perfection! However, since we have sent this message to the earth with love, we have presented to those members of humanity that if the ember of divinity could be fanned within the heart, perhaps there would be those who would serve the nobler cause. Perhaps there would be those who would come forward and disallow the state of competitiveness within their being. Perhaps there would be those who would allow the spirit of cooperation, Brotherhood and Sisterhood, that of the unity of *One Family*.

It is necessary that humanity hears this message!

It is necessary that all practice it.

It is necessary that you begin to live it. How else will you achieve the discipline but by practice?

As you have said, "practice makes permanent." Is now not the time for an Age of Grace to become a permanent age, the permanent factor by which this beloved Terra is known? As you have known, beloved Terra has never held the position of a sacred planet. However, it is known as a servile planet—a planet that offers a service, a place where many throughout the universe and the galaxy could call home. Terra, much like the destiny of the United States, has been the cradle of many members of [intergalactic] races, societies, and religious sects who no longer had a home where they could freely practice and speak their beliefs. The United States and America has also been known as this type of *melting pot.*

The *entire* planet of Terra is a melting pot. Yet, when we allow a special interest to overcome, be that special-interest greed or competitiveness, we are no longer the Vibration of a Melting Pot. And what would happen? Then naturally, all patterns that have set up [created] this planet fall, one upon the other. Why do you question change? Balance must be restored.

Answer: "This is understood. When we speak of discipline, we speak of choice. And at some time in the future I would ask that you elaborate upon a day of discipline."

First, discipline comes through the way *you see.* Discipline comes through the way that *you hear.* When beloved Brother Iamblicus delivered the Prophecy "before the eyes can see, they must be incapable of tears..." He was teaching the greatest of all disciplines. It is time that you discipline your emotional responses. "Before the ears can hear, they must have lost their sensitiveness."

The motivation of competition comes toward you as an energy—a rush or a blast—you must not react to this with *more* competition! Simply *allow* the [message to come] through that Mighty Law of Cooperation. "Before the voice can speak in the presence of the Masters, it must have lost the power to wound."

When we speak injurious words toward Brothers and Sisters, we utter energy forms. They [energy forms] take on a life within themselves, and attach themselves energetically as you have directed that word and that thought. Oh, if humanity only knew the power of the words it speaks. That is why we have spent so much time with you through the rhythmic patterns of decreeing, through the rhythmic patterns of prayer. It is important for you to understand, my Dearest ones, how important the Violet Flame is at this time. For you are calling forward through voice and sound vibration that Mighty Law of Perfection. These words do not injure; these words heal.

A Time of Healing comes to the planet. But the healing must be carried in your hands, in your ears, and in your words. During this Time of Healing, bring yourself forward in service by the laying of hands. Don't forget to lay your words carefully, too—and your thoughts: lay them so carefully. All that comes from the center of your divinity empowers cooperation. So be it!

I AM a being of Violet Fire!
I AM the purity cooperation desires!

So be it, Dear ones. Let us now raise our Cups in celebration of the times to come. Let us now raise our Cups to the love we are and share. Hitaka!

7

Weaving the New Web

Saint Germain with Two Students

GREETINGS MY BELOVED CHELAS, I AM SAINT GERMAIN, AND I REQUEST PERMISSION TO COME FORWARD.

[Both host and students respond] "Please, Dear one, come forward."

Greetings in that Mighty Christ, I AM. Dear hearts, it is with much pleasure that I bring this discourse to you; for we have found that on the Earth Plane and Planet the New Time arrives, a New Time for the activation of the Golden Cities of light and sound.

For you see, Dear ones, these Golden Cities will birth the planet into its new state—into that state known as Unana—which is the activated Christ. Dear ones, facing you is a Time of tremendous Earth Change, but also a time that births a New Millennium of light and sound; a time when we will see many changes not only on the earth herself, but *within* the earth.

Her whole crystalline structure is taking a new form, and she shall occupy that shining light throughout the New Universe. This is a Time of Preparation, a time when we'll prepare the Cup, that Holy Grail, for the light shines on in Mighty Magnificent Consummation!

Dear ones, at this time we ask you to consider that the earth's grids are also changing. The belt of Golden light, which swept around the planet in the early part of this century, is also transforming. We have found a collective census of light workers who have held this light in constant consciousness. We can now remove this band of light to allow the activations of these planetary cities. The Golden Cities are part of the Prophecy that is brought for change; for change comes not only in the heart and in the mind, but change must also be an *active cause.* And today, we ask you for your service and unite you with this active cause.

Each of the Golden Cities will be activated in a sequence. And as you already know, it is that Golden City of Gobean which was activated almost 14 years ago. And now, stalwart light workers have come forward, chelas and students of that Mighty I AM, to carry that Cup of Service throughout the world!

For more information and study topics on *Weaving the New Web,* see Appendix G, page 205.

The second Golden City that we have asked for in the activation process is Malton, which holds constant fruition for mankind, humanity, and her people—that they may attain and complete certain goals held in the mind.

The third city is Wahanee. This is where I serve, arching energy to beloved Portia who serves in that Seventh City in Canada, known as Eabra. It is there that freedom shall be served as that *cause on high*. And also, the third activation is most important. And we ask for [Wahanee] to be completed as soon as possible. However, Dear ones, if this is impossible, we ask you to hold ceremony at the apex center of Gobean and arch energy over to the Golden City of Wahanee.

The fourth Golden City that we would like to see activated is Shalahah—it holds continuous consciousness of abundance and healing for mankind. This is the Golden City served by Master Sananda.

The fifth Golden City called into action is Klehma, held by the continuous light of beloved Serapis Bey. It is this city that holds the continuous consciousness for Ascension of humanity at this time. It is also the city that marries the energies of east and west, and both may meet in one continuous consciousness.

Dear ones, there are specifics that I would like to share regarding *ceremonial activations* of Golden Cities. As you have known in the past, we have taught that it is the principle of sacrifice that brings about any activation. However, in this New Time, we would like to teach that it is discipline and hard labor that brings about activation. We do not see this work as a sacrifice. And it is our intent and our hope for you, that you do not see this work as a sacrifice. However, you and many others realize the hard labor and the discipline it takes to bring this type of work into action.

We have always taught that all things come forward in the Mighty Three of Thought, Feeling, and Action, and you know, as well as we have taught, that [the end result of] action brings a noble cause. And from that noble cause, is thus the goal achieved? Is then focus realized? To bring about this focus into manifestation, all must work with discipline and hard labor. And so we ask, Dear ones that before the activations of Golden Cities occur, that ceremonies are performed on two points of the *Northern Door*. For Northern Door locations [geophysically] birth the New Humanity! These locations also contain a continuous consciousness that is a substance throughout the entire Vortex. [The Golden Cities] allow a leap in consciousness, shall we say, a *Star seed consciousness*. We ask you to locate these two [Northern Door] points at will, sensing first through your geophysical or geo-sensitive capabilities. Or, I would also be willing to give you these [Northern Door] locations as we have pointed out the width and circumference of Golden City Vortices and their action.

These two points are important [to locate and visit] so that the intent of hard labor and discipline is held by all chelas and all disciples of this work. [These disciples] will understand that discipline and hard work will bring forward this mighty action.

The time that comes to the Earth Plane and Planet is a glorious time, Dear ones. A time when new plants and birds, new animals, and yes, indeed, you too, shall receive a New Body. This New Body we have spoken of as the *Eighth Body of Consciousness*, aligns to the Light Ray vibrations of aquamarine and Gold [light]. This light body holds in continuous consciousness energies for transfiguration. And, as I have stated before, this light will bring about the transfiguration of the consciousness to prepare for the times to come. For this reason [alone], it is important to reside in Golden Cities.

We have long asked for many of the students and chelas to come forward and live in Golden Cities. However, very few have taken this call seriously. But those who have come realize the great benefit of living in the *lighted stance*. We have prepared humanity for eon upon eon, readying them for this time; for you see, Dear ones, we've spoken of *Time Compaction*—when time will slow down and compact, then slow down and compact again. These are known as *Cosmic Wave Motions*. A Cosmic Wave Motion readies the earth for the birth of her New [light] Body, known as *Freedom Star*.

This New Galaxy that she shall be birthed into is known as Unana. She [the earth] will travel through a crack in the universe that you now know as a *black hole*. This is a Time of Dimensional Leaping and this type of movement is essential. Conventional time-keeping systems [that you have known] will no longer be used. These perceptions will be changed!

Many Brothers and Sisters who come from other galaxies are [present] on earth at this time to experience, or shall we say, *ride along* on the back of this movement as the earth prepares to enter into that *Lighted Shaft of Consciousness*, birthing all into a New Time, place, and a New Beginning.

Many upon the Earth Plane and Planet sense this as a time of hopelessness and despair. However, as you well know, it is the strongest of steel that must go through the fiery furnace. And this furnace, as we all know, is a Time of Testing, a Time of Initiation, a Time of Hard Work, and a Time of Discipline.

But not one of these labors will be lost, for each one of these labors prepares you for this time!

Embodiment after embodiment has also prepared you for this time, for this is a monumental time when the earth itself leaps in consciousness. The Earth Plane and Planet has experienced these dimensional leaps many other times. However, the current history does not record them. It is important to understand this, and how important and monumental this occasion is. It is also important and monumental that each one of the Golden Cities is properly prepared [accessed by chelas and students] for this monumental leap in consciousness.

Through entering the Star—the center of each Golden City Vortex—we ask you to [ceremonially] activate all Golden Cities. For the apex carries the focal point of energies. Within a twenty-mile radius of the apex are the locations where your Brothers and Sisters of this Great Lodge hope some day to manifest, and to [physically] bring forward their *teachings in action.* Until that date, Dear ones, it is important to prepare these places to assure that they are ready for this great time, this leap in cosmic consciousness.

Are there questions?

Question: "Yes, beloved Saint Germain, there are questions. We have come in conscious awareness to offer ourselves as pillars of light to activate the Golden Cities as you have requested. And we wish to honor the instructions that you are giving about how to go about in the activations. You have mentioned a sequence, first of Gobean, second of Malton, and third of Wahanee. At this time, there are students in the state of Colorado who have come forth and offered this June 9th or 10th, something to that effect, to activate the Golden City of Klehma, making it the third. Is this acceptable, or do you prefer that we wait on that and do Wahanee as you had requested being the third, and then Shalahah, as the fourth and then Klehma? Because I am here to offer service in the way that would be best for all, and I don't care which one it is, but I just want to do it correctly."

As you know, Dear one, all is in within that limit of free will and how well we know this upon that Plane of consciousness occupied by the human. Free will adjusts all things, and what we've laid down in terms of activation is the most perfect and serves that greater good. However, we must not tarry in this work; we must work with what has been given to us.

Do you remember that phrase, "turning a lemon into lemonade?" Now's the time to move forward with the work at hand—with the plow in our hand and the field in front of us. This is a time, Dear one, when we must work with what is before us. If we were to wait for the most perfect circumstance, we would wait forever and a day!

Dear ones, work with what is presented to you; work in that Law of the Best and the Highest Good. Work, also, with a plan of ease. When things fall in front of you, one step at a time, follow that plan! Like each rock placed in front of you as you cross a brook of rushing water, you must navigate your next step.

We ask you to consider this on the path of service. If you feel discomfort or resistance, settle back and allow the laws to play out. Do you want to enter into the storms of unreason? We ask you, Dear ones, that if activation [a ceremonial activation] of a Golden City becomes filled with discomfort and disharmonies, retreat to the apex of Gobean, which was activated years ago by another being of light who understood this seed of work. Then, it is important, Dear ones, for you to *arch* the energies

Do you remember the lesson I gave you of *source and destination*? Use the center of Gobean as your source, for you can project those energies to activate another Golden City. Use again, the same formula: seven devoted chelas, dedicated to this work, stating their intent in ceremony. As you have been taught, and as you know, *the thought* creates. You know too, that there can be another group centered in the apex of Wahanee or Malton. These cities at this time seem to be more difficult for one to access and activate.

Pick a time you may hold together; pick that time to hold your thought in the collective. And there, activation too, can occur. Dear ones, it is important to keep harmony at all times and avoid the bite within your pocketbook. It is important that abundance and prosperity stream in, through, and around all of your [ceremonial] work. If you don't have enough money to go around, it is important to understand that the timing isn't right. Or perhaps [it is better] to call that Mighty Law in to action and ask that Mighty I AM Presence to bring forward all that you need and all that you would require.

Dear ones, I bring this teaching in hope that you will understand that activation can also occur without your physical presence in a geophysical location. However, it is important that you hold the *immaculate concept* as beloved Mary has taught. Those who have come to be gathered in ceremony and ritual at the Golden City of Klehma are called. This is their duty and this is their service—an agreement many of them have made prior to this embodiment. This must be understood. [Those who have come to celebrate] have aligned with the collective will and that vehicle of choice; they now *choose* to bring forward this active service.

Dear ones, worry not if you get off schedule. All has been laid down in the most perfect of plans. However, as we all well know, at times mankind is not receptive to the plans of God. It is, however, important at this time that we allow the Divine Intercession of free will. In the understanding of the Law of Opposites, each of these cities can be activated in such a manner that will circumvent certain Earth Changes. Each of these Golden Cities can be activated in such a manner that will bring a balance to the earth, the beloved planet.

Dear ones, understand that at this time all will be laid down in front of you much like those stones over the rushing brook. Worry not if activation comes out of sequence. My only request is that we hold the focus first on the United States and carry the Freedom Flame, onward through Canada. We shall give you further instructions on how to carry this Flame of Freedom, which will sweep from the South to the North Pole, covering all of America. America's destiny is to hold the focus of this Mighty Cup of conscious light! This service will travel from the heart of her lands to other lands of the world, and it will touch the hearts of many.

This is the intention; for America is not only the return of many of those peoples who graced the planet once known as Atlantean, but many Lemurians have returned in physical form [embodiment] to bring about a final service for the beloved planet. Many have returned at this specific time, so they can birth this planet into this New Dimension of Light and Sound.

While it is a dimension of planetary Ascension, creation will continue. For you know, Dear ones, you are created in that mind's eye—the thought of the beloved Creator—and you carry within your heart the same spark of divinity as the Mighty Creator. You are a part of God and cannot be separated from God.

And so Dear ones, even if you were to give up this physical shell, this temporary house—home to your mighty Monad, the individualized Jiva of consciousness—it is important for you to also understand that the evolution and the continuation of the beloved Creator extends into other realms of creation and consciousness.

The physical body is not needed to achieve this planetary Ascension. However, there will be those who will opt to take the body with them. This too, can be achieved through hard labor and discipline. The electromagnetism and the vibrations upon the Earth Plane and Planet at this time, and at these geophysical locations known as Golden City Vortices, greatly enhances and assists the physical, emotional, mental, and spiritual bodies into the synergy of Ascension.

Ascension is the free gift. It is the Law of Grace. This is the time, a Time of Awakening. Dear ones, will you come?

Answer: "Yes, we will."

Do you have questions?

Question: "Thank you beloved Saint Germain. That brings great clarity. We will go forth as you have directed. The other question: You mentioned in activating the Golden Cities, two points, the first being, the North Door. Did I miss the second point, or, were you speaking of the Vortex?"

Dear one, these are the two points of the Maltese Cross located on every Golden City Vortex. Should you need assistance, I would be glad to point these out to you later.

The Southern Doors are locations of retreats of healing; the Eastern Doors serve as Lodges, and areas for the gatherings of families and tribes. Western Doors are locations of teaching and information. The Star is a place of ascent.

Question: "Thank you, beloved. I understand. I would also like to speak about what you have said regarding the apex of Gobean, which is fully activated. In the two who have come forth this day to offer ourselves of service in activation of the other fifty—other Golden Cities or fifty-one, total—am I to understand that we can begin this work in the physical location of the center of Gobean? We may begin then, as pillars of seven, to do the activations?"

This is so, Dear one. For as I have taught so many times "hold the thought, first. As a man thinks, so he becomes." This Golden Age will be birthed on that vibration, that wave of thought. The Age of Aquarius is an age of thought-vibration when man will learn to discipline his thought as the mighty Co-creator of life!

Answer: "Thank you beloved. Then we will call forth our Mighty I AM Presence to begin that wonderful opportunity to serve and to activate the Golden Cities. And we would call forth your help and your guidance."

Call forth the Golden Age, the paradise of Utopia. Call it forth in prayer and song. Call it forth in your conscious intention. Call it forth in your consciousness. Call it forth in your thought and your feeling. Call it forth in your actions of ceremony.

Dear ones, these are the components that will birth this New Time; consciousness creates an electromagnetism, and thought is directed as a wave. This is how the Golden Band [Belt] was woven [constructed] around this earth. And we ask you, Dear ones, to weave a New Web, the *Galactic Web,* around the planet. Of course, there will come a time when we will appear for planetary assistance. However, until that time, you are our hands; you are our feet; you are our ears; and you are our mouths. Dear ones, go forward in service; weave this web!

Answer: "It will be done, beloved. Thank you."

Are there further questions?

Answer: "No. Thank you beloved."

And now I would like to close with instruction regarding the rose. It is important at all times to present the rose in all ceremonies of activation. For this [purpose], the rose symbolizes the *ancient lotus of the east* as the *lotus of the west.* We ask for its presence because we have always relied on our symbols to teach. The opening of the rose will open the minds of humanity. Understand that creation is held in thought. Understand the paradise to be birthed.

A New Time awaits all of you, Dear ones—a time that is *beyond* belief. It is a time long awaited. This time shall come. Hitaka!

8

Golden City Classes

Saint Germain Answers Questions

GREETINGS BELOVED, I AM SAINT GERMAIN, AND I REQUEST PERMISSION TO COME FORWARD.

"Please Dear one, come forward."

In that Mighty Christ, I AM. I stream forth on the Violet Ray of Mercy and Forgiveness. At this time, Dear hearts, many have gained an interest in the work that was sent through you. This interest is in the messages of the Earth Changes and contained in the Golden Cities.

In this discourse, we would like to present a template; so you will understand the work of the Golden Cities in the United States, and how they help form a New Consciousness in the Time of Change. You have understood that Prophecy comes to awaken not only your eyes and your ears, but your hearts. You will now learn that Earth Changes will lead mankind to begin to understand the Great Reason and the internal being of our soul.

This has been known through teachings as the *metaphor*. However, we like to present it as the *awakening of the heart*. Once the heart is open and present in these teachings, then the soul is ready to stand at the foot of the Master and receive the instructions that will change his or her being forever.

All are interested in and readied for this teaching when they begin to understand the Golden Cities. Each of these structures has been presented as a template for the understanding of global Ascension. Global Ascension in itself is only obtained when a certain percentage of those whose eyes, ears, and hearts are open, and ready to walk on the spiritual path, face each day anew, and follow the path of the seamless garment.

The seamless garment is woven in, through, and around you as an aggregate body of light. However, it is not woven entirely through thought, although thought is a component. Each stone of the aggregate body of light is woven through an action taken with intentional consciousness and conscience. It is each of these actions that stays within that aura of electromagnetic energy.

For more information and study topics on *Golden City Classes*, see Appendix H, page 219.

Always, each and every one of your actions is subsequently recorded in the Human Aura. Understand that the aggregate body of light is woven through each of those actions that are taken with intention, with consciousness, with conscience. This is known as the *alignment of the will*, or the alignment of that Mighty Will to the Light of God which never fails!

There are five Golden Cities that will exist in the United States during this Time of Tumultuous Change on the planet. Each of these cities have been formed to help assist in the spiritual awakening of humanity.

Dear one, we have given the exact geometrical locations of these Golden Cities. And each of these Golden Cities and their location are important in terms of the electromagnetism of the earth during this Time of Change. You are now beginning to understand that the many-ringed map represents a worldwide creation grid. The intersections of these grids help to birth new creations which will assist the New Age that follows the Time of Transition and Change.

The Time of Transition and Change may be as short as six years or as long as 1,000 years. This again, Dear ones, will be determined by each choice you make and in each action that composes your aggregate body of light. I have said before, "Gather your aggregate body of light around you, Dear ones and Dear chelas of mine. Each day, take a new action filled with the hope and faith of the spiritual awakening." Follow your heart, as I have always taught you Dear ones. Following your desire leads to that greater union, that unity of the ONE—Unana.

This is the full activation of *your* body of light. Many chelas say, "Let us turn this in to the light, or let us turn this over to the light." I say, "Let us *take action* in the light, Dear ones." For then and only then is the light brought forward in full activation.

The five Golden Cities upon the Earth Plane and Planet in the United States will ideally affect the whole planet. Each of them holds the first seeds of consciousness that will awaken the entire globe to a New Time, a New Era, and a new way of being.

The first of these Golden Cities is known as Gobean. [Gō'-bee-on] Its energy aligns not only to that Vortex of energy known as Shamballa, but to the Middle East and to Egypt—the heart of the beginning of *this* time. This Vortex will be held for transformation. It is served by that Mighty Master of the Blue Ray known as *El Morya*.

Beloved El Morya's teachings are to be understood within this Vortex. This Vortex Golden City, which was activated eighteen years ago, was held in continuous consciousness so that a spiritual awakening *would* come. It has held the consciousness that a spiritual awakening would happen in the United States. And therefore, many of the cities located outside this Vortex have also held consciousness. Do you not see this to be so?

Answer: "Yes."

Now let me explain the higher purpose of holding consciousness in a geophysical location. When you gather for the intent of holding a perfect out-picturing of crystallized consciousness, this form of consciousness takes action, and gathers and collects on a focal point. That point becomes imbued of the characteristics of that specific crystallized thought.

When crystallized thoughts gather in one area, as beloved Sananda has often said, two or more (persons) will form a collective consciousness in that area. And when Sananda speaks of consciousness, he means the collective consciousness in which all partake. The unity of consciousness is found in the concept of Unana: beings of the Deva and Elemental nature, trees, birds, rocks, angelic hosts, and human beings. All these entities participate in the collective consciousness imbued within an area.

You are the *HU-man* beings who have been given the God-characteristics engendered in your will; and since you carry the momentum of choice, you Dear ones, are known as *Co-creators*. The Co-creator can activate a choice for a greater and a higher good!

Through the activation of choice, imbued with the crystallized characteristic of a focal point, consciousness fills or penetrates all of creation. When a group of HU-mans aligned to the Great and Mighty Will of the I AM gather, and align their focus and their intent for a certain comprehensive characteristic, this allows a consciousness to inner-penetrate this area.

I have instructed you to gather in Golden Cities and intentionally share ONE cosmic consciousness to hold ONE focus. In this out-picturing, the Rays of Light and Sound attract. They gather to an area and to that command of the Mighty Will called upon in the name of I AM. At that point and time the Ray penetrates the area by first following the middle structure, as explained in the Prophecies of Earth Change. This extends to the locations taught in terms of mileage or kilometers.

It is important to understand the scientific reasoning of *how* and *why* this would happen, and the impact it will have on the world in the future.

In that mighty Vortex gathering of Gobean—the crystallized out-picturing—the mighty focus is on harmony and cooperation. Harmony and cooperation require a great transformation of will and choice.

Many of you have discussed organizations and how this work should be organized. Worry not, Dear ones. For it was organized upon its conception. However, if you would like to gather and learn to further feed your mind for the out-picturing of this Mission, we ask that classes be formed in each of the Golden Cities. These classes follow a structure of each of the characteristics and out-picturing. Do you understand?

Answer: "Yes."

Now, let me move forward and give you further details. In the city of Gobean, the structure shall be as follows:

1. Classes taught on the nature of harmony.
2. Classes taught on the nature of cooperation.
3. Classes taught on the nature of choice.

This will help with the out-picturing of consciousness and will help bring structure to the confusion. Many who come to Gobean do not understand that they are aligning their will to the Mighty One Will, and in that alignment comes a disciplined focus.

Beloved El Morya has always taught the path of discipline as the way to achieve. In this Golden City Vortex, many will be brought to a more disciplined approach and an understanding that cooperation is the law that heals all. Cooperation is the law that leads to harmony. And only in harmony, Dear ones, can that Mighty Law of Love be understood and acted upon.

The purpose of Gobean is to transform the choices of humanity. It aligns its magnetic energy to the teachings of the ancient Egyptian mystics. Also, it is important to understand that the electromagnetic grids of Gobean align not only with Shamballa, but to the direct (Akashic) teachings of the Mighty Masters of all eons who have existed upon the Earth Plane and Planet. Geophysically it also aligns its energy to the central point of earth at its creation and inception known as Giza.

Now Dear hearts, unless there are any other questions, I shall move on, to the city of Malton.

Answer: "Please continue."

Malton is a (Golden) City that has been brought forward to help cleanse the Deva and Elemental energies at this time. Therefore, beloved Kuthumi has been brought forward as the Master Teacher for this area.

We have come to understand that the earth's purification at this time is a cleansing and a purification of *many* systems. This is also a cleansing and a purification of the inner self and those who seek this inner cleansing will realize great fruits—an attainment of the Mighty Divine Mission!

When one understands this, their hearts, their minds, their intent, and their conscious out-picturing aligns with the energies of Malton. It assists the healing and purification of the Deva and Elemental Kingdom. When I speak of these Kingdoms, I speak of the Vegetable and the Flower Kingdom, the Mineral Kingdom and the Animal Kingdom.

We seek a harmony with these Kingdoms in Malton. Not only as they can express within the human body, but their *individualized* expressions. It is in the Golden City of Malton that the greatest harmony of these Kingdoms will exist after the Times of Changes.

Great gardens will flourish in these areas. I ask that this be a focal point for the chelas who align their energy to beloved Kuthumi. Again, the aggregate body of light is built on action. Light is indeed *love in action*. Those who take the hoe into their hands with earnestness for the attainment and the fruition of the soul, walks the path of self-actualization and integrity.

Beloved Kuthumi will guide and direct those toward the gentle purpose of this time. Gentleness is the Divine Mission and the purpose of Malton, and it aligns energies with that of the great Vortex above Glastonbury [England]. It also holds a relationship to the Druid cultures, and to those who understand that the Sun and the Moon [the luminaries] rule all.

Dear ones, those who come to this area of Malton, instruct them in classes that enhance knowledge of the Vegetable, Mineral, and Animal Kingdom. For this is where they will understand they're connected to beloved Babajeran [Mother Earth]. This is the service of Malton. Do you have questions?

Answer: "No, I understand."

Now, let us proceed to the third Golden City known as Wahanee. As you have most recently traveled there, you have now felt the great strife that exists in this area through past inequity and hate. It is important that we understand the nature of freedom and how freedom is attained—only again, through action.

First, the out-picturing of perfect freedom must be understood. Perfect freedom is indeed pathless, *and* perfect freedom is organized. It is organized first, in the individualized heart. Teachings on individualized freedoms must be brought forward in this Golden City of Wahanee.

Teachings of justice, and individualized freedoms will help humanity and the earth understand continuous consciousness. It is important for all to understand how governments function on the earth. It is important to understand the history of humanity. I ask for these classes to come forward from Wahanee:

1. Classes in understanding the governments of the world.
2. Classes in governments, and their relationship to individual rights and freedoms.

This is the focus of Wahanee. Only through the past can the future be understood. Only in the marriage of the past and the future can we *live* in the present. Only in the present will we understand the infinite, immortal truths.

These teachings will change the heart and the mind of the collective consciousness of the world, and these teachings will set men free. Is it not unconditional freedom that we are all seeking at this time?

Dear ones, this Golden City is where I shall serve personally; and I align my energy with my beloved Twin Ray, Portia, who holds her energy in continuous out-picturing in Eabra, in North America. It is important in Wahanee that these classes are held without judgment and without prejudice. These are classes that hold in continuous consciousness the idea of freedom—freedom of expression, freedom from fear. Do you understand?

Answer: "Yes."

Now, let us move to the fourth Golden City known as Shalahah. We are well aware that you are all preparing yourself for a ceremony of activation in that Golden City. I have taught activation in this material that is presented, and it is important that these activations occur. However, once a Golden City is activated, it is only again through the (continuous) conscious out-picturing and aggregate actions that allow the Golden City to (consciously) exist!

One cannot simply travel to a Golden City, (ceremonially) activate it, leave, and then say that it is activated and working.

All things work through consciousness. All consciousness moves through the conscious will or choice. The will chooses and creates an action. It is important that activities stream forth from each of these Golden Cities once they are consciously activated.

The fourth Golden City of Shalahah is to be of major importance, particularly during the Times of most Tumultuous Change. That is why so many are now moving to this area, for it is an area that holds in the continuity of consciousness, healing, and hope for humanity. And dear Sananda, who understands the constant, vigilant out-picturing of the Christ, will be the teacher.

I ask that classes on healing are taught in Shalahah. It is here that classes be held on the understanding of the Human Aura, the understanding of the body-mind connection, and the understanding that joy is lived each day as chosen.

Dear one, this is the perfect location for any school of healing to be held. And I am sure that you understand those who come, must *first* choose.

Now, let us move to the fifth Golden City known as Klehma. Klehma is held in continuous consciousness by beloved Serapis Bey. He understands the Ascension Process requires complete cooperation—cooperation in the body, in the thoughts, and in the feelings.

It is here that the cooperation of thought, feeling, and action will come forward for the sole purpose of the perfect out-picturing of harmonious Ascension.

In the past, most Ascensions were obtained by men and women who isolated themselves from societies, and found, shall we say, that highest mountain peak. They became hermits of sorts, to understand the wisdom and secrets that existed in the timeless and in the immortal.

In this area [Klehma] and during the Time of Great Change, many people will begin to understand this wisdom and it will exist on a global scale. These are the principles that will rule mankind at this time; these wisdoms are timeless and immortal. And in this area, I ask for these Ascension teachings to come forward. Beloved Serapis Bey will hold his timeless and immortal consciousness in this area.

This Vortex is held or aligned with the teachings of Native Americans, who traveled from the mouth of the Indus River across the Aleutian time-bridge [Aleutian Islands], and are now known as the tribal indigenous people of North and South America. Their teachings must come forward in this area and bridge again the eastern and western worlds. These teachings demonstrate the timeless and the immortal.

Again, let these teachings have action! Let these teachings carry forward in all societies. Let these teachings carry forward in all man-made governments. Search for the timeless. Search for the immortal. And there you will find the natural cooperation of *all* structures.

This is the teaching of Klehma, and it holds the consciousness for Ascension. Ascension attaches to what is real and disconnects the unreal. Ascension is an activity and an understanding that is the truth.

It is here in Klehma that classes on truth and the truths contained in all spiritual teachings be brought forward. Beloved Serapis Bey will serve this focus and those who wish to align their will to his teaching.

This is the network that covers these five Golden Cities. Let me go over these again, in case we have missed any details.

The first Golden City of Gobean aligns itself to Egyptian teachings.

The second Golden City of Malton aligns itself to the teachings of the Druids [Celtic teachings].

The third Golden City of Wahanee aligns its teachings to that of the African tribal peoples.

The fourth Golden City of Shalahah aligns its teachings to that of the eastern India [Ancient Kingdom of Magadha].

And that final Golden City Klehma aligns itself aligns itself to the teachings of the Native Americans [Indigenous people of North America].

Now, I shall step back from this lectern and you may ask questions.

Question: "It would seem that the outlines for each of these cities, is comprehensive. And even though short in detail, extremely long in action and activity of fulfillment. Occasionally we have those who ask us questions. And we have one from an individual who we know well. His name is Bob. Bob has a question. He asks about the project we're working on with the celestial teachers Morgan and Rachel who are working through Daniel and Alara. The work and wisdom seem excellent. But Daniel and Alara are concerned that they may be filtering information. Could you please check with Saint Germain? Is our work on the right track? Are Daniel and Alara conveying their channeled information without distortion?"

All channeled work seeks to understand the infinite internal, and it always leads one further along the path, does it not? Daniel and Alara who say that they are receiving instruction, are indeed receiving instruction from the assistance of beloved Serapis Bey. At times, they might want to call upon the Master Teacher of Klehma, and ask for the teachings to come forward.

As in all cases of work given to a heart, and then spoken through sound and vibration, a human element is always present. It is important to understand this and the human who will put it into action! It is important to put teachings in action or, they are not teachings.

Teachings come forward to instigate action, crystallize thought, clarify feelings, and bring motion forward.

Ask of yourself, am I moving forward? And then you will know the truth of the teaching. Am I moving forward? You must ask that question of yourself in all teachings you receive. Even those from myself! If you are not moving forward, then you must take the appropriate action.

Question: "Are you saying that all teachings come to a place of being and living, breathing activity of your life?"

The adept is one who not only understands the perfect out-picturing, the crystallized focus of the teaching, but *lives* it.

Question: "That is clear. Thank you. We have some other questions. Friends of ours, Theresa and George, would like to know what their highest and best service would be during the Earth Changes?"

To align their wills at this time to the teachings contained in each of the five Golden Cities. Both of these life-streams have been brought forward at this time to help serve at this Time of Awakening. These two beings have known one another throughout many embodiments and have served in many levels of organization. Now it is important that they balance and harmonize their energies. One understands the Elemental nature of this work. The other understands the more practical and more organized application of this work. It is important that they help and assist in the organization of classes in each of these five Golden Cities.

One is more directed toward the healing arts. The other is more directed toward the healing of the earth. It is important that these two energies know they are *arching* energy back and forth for the purpose of activity.

Question: "When you are referring to classes, who are you asking to teach these classes?"

Those who have aligned their wisdom and their understanding to the crystallized focused out-picturing of each Golden City. Do you understand?

Question: "How does one know if one is aligned?"

Do you not see? Do you not hear? Have we not worked with discernment? Do you understand?

Question: "Another question that they have is about the date and their participation in the Shalahah activation?"

Again, as I have stated, activation is important. However, it is the continuous out-picturing of that crystallized thought through action that is indeed even more important. Activation is the seed; it is the Start, it is the beginning, it is the birth. It is important then, that all things that are birthed, grow and mature.

Question: "Another question comes from Spotted Pony, and she asks, what is the definition of a soul mate?"

A soul mate, or shall we say, soul mates, are beings who have been together in many embodiments, and through the course of several embodiments, have decided before the current lifetime to take on a certain Mission together. That Mission may be achieved through many means.

Missions accomplish perfect out-picturing.

Sometimes, soulmates are the blending of opposite octaves. Sometimes they are the harmonizing of a focus that is similarly aligned. It is important to understand that soul mates may vibrate at many different levels, and it is also important to understand that soul mates often vibrate at compatible or harmonious levels. However, they are brought together in a union to achieve a desired result—one that was chosen before the embodiment.

Question: "Since we have just discussed how soul mates work together, we have another question. What is Lee G.'s role in Earth Changes?"

This being has come forward with an understanding of the nature of crisis. And as there may be times in the days to come times when many people will feel a sense of cataclysmic crisis; this person understands how to help others overcome crisis consciousness and see that every lemon is made into lemonade!

Question: "What is the highest and best communication for those unaware of the Earth Changes?"

Of course, this too has been a concern for us at this level. First, it is important to teach the spiritual way. It is important to teach that hope, faith, trust, and love are the most important attributes to develop. For only through the development of these attributes can anyone circumvent both cataclysmic and personal destruction

This should be taught and placed at the forefront. Yes, it is important too, to deliver the message. For sometimes, those who have hardened their hearts and closed themselves off to the message of love will hear first the message of losing something to which they are so attached. It is important to blend the spiritual and material, and bring *both* forward, as I stated before. Much like soul mates coming together as opposites, yet opposites sometimes produce attraction. This attraction can stimulate a desired result.

Answer: "Yes, I understand. We have further questions. This is from Shanti: do human archetypes play a role in how people perceive Prophecy?"

Prophecy is Prophecy. Prediction is prediction. Love is love. That is the most important thing to understand. Prophecy strives to unite love and hate or fear, so that one may come to a point of conclusion. That is the *inner* work that must be done. Prophecy helps bridge the gap of two worlds colliding. Do you understand?

Answer: "Yes. I do understand that. How do we change the archetypes of man to allow this New Era to come forward?"

There is no archetype of man, for man is individualized! How can you archetype a snowflake? How can you archetype a thumbprint? There is no archetype of man. Man is here to *take* his identity. That is the path.

Question: "Understood. What is the relationship between psychic predictions and prophecies?"

Psychic prediction relies upon the electromagnetic currents of the present moment. Also, it relies upon the interchange and the interaction of *that* moment. Prophecy is a philosophy and a spiritual teaching.

Question: "Understood. What is the relationship of free will and future predictions?

We have always taught that your future lies in the moment of your choice. Will is choice. The choices that are made today create the future. You are now living the end result of a great line of your choices of the past. Look carefully at your life and you will understand this.

Question: "Yes, I do. What is a person to do with the fear that is generated by psychic predictions?"

He who knows himself and functions with love, faith, hope, and trust. Does he worry?

Answer: "Truly not. Prophecy is a philosophy of spiritual teachings of actions chosen within certain life experiences. Many people who consider the life experience of death as the end will see more death as a result of an Earth Change on the planet. How would you ask people to deal with this in their hearts?"

You, as light bearers, forbearers of the future, Prophecy has been given to you so you will become teachers and pillars of consciousness! Prophecy has been given to you so that you understand the cohesiveness of natural law. Prophecy has been given to you so that you understand balance and that both sides exist simultaneously.

These times will come, as all cycles must come to an end. All cycles travel the sequence of birth, growth, maturity, and decay. You are now in a cycle of decay, and because you are in a cycle of decay, do not forget who you are and your Divine Mission! Death is part of this cycle. Understand through death comes rebirth. Do you not see this exampled in nature? Do you not see this exampled in your own life? Think of a time when you experienced spiritual death within only to be reborn again anew! This teaching of the Christ consciousness exists as *super-consciousness*, ready to birth itself out of death!

Follow the teachings, Dear ones, forbearers, light bearers, and pillars of light! Understand the warning contained in the spiritual teaching of Prophecy. You must always live with an understanding of the cycles and the warnings. Understand how important each choice *is* that you make.

Question: "Can we alter these prophecies with our choices?"

We cannot alter the cycle. However, we can alter outcomes of cycles. We can alter many things through the ways we see them. Is this not true? Is the glass half full? Is the glass half empty? Can we make lemonade from a lemon? These are all things we must begin to understand to alter any situation. Have you not met two Brothers: one who sees only the bad and one who sees only the good? Have different things happened in their lives? On the surface, they've probably lead similar lives; however, the difference is how they see their lives. One sees what they *do not* have, another sees what they *do* have. It is through the blending of these two perceptions that we begin to understand and Master duality.

Question: "Understood. Is there anything for those individuals who are agnostic or atheistic, or those who don't necessarily have an opinion one way or another to consider about Prophecy?"

Live each day with a personal sense of Prophecy. Understand that you create *your* Prophecy each day of your life. Understand that Prophecy is part of you as the Teacher and the Healer. Prophecy is the Mystic that exists in all of us. Prophecy is created each day *as we choose* to live.

Question: "Does a cause-and-effect relationship exist among the gradual deterioration of the environment, humanity, and the Earth Changes?"

It is part of the cycle. It is part of this time. It is the completion of a time for mankind to grow and to learn; this cycle must be completed. To circumvent this completion is moving backward, and such energy would be counterproductive.

Do not fear the times ahead of you! This is a time to practice what you have learned and know.

Question: "Do survivalists or paramilitary groups have an appropriate answer to the future?"

They have the answer that is for them. Again, truth is pathless when we begin to understand choice and freedom.

Question: What is the relationship of Christian Biblical Prophecy and the Ascended Masters' Prophecies?

Those Christian Prophecies were the prophecies given at *that* time. Prophecy is always for the present moment. Prophecy is given for those cultures to understand at *that* given time. Is it difficult for you to understand the prophecies of those times? Those were prophecies given to the people of that culture, of that time.

These are prophecies given for people of *this* time.

Question: "Do prayer, meditation, and acts of charity affect the future?"

As always, those out-picturings of trust, faith, hope, and love change all things, and make a day much brighter and more useful. Isn't it more pleasant to live the Law of Love than to live with fear? Only those who have experienced this would understand. Of course, they do!

Know that we are with you. Know that our vibration is there in service. Know that you may call upon us and we may assist you. Have we not proven this already?

Answer: "This is true. I thank you for your guidance and counsel."

9

Vibrational Shifting

Saint Germain with a Student

GREETINGS IN THAT MIGHTY CHRIST, I AM SAINT GERMAIN, AND I REQUEST PERMISSION TO COME FORWARD.

"Dear one, please come forward. You have permission."

Dear ones, the work upon the Earth Plane and Planet is one where I say again, tarry not! For the accelerations in the dimensions, in the sheath that exists between the Third and the Fourth Dimension, is thinning on a daily basis. As you know this is a Time of Transition; it is also a Time of Tumultuous Change. We have come forward to bring our service, our vibration, and our energy to assist you, Dear one, in taking the next step towards that mighty gift of the Ascension.

It is a time when things are changing rapidly. And many people around you are changing, too. Have you now had lessons of experiencing another who is in the process of losing bits of their reality? You call this insanity. However, we know this, too, as only a symptom of vibrational-shifting, rifting, or tearing. The energy is so impacted on and within the individual that they can no longer deal with their own centers of energy.

This is why we have given you so many instructions in the different centers of energy—your chakra system—so that you can understand. There is also much energy flooding the Earth Plane and Planet at this time. The chakras or energy centers are imploding upon themselves, as if the chaotic energy does not know where to go. The individuals do not know how to qualify or use the new energy. Do you understand?

Answer: "Yes."

This insanity, along with increased drug and alcohol addiction, will become more common in this Time of Change. Because, Dear ones, these are people who have simply failed to understand choice. We have said over and over again "you, yourself, are doing the choosing." Although we ask you to make a decision, you are actually the ones who align your will to the Divine. Your choice to stay in that stalwart commitment—commitment to the Mighty I AM—allows you to awaken and utilize these centers of energy for the service of all.

For more information and study topics on *Vibrational Shifting,* see Appendix I, page 229.

As we have stated, the way to take the next step up this evolutionary ladder is to be of service to your Brother and Sister. This will help you abandon self-aggrandizing ideas while allowing you to access the energy of unity.

Only in compassion are all things united. Have compassion for those around you, even though they are a bit insane at this time! Have this compassion for them, Dear ones, for indeed it has been stated before, "They know not what they do."

However, in this time and with this acceleration of energies occurring, there is also a higher law. And we ask you to consider using this energy influx to help lift you to that next step—that new level of understanding.

At this time it is important to spend time alone in the Violet Flame. This calms and centers the activation of your energy centers. Apply what we have taught, Dear ones, to awaken your cellular energy.

It is important to take calming baths in a saline solution. To create a saltwater bath, mix one cup of salt, along with the essential oils of violet or jasmine, in your bathwater. Also, adjust your dietary standards to align with thoughts of harmony and beauty within the body. [Editor's Note: this is in reference to a conscious diet.] These molecular adjustments are planetary in nature, and they do affect the earth and sun through waves that reflect from the moon.

You have heard that the earth affects the moon. However, this is the reflection of energy from the moon to the earth. And so, it is important to understand that these are planetary influences; learn to integrate them into a higher nature or energy.

This is also a time when the earth may go through tremendous upheaval and geophysical changes. Therefore, it is important to understand that before such great movements happens, the psychological body of humanity must go through many changes and upheavals, too.

Over the next five years, you will see many changes in the political and social systems of the United States. As stated always in the prophecies of change, it is the United States that will first go through these geophysical changes. And therefore, many of the social and political changes will begin in the United States. It is important to observe the next presidential election. For in this election, you shall see the coming together of the inevitable flurry between light and dark forces. It is important to watch this, to understand it, and to identify it. For its outcome will determine the extent of many Earth Changes.

As we have stated in the Six-Map Scenario, it is up to the collective choice of humanity to determine what will become of the earth and her peoples, and to decide the inevitable outcome of these times. Some outcomes can be predicted by taking a look at the current political and social unrest of the peoples of this planet.

It is important to pay attention to social systems, and it is important to understand that their breakdown is inevitable. Why many of these changes are inevitable is what we would know as a type of "death-cadence. It is important also, to understand that through death comes birth. Death allows the new cycle of birth.

Perhaps you have realized, Dear ones, that as you let go of an old idea—something that no longer serves your needs, even if it's an old piece of clothing, or a way of thinking or doing things—a new way of being emerges in your life. Have you not noticed that when you discard an old piece of clothing, a new garment comes quickly?

It is important, Dear ones, to understand that at this time death-cadence [decadence] is all around you, but a birth awaits you. This birth is cellular and physical, yet filled with the majesty of the heavens! It's a collective birth that coincides with the system of the Earth Mother. You are of it, and it is of you. You are all connected to that Mighty ONE!

As we have stated in other laws, specifically, in the Law of Rhythm, unity is in all, and corresponds to those Laws of Rhythm.

You may experience a time in this energy shifting—what we refer to as dimensional planeing—a time of one dimension slipping into another. Time seems to fall backward, and then it may move forward. Whatever way you move is your choice, Dear ones. That is why we stand here in support, and hold at all times the thought of the Mighty I AM. We stand with the out-picturing of thought, holding you in perfection.

Dear ones, during this Time of Dimensional Plane-ing, a tunnel is created between the Third and Fourth Dimensions—you may enter it. Think of it as a staircase: one step up at a time.

You have been studying the Laws of Octaves, and it is important to understand that this barrier you are entering is known as shock. In these times, energy may slide back and forth uneasily and easily. Do you understand?

Answer: "Yes."

The laws we have given you are important. Pay attention and follow the energy.

This energy fluctuates: it can force you backward, catapult you forward, or keep you in one place. Again, these are your choices. You have witnessed those who have used drugs and alcohol. They are people who now use their voices within the theater of the mind to create insanity.

You too, have the same choice to align your will. Dear ones, are there questions?

Question: "How does it affect your mind when this energy slides back and forth?"

It is unsettling, of course, to the mental body. However, as we begin to understand the Laws of Pitches or Laws of Octaves, it creates a sound vibration within the mental body. The disunity of bodies abrasively corrodes the others, causing an overlapping—which is not transmuted—of emotional substance. All the emotions not yet transmuted or transformed into a higher purpose overshadow the mental body. There, the mental body, or that which is the thinking body, is overwhelmed by emotion. Its purpose loses definition.

Question: "Does this cause memory loss as well as insanity?"

Not only memory loss, but mental loss—corrosion of the mental body.

Question: "How do you heal this so that you can remember day to day what's going on?"

It is important to watch the vibrations of those around you at this time. Do not engage in their emotional outbursts. It is most important to stay within the focus of your own being—into the center of your own I AM.

It is important to spend time in silence, and you personally require this. There, your mental stability can regain its footing. Spend your time in nature, especially in wooded areas and near running water.

Question: "So my mind has slipped on the ice. Can I help my emotions? Will silent time help my emotions also?"

When an emotion comes up and begins to crowd the thinking, it inhibits crystallized thought. It is then important to use thought to contain the emotion. Emotion is quite different from feeling. Feeling comes from the instinctive body. An emotion, however, comes from a higher frequency of the emotional body; and is closer to a crystallized thought. Emotion bonds thought to action. Emotion, which allows action to take place, is related to the fields within the sphere of the Human Body.

It is important to understand that emotion is like an adhesive glue of thought to action.

Question: "Then, would the new energy affect the Dream World in a different way also?"

The energy you carry about your being is what you use to travel at night. This is known as the higher emotional body, an astral body often used at the Time of Dreaming. However, some people have developed higher mental bodies. They use them in alchemic marriages—

the fusing of higher emotional states with higher mental bodies. This forms a stronger body for astral projection into the dream state.

Sometimes in the dream state you may feel as if you are being attacked. You may feel a sense of impending doom. This is, of course, being carried out through the emotional body. These residues have not yet crystallized into physical action.

Question: "Can I ask about my Sister's dream of sliding in a house and finding firm ground, she and her daughter?"

The location where she is presently living is geo-physically unsafe. And she is currently feeling the geophysical residue [Earth Changes] that may occur in the future.

Question: "Will Nevada be a safe place?"

This of course, is contingent upon the choices of humanity. However, the area she's considering moving to is filled with environmental pollutants. Her energies are conducive for the states of Wyoming and Montana.

Question: "Is all of Alaska unsafe? What about the Aleutian Islands?"

Much of this area, of course, is affected by the Pacific Ring of Fire. And, if the planet as a system enters into the Time of Great Change, this area will experience many shattering earthquakes. It is important to live in an area where you feel called, and are able to fulfill your destiny or your service to humanity. For at this time, many people will be called to live in areas that will inevitably end up under water. Yet, it is important for these individuals to move to these areas as they feel called. This is a Time of Completion and the ending of cycles. It is a time when we must remain committed to the choices that we have made.

It is important now to play every last note of this octave. It is important that we allow our choices to play out the last crystallized activity. It is also important, Dear ones, to remember that at this time, only a few will have the ability to move or live in a safe place. It is important to act on every desire, so a New Time can enter.

This thinning of the Veil is indeed, purposeful. One may ask, "What is the purpose of this, and wouldn't it be easier to stay with what we have already experienced?" Dear ones, please understand this: the Time of Change will move humanity forward and reshape the entire planet.

This is a Time of Unana, a Time of the Activated Christ. This is a time when we will experience Oneness and unity beyond the Earth Planet—this is a Oneness and a unity with the universe.

This area you question, Alaska, is an area that will go through many geophysical changes—not only earthquakes, but volcanic activity. However, if your Sister is called to stay in this area, it is important for her to be trained with medical knowledge. She has an aptitude for this; she received preparation in previous lives and in other schools of understanding of the workings of the Human Body. She could be of great assistance in the Time of Change by helping many in medical clinics and hospitals. Is this not true?

Answer: "True. And possibly she could do the same even in Nevada or California or any place."

It is possible indeed. These are the choices. I am only sharing knowledge with you at this level, so she may use this information to assist her choice.

Question: "When everything is based on a group rather than an individual, how much individual free will or protection can we generate? Or, are we bound by the group, the group consciousness, compared to the individual? How much free will does the individual have? Can you protect yourself and be guided to do what you need to do?"

It is important to understand the energy contained by the individual. Take for instance, a pool of water. Dip a glass into the pool. Hold the glass away from the pool, and let it sparkle in the sun. Is that not the individual—who is like the glass—contained of that one pool? The pool and the glass exist independently. Yet, the pool and the glass contain the same water. Is this an example of the ONE? Inevitably, yes. But the glass alone, is it not the ONE? It is not the ONE, but of the ONE.

Individuality is, shall we say, the pooling of many forces! Please understand—we are all connected as ONE. Even we, in this dimension, are connected to you at your dimension. This connection extends to plants, vegetables, insects, and minerals—they're all connected within and as ONE.

However, on the path this is a discipline—understanding individuality. Every soul that comes to this planet seeks embodiment or pursues a path to understanding their individuality. Once individuality is completed, other courses are available to explore, or shall we say, to co-create.

However, at this moment, you understand the forces within the individual; you are Mastering the forces—those commonly known as thought, feeling, and action—within. You will first work with, gain an understanding of, and contain these forces. Once this is achieved, other courses will be given.

At this present time, however, Mastering these forces is as simple as thought. The union of all three—thought, feeling, and action—produces an Alchemical Marriage, and unites the masculine and feminine forces within the body. This initiates Unity Consciousness—the

Mighty Unana, as we have spoken of before, Dear ones. However, at this time it is important that we put our focus, and our attention, on what we must Master first. That is, individuality. And then we will focus our attention on the universalities of all things.

Question: "Is there any way that we are going to alter, as an individual, alter anything . . . or is it now set what will happen?"

Of course, there is collective free will—collective choice. There have been many moments throughout the history of humanity when choices were made that altered destiny. However, destiny is more or less, unalterable.

Each and every person has played out a destiny in previous embodiments—a destiny may play out in this embodiment or future embodiments. This destiny is like a web; it is part of a line that exists in the Plane of consciousness known as time. Each embodiment resembles a dot that encapsulates moments of destiny.

Men often refer to this as fate. However, we would like to refer to it as self-awareness. It is important to understand that all things work for the common good. It is also important to understand that the good and the light—the right way—is always coming forward, even though it seems to be left-handed or a wrong way. Always see through self-awareness that the right way or better way is an evolution happening before your eyes.

As you understand that all things work together for the good of all, you will then begin to understand that everything is somewhat predestined. Yet, free will is present. Individuality is present. Free will and individuality are working in the harmony of mixtures and balance.

Question: "What else can you tell me about my Sister's personal life? Can I do anything to help her find peace of mind? Since she quit drinking, she doesn't seem to have a life of her own, other than her children. What advice can I give her?"

As I have said before, she would do best by giving service to others. This service may or may not be given to the family. However, it will most likely be found in medical institutions, for there is a natural aptitude that has been gained in other embodiments. She also has an aptitude toward natural healing, and understands the application not only of acupressure and acupuncture points, but of herbs and the healing of the body.

It is perhaps to her best advantage to study these things and to reawaken the memory obtained from many lifetimes. It is then important that she utilize her knowledge for the service of humanity. There will be many who will appreciate the service that she could offer.

Answer: "Thank you. I have no more questions."

I shall close and will be most happy to return in the service of the breath, the sound, and the light . . .

Response: "Thank you very much."

10

Closing the Circle

Saint Germain Helps a Friend

GREETINGS MY BELOVED, I AM SAINT GERMAIN, AND I AM HERE TO BRING DISCOURSE AND GUIDANCE.

Do you have any questions before we proceed?

Question: "I need to know about how I got into this jam that I'm in. Why am I experiencing all this fear? What can I do to make peace with this person who is stoned out of their mind?"

Again, let me remind you of the Laws of Attraction and Repulsion we have taught so many times and of which you are aware.

These laws, which are the Laws of Duality, govern the world of form. The Laws of Attraction and Repulsion continuously serve the evolution of the soul on the Earth Plane. The evolution of the soul is always compelled or propelled by the Laws of Attraction and Repulsion.

The soul takes in its journey a series of lessons to be learned. Some lessons are brought through a natural course of action through the Law of Rhythm; sometimes through the Laws of Octaves; sometimes through the Laws of Death and Rebirth; and sometimes through the Law of Love. And in this case the lesson is learning the Laws of Attraction and Repulsion—a Law of Duality, of opposites attracting. This also allows a fusion of Universal Laws to serve for education. In this case, one, whom you have known in many other embodiments, has been brought to your path. Not only as a Brother but as a father. You have known one another many times. Does he not carry energy, a vibration, of your own biological father in this embodiment?

Answer: "Exactly—totally."

This is the purpose of this lesson: to close the energy so you may move on for the evolution of your own soul. It is important that this has happened at this time in your life. For after you jump over this hurdle that is in front of you, brought by the Law of Repulsion, this allows the Law of Attraction to come forward in your life.

For more information and study topics on *Closing the Circle*, see Appendix J, page 233.

This too, serves the greater cause and the greater purpose. It has been said, "In the best and the highest good." This means that in the greater law of all things comes the harmony of all voices. There is a harmony in mixtures when light and dark meet together in one homogeneous manner, and a unity of consciousness is achieved. It is a way that one is brought forward in evolution. It is a way that one is brought to a greater understanding.

Dear Sananda has taught that all points comprise the circle. It is a time, yes, for the circle to close; it's also a time when the spiral within the circle comes forward. This is the lesson in front of you.

Question: "Why are so many people using drugs?"

Answer: It is, of course, a time when society is de-structuring. A time when many people are escaping from the reality they will be facing in the next ten to twenty years. This reality is hard for them to understand. Again, it is the Law of Repulsion and the Law of Attraction.

Addictive substances create subjective bodies that many people in these induced states clothe themselves with. For instance, have you noticed that a person who is using an addictive substance suddenly becomes another person? It is as if they have changed into a whole new set of clothes, placing them on, and of course, coloring this person's personality. One minute the personality is happy. The next minute, the personality is angry. This is what an addictive substance does. These subjective bodies, of course, remain long after the death of an addict. And even if that being or soul decides to no longer use or abuse a substance.

These subjective bodies float in the [lower] astral plane. In this case, this area is located between the Third and Fourth dimensions of your planetary sphere. This is an area where disembodied spirits and beings without mind substance, also known as ghosts, reside. They are all mindless, like a rack of clothing a wardrobe hanging in a storefront.

This is one way for you to understand addictive substances. They each contain an element of lower octave consciousness that creates the addiction. However, these creations only work within one mind focus; this one mind focus is of one plane and one element. Therefore, addictive substances are *very* limiting, though they provide an escape in that moment. They are *always* limiting.

One who has used addictive substances soon realizes that these substances limit their freedom; their ability to make sovereign choices; and their ability to express the true nature of their being. This is often the reason why the addictive substance is discarded. However, the addictive nature—the subjective body—that is created through the *use* of addictive substance is never removed. Or shall we say, never leaves that sphere of consciousness. It is always there, waiting for you to put it on. It's much like an old sweater, an old pair of shoes, or an old pair of socks, ready for you to wear again, ready to color your personality. Do you understand?

Answer: "Yes. How can I escape, get away from this, or stop? How do I stop this mirror that I have brought to myself? How do I get out of this condition where I am so full of fear?"

Recognition is, of course, the first element. Recognition and diagnosis of this condition are always first. The second element is the understanding of the will and the choices involved. It is also important for you to complete this cycle, this inner cycle where you must deal with the male energy held in torment through anger and rage. This was present with your own biological father, and now with this person who wears the same pair of shoes as your father! This is the same type of consciousness, as I have explained in addictive behavior.

Never engage a person when they are thus clothed, for they are under the influences of a dimension that are not at all friendly toward you!

Question: "Like walking through the valley of the dead souls?"

It is known in some instances as a *dead zone*. However, sometimes it is important to experience the dead zone to understand the gift of life and to experience the difference. Sometimes, it is important for the evolution of the soul to receive the lesson as *mirroring;* and once again the soul faces an apparent opposite. However, the experience of the dead zone and the understanding of the gift of life allow a synergistic movement, as I have mentioned before, that brings a unity of consciousness and a unity of purpose.

In this case, recognition of and closure with the energies of your father allow energy to move forward. It is important that you cut all ties you have had with your father, in terms of energy, on the other plane. It is important for you to enter into the ceremonies that you have been taught by your spirit guides. For they too, understand the torment that has tied you astrally and spiritually.

These energies are draining you. These are the energies of fear that you are looking to heal. This has allowed the attraction. It is important for you to bless your father and send him on his way. For this allows final closure. Do you understand, Dear one, that the situation you chose to live during your early years on the Earth Plane and Planet now gives you strength of character? Do you understand that this recognition and closure is a rite of passage?

The ceremony, itself, does not imbue your character. For the quality of character was gained *through* your experience. However, the ceremony allows for a closure of the circle. This is a closure of energies of learning through abuse, of learning through a nemesis, and learning through opposition.

There are many other paths you can now follow for knowledge of the soul. And the contrary path is one path that one may follow. However in this case, it is now your choice, for you have completed the path of learning through the Law of Opposites. And now, should you choose, you may learn through the Path of Unities. You may learn through the Path [Law] of Attraction—all that is magnetically drawn to you, because energetically it is *similar to* you. Do you understand?

Question: "I don't need to be the contrary any more?"

Yes, it is important for you to understand that, again, through your will and through your choice, these lessons have come to you personally. You chose this situation before you chose this embodiment. You chose in this lifetime that you would Master the contrary laws, the Law of Repulsion. You learned what you resisted the most! You learned through the dark side or the opposite side of yourself. Is this not so?

Answer: "Yes."

And now, a closure comes to this circle. This is a time spiral, as you would understand it. This is a time for you to see again; it is your choice if you continue along this path. This is what this other soul has brought to you. Does he not represent all that repels you? Does he not represent everything that is against what you have learned and chosen?

Answer: "Yes."

And now, if you continue in the evolution of your soul, you too may choose to learn through new laws. You have achieved, as a rite of passage, a new understanding and a clear understanding of the Law of Repulsion. The ceremony given to you by your spiritual teachers—your spiritual guides—shall be done during the time of the full moon. It shall be done, if at all possible, near a body of water. It shall be done in such a way to allow the magnetism to properly attract. The magnetism is also created through sound vibration, as you have been taught in Native American drumming. Through this you will change and choose new ways to evolve. Do you understand?

Answer: "Yes."

And so, you must make the choice. Will you continue to learn through the contrary path or will you go forward through the active gate [attraction]. This again, is your choice. All embodied life on earth contains the blend of conscience and consciousness; these souls learn what moves through the will and the choices. It is choice that brings every soul here. It is choice that evolves intelligence into wisdom. It is choice that allows life *to be*.

Question: "When I do the ritual to let all this go, to pass it off, and to understand it, will he then feel no energy elsewhere and move on?"

Answer: This is so! He fulfills his own destiny with those he has come to serve. Do you not see the same pattern in the life of your own father? Do you not see that he helped many to make certain choices and to continue along a certain path?

Is it not apparent that your mate has chosen a path of nonviolence? And so therefore, do you not act with nonviolence towards him?

Response: "Yes."

So, this is true. In your choice the Law of Attraction exists, as exampled by your present life of nonviolence. Every day, you are choosing your destiny! If humans would understand only this, they would no longer see themselves as victims of circumstance. Instead, humans are choosing every day of their lives; and at any moment, they may also change the course of direction through the wind that generates in the soul.

Answer: "It felt like I chose the path of fire."

Fire transmutes quickly and allows one to understand how to bring something from the lessons, and find Mastery swiftly and rapidly. Wind feeds the fire. But it is the earth element that allows you to take the steady and stable ground. You might consider that it is time for earth within your life.

Answer: "In the ceremony, I feel like the ceremony has to be fire as well."

Saint Germain: Ceremony represents symbols. These symbols speak a language that is more direct than words or mind substance. Symbols unlock the potency held in universal languages and are able to transverse states of consciousness. The symbol holds these things, so choose the symbol carefully as you would choose the name of your child! For these symbols will repeat the *New Law* you choose.

Answer: "I see. I've got to meditate on that. I want clarity on this to the point where I never have to walk this path again. I don't ever want to be in the path of someone who is insane. I don't ever want to draw this to me again. I want to find a more peaceful, creative space. I feel as if I've paid my dues. I want a rest."

The soul knows when a lesson is completed. The soul itself knows when it is time to change the path. The fact that you are now ready indicates the soul has recognized this willingness. As I said in the beginning of this session, the first element is your recognition of the pattern, and the second is your will or your ability to take action.

Once these two things have been achieved, change will happen. This is the Mastery again, of those three components: knowledge, willingness, and expression. And in this instance thought, action, and then feeling. This has been taught in prior lessons in the sequence: thought, feeling, and action. In this case, we will temporarily remove the feeling body, as often times the feeling body is housed in astral levels. Since we are asking for a change of the evolution of the soul, it is important that we work *first* with the *thought*, and then we will work with the action, and finally the feeling. Do you understand?

Answer: "Yes. I feel as if half the people on earth right now are hiding inside drugs—the dead zone. The other half is out challenging life with dangerous hobbies such as mountain climbing, trying to prove they're alive. Why are so many people testing death?"

Saint Germain: It is true that there are those testing death who are dead themselves—so many among humanity are not even awake! They slumber in the dead zone. They slumber in this Time of Spiritual Awakening. A bell rings to awaken them from centuries and embodiment after embodiment of sleep.

However, it is *their* choice to remain asleep. It is their choice to be dead. But then, there are those who have made the choice to be alive and make daily choices, fully awake, resulting in full consciousness and conscience in all of their activities. It is important, Dear ones, to understand at this Time of Transition that this is a time when choices awaken the will. It is the awakening of spiritual laws that all *is* contained within and without. We have always said, "as above, so below."

What does this mean Dear one? The laws are contained within every cell, from microscopic organisms to the most complex organisms. All contain within the Laws of Unity of all things. When we speak this way, we speak in an older language that is hermetic in origin. It is also universal.

The world is asleep. It is so! It is time for universal awakening. There is indeed a connection between the body and mind. It is the mind that creates the body. There is also a connection between the collective mind and the earth. The collective mind is collective consensus, and you now know this as the one-hundredth monkey. Perhaps it will only take one more for the collective awakening!

Are these possibilities? Are these probabilities? Of course they are Dear ones! There are laws which govern, "as above, so below." These are the Laws of Momentum, and you understand them in your science of physics. And now we offer them through the understanding of psychology, religion, and beliefs. It is important, Dear ones, for you to see the importance during this time to stay awake and conscious. It is also important to use your conscience. Every day make intentional choices with knowledge and understanding.

Question: "If you are awake and your collective essence or energy is directly related to the earth, how do the dead, the asleep, drug addicts, or other abused souls affect the earth? Compared to how the awake affect the earth? Does it take a lot more, or is it half and half? Is this going to make a bearing on how soon the earth crumbles and is destroyed? Does the earth need the energy of awakened people?"

Answer: There is a percentage of people who sleep; there is a percentage of people who are awake. And this has *always* been and always shall be. However, for the New Dimensions to be opened, and to traverse through time with a leap in consciousness, a certain percentage of wakefulness is required. This of course, must be subjective first, and then understood and experienced on an objective or collective level. The individual choices that you make become choices made for *all* of humanity.

If one person, one individual, subjectively awakens to this objective ideal and begins to understand how individual choice affects, in essence the whole, then in one small way an opening, a portal, a window for consciousness grows. This is achieved day by day through the holding of thought, visualization, and an understanding of peace. However, there are still those who will remain in a dead zone. These are those who must be left, they must be discarded, as was spoken in the Book of Revelations: two are standing in the field, side by side; one will go, the other will stay. Do you understand? This choosing is not by [a] God. This choosing is through the will, the developed will, the conscious will as God in man!

It is a choice and a commitment to stay firmly rooted. Recognize that when someone is asleep it is not necessarily your responsibility to awaken their slumber, but to *allow* their choice. For within their dream, some day, they will awaken to the ONE reality, the ONE truth, which *is within*.

Question: "Why do churches ask all their people to apostatize as if they want to awaken and bring God to everyone around them? Why do they do that?"

It is again, a slumber within the sleep, another illusion, another dream created within the dream. It is fear of awakening, fear of what would happen if the slumber is removed. [Then] One would be free. However, it is important to let those who sleep to remain in slumber. For those who are awake, stay awake!

Question: "With Lee, is it best for me to do my ritual and just stay out of his way, and send him love?"

It is important to understand the completion of the spiral of energy. For you carry this in your DNA as well as your electromagnetic aura. It is important for you to understand that this is the completion of a major task of your life's work. This is a completion of a major portion of what you have come this time to learn. Does this speak truth to you?

Response: "I find myself leaning toward the shaman's answer of healing and peace: cast him into the winds to do his own thing. Meanwhile, I don't need it anymore."

Saint Germain: That would work, Dear one. As I have said before, call upon your spiritual teachers, your spiritual guides and friends. They are with you and will help you to bring this to full fruition and completion.

"I thank you. I understand."

So be it! In that Mighty Christ, I AM.

11

Doomsday—Peace Day

Saint Germain Shares Prophecies

GREETINGS MY BELOVED CHELAS, I AM SAINT GERMAIN AND I REQUEST PERMISSION TO COME FORWARD.

Answer: "Please Dear one, you are most welcome."

Response: "Yes, please come forward."

In that Mighty Christ I AM, I stream forth on the Violet Ray of Mercy, Compassion, and Forgiveness. We ask you Dear chelas, Dear students of mine, that you remember this Violet Flame in every endeavor. It is important that you always use the Violet Flame in, through, and around all requests for financial abundance. For the Violet Flame can transmute the cause, the record, and the effect of any problem you may be having, whether it be with others or through the movement of consciousness itself.

The Prophecy Conference is an important event, one that many members of our Great White Lodge will be observing. Indeed, it is an important event, for it is near the great pattern of freedom, that was focused for the birth of the United States. Near that area where at one time the patriots, who so longed for freedom wrote a Constitution that enabled them to uncover a New Time, to see a new country, to discover a new world.

Now the Prophets gather to see a vision for the future: what humanity and the collective consciousness chooses and is about to create.

We have said before, many ears are ready now to hear and many eyes are now ready to be opened. There is a message that is to be given, and now this message must be heard and received, and put into final plans. It is this final plan that we shall talk about, for Dear ones, the countdown has begun, and we would like to inform you that it is important that you pay attention for truly these are the final days!

In the beginning of this work, when it was decided that the I AM America Map would be dispensed to humanity, it was also decided that humanity would be given time. Not only

---

For more information and study topics on *Dooms Day—Peace Day*, see Appendix K, page 237.

would they be given several decades of spiritual preparation, they would also be given a time period to heed the warning. Our original work of preparation began in the early 1950s. At that point many messengers were prepared. Some of them came to the Earth Plane and Planet at that time, as well as many who developed their voice, and were ready to give the message of the Great White Lodge. From there the work matured, and in the eighties [1980s], we knew it was time for the map [I AM America Map] to be dispensed to those whose eyes and ears were willing and open.

We have now given approximately fifteen years to this work; as well as seven full years to publicly distribute the I AM America material. It is important that you understand this final countdown; it is important for you to pay attention to events as they occur. We relayed the prophecies as they relate to geophysical change; we are also ready and willing to give prophecies as they relate to social and political change. For these will be the first changes that will be the undoing of one large ball of yarn! Yet, at the end of this entanglement *is* peace. Peace begins with each heart, Dear ones, as you well know, and it is for peace that you have come to listen. Peace is first in your heart—peace that is first and foremost in all that you do. We have always requested that this work is never brought forward to instill fear, but is given so that those who are ready may take an action *with us* in our Mission of peace.

Through the Mission and intention of peace, these prophecies are dispensed, so there is an impetus to do something, to take action, to change the situation as it is now, so a greater and a higher good may manifest.

At this time, there are those who think, "Why should I do anything? Why should I even take an action? It matters not." The foolish man is he who will not put the hoe in his hand or will not shovel that first spade of dirt. Recognize, you are all in this together! Place all of your hands on the shovel and dig the foundation of this new building. In our mind's eye, now we know that the time has come for the capstone. This is a capstone of peace; grace is revealed.

Dear ones, there will be many changes in the state of California, many changes that will Start through civil unrest. However, within the next nine to twelve months, escalation among the races will be even more pronounced, for there is a dark force that is exploiting this energy and allowing it to be brought forth through the media. It is there that this war is played, and it is there that we see the first of seven plagues. For the media at this time is filled with disease, and a greed and a lust for sensationalism. This lust is not truth or justice; it is what *makes money*.

These types of activities [racial unrest] will influence the Phoenix area, and there may be violence and unrest.

It is important that you understand this as polarity. Even those who stand at this time as white or black separatists, stand at any time to raise their swords at one another. Put down your swords! In that name of Mighty Justice and in the name of Mighty Freedom, peace is where all shall lie!

And now I will begin the Second Prophecy; it is important to note that in the next twenty-four hours, you will receive notification of another Earth Change event, and this Earth Change is a smaller activation of the Ring of Fire. It is important, Dear ones, that you understand that as quickly as things are changing, you must keep an even footing. After the complete activation of the Ring of Fire, it is important to know that there will be price wars for gas and oil, followed by price wars for food. These are again, notations of the days to come. In the next two to three months, changes in food pricing [occur], as there have been tremendous crop failures in Canada and Australia. It is important to understand how sensitive your global world is.

Dear ones, do not sigh heavily, but rejoice! A new day is coming; the dove is ready to land. Peace is ready to burst from every heart. If only you could know how happy we are in this Lodge! The happiness we feel, for we know the chains that bind mankind to the carnal, to the human bondage of flesh, will soon be broken. This chain is broken by the initiation of understanding, and the initiation of experience.

It is important that you observe the civil unrest that exists among the races, and the civil unrest among the youth. For the youth has little hope, and many have incarnated at this time so they may experience this Time of Great, Tumultuous Change, and learn about choice. The choice is simple for infinite, eternal peace!

It was dear Sananda who said, "As I walk through the valley of death, I fear not, for the I AM is with me." Know Dear ones, if you walk through a valley of despair, or sorrow, know that I AM always with you. Remember, and use the training you have received from this Lodge and put it into action.

I remind you to use the Violet Flame always. The Violet Flame can transmute and change any violent situation into a situation of peace. Should you encounter violence at any time, invoke the Violet Flame.

I warn you Dear ones, for these things are coming: increased violence, crop failures, and societal changes that institute and constitute the final countdown. While this would appear to be a doomsday speech, it is also a speech of hope for the future. For unless we break the chains of materiality, how will we ever understand or realize the paradise revealed within?

Dear ones, it is also important that we constantly hold the vision for a New World, and vigilantly see that the New Millennium of Peace and Prosperity comes for all of humanity.

Dear ones, the next prophecies that I shall share will be overseas. There will be increased violence, not only in Bosnia and that area of the world, but it will creep into Russia with the threat of a nuclear explosion. This possible threat of a nuclear explosion is located off of the Sea of Okhotsk between Japan and Russia. It is important that we keep a vigilant prayer and uphold the use of the Violet Flame for these peoples, for they are now beginning to understand what freedom is and its gifts. However, you've all understood that often a sacrifice must first be made for freedom to be realized or understood. These people now stand in the middle of that sacrifice. Pray for your Brothers and Sisters, Dear ones. Pray for your Brothers and Sisters that they too hold the vigilant torch of liberty!

Dear ones and Dear hearts, there will be increased monsoon activity and rainfall that come to areas of Europe in the next two to three years. These rains, related to global warming, will affect the entire area of Europe. We are also quite concerned over the nuclear testing that is occurring now in France. It is important to pray and hold the vigilance of the Violet Flame in, through, and around this country and her peoples. For again, this is a dark energy that misuses technologies and misunderstands the importance of this time.

Now, for your preparations . . . I have revealed a few of these, though I see I can invoke much fear in your heart. It is important that you always understand the love from which and for which you are created. I have released information regarding the apexes of the Golden Cities. This apex information is given to you so you may understand its importance. There is an intricate relationship between geo-energy and bioenergy that is designed to serve and assist you at this time. We have discussed the Cellular Awakening and introduce the Cellular Acceleration. It is important to live as close to the apex as possible, for it has always been prophesied that these are areas of acceleration, areas where water and air are accelerated and prana, [chi, energy] is deeply encased.

The new bioenergy that will be produced during this time is of great import and benefit to those who wish to achieve physical Ascension. We have always stated in these prophecies that physical Ascension is indeed an important part of this work. The physical Ascension joins the spirit forever with its true identity—the soul and full consciousness overtakes all bodies [light and physical]. This allows a momentum of energy to raise the physical body out of this dimension and into a New Dimension where it is freed of physical limitations. The soul then becomes individualized through the spark of freedom and gains a Mastery over the physical dimension. This physical Mastery empowers the individual to come forward as part of this Great Lodge [Great White Brotherhood] in Divine Mission. Ascension is not given to those who wish to be freed of burdens; Ascension is given to those who wish to fulfill a meaningful Divine Mission. Are you prepared for this?

Answer: "Yes!"

It is important Dear ones to understand that the Divine Mission is present for those who desire the Ascension. There is also the benefit of living in these areas to stabilize and balance the energy that is now coming forward. This grid of energy, the Golden City [Golden Cities], or as we refer to it—the Galactic Web—is a web of protection that covers the entire planet during the Time of Change. During physical and Cellular Accelerations, the Law of Balance is present in the Golden Cities.

They are present for you to utilize if you so choose. These are locations during the Time of Change that will experience a lessening of polarization and of energies of balance. If you are to have a business, build a home, and raise a family, you can continue your life during this Time of Great Change. Dear ones, we ask that you live within a forty-mile radius of the center of the Star. It is also important through this knowledge, that you use the apex of Gobean for the ceremonial work of the Great White Lodge. Make this decision with a pure heart and a pure intention. There are many other things I need to share; however, I sense at this moment there are several questions.

Response: "Thank you, beloved Saint Germain. I'd like to ask your assistance regarding the property I purchased in Nutrioso, Arizona, which I believe is inside the forty-mile radius of the apex. I need help finding a way to accomplish this, including putting up the house and acquiring the various things we need to make the transition."

It is important always, Dear one, to use the Violet Flame throughout preparation and planning. It is also important that you make this move as soon as possible. Call upon me, and I shall lay the foundation down. Call upon me, and I will see that your move is effortless. It is important too, that you raise your own food in this location and have storage for water. For you see, Dear ones, during the Time of the Fires, should they arrive, there will be a time where the water supplies of Arizona will be severely affected. Do you understand?

Answer: "Yes. I do, thank you."

Questions?

Question: "How much water will we need and for how many years?"

It is important that you have storage for at least six to nine months. However, we are hoping through the assistance of members of the Lodge, and through thought, prayer, and meditation, that many of these most cataclysmic changes can be averted. However, as I have stated before, the ultimate destiny of this time still remains in the choices of humanity.

It is important to understand, as you see, that at this time many things will happen that will be difficult to understand. These are the choices and the experiences that cannot be denied to the groups of souls that are having them. Should you see a child suffering, understand the choice of the soul. Should you see an elderly woman suffering, understand the choice of the soul.

Know that this is a time when balance will be achieved. All will be put into proper order. It is important to understand proper order and destiny.

You need to understand, Dear ones, that not all are ready to hear this message. There will be those who will hear and be awakened; many will [hear the message] in the twilight hours. However, Dear ones do not lose faith, do not lose hope.

Now, Dear ones, as I have explained to you, it is important to understand that in one year's time you will be established in the location where you will spend the next twelve years. It is important to understand that the Time of Change—of geophysical change—as well as social and political changes, are now coming.

One droplet of a terrible vial has fallen upon the planet, and this drop will spread disease and sickness. We will see many new diseases appear on the planet, and it is important that you pick a location with winds blowing from westerly and southwesterly directions, for these are winds which help to purify certain types of diseases. It is important that you know this Dear ones. It is also important that you continue in meditations for the best and the highest good, and that you constantly and vigilantly chose connection with your Mighty I AM Presence. Disease is dis-ease—a lack of harmony among the body, mind, and spirit. However, in the times that are to come, many challenges will be placed in front of you. Know this as I speak it.

While there will be many choices placed in front of the course of history and the destiny of humanity, inevitably time marches on and changes all things.

In this case, Mother Earth becomes time's servant of change. Dear ones, it is important to make the proper changes and adjustments. It is important to place the capstone on the house you have built. If you still doubt, if you still question, examine each wall of the home you have built, see whether it is sturdy, whether it is sound. Shake it and ask, "Am I happy with this? Will I keep this?" This is a not a time of discernment; it is a Time of Choice! It is also a Time of Common Sense. Place the capstone on your house, your mansion, and ask, "Is this sturdy?" Are you ready to stand the times to come?

Are your vehicles [light bodies] purified and ready for the service that is ahead? Are you ready for those who will come, asking, "Where is the Cup? From where do I drink?"

It is important to prepare locations, for is this not your service? Offer your hand to your Brother [and say], "Yes, I am here, willing and able to serve!" Questions?

Answer: "I'll make effort then to begin preparations, to go to the two and a half acres, I've purchased. I feel that this is what you're asking and this is what I want."

Question: "Thank you. Our friend Russ wants to know how he can better serve the Brotherhood."

Of course through use of the Violet Flame! However, this soul is one who has served the Great White Lodge in many other capacities before. It is important that he aligns himself in service to the Master Teachers, and ask for the appearance of one Master Teacher to give him guidance and direction.

Of course this is best achieved while living in a Golden City. However, it is best that he not live at the apex to begin with. As you have noted, when you were sent to this Golden City, you were sent first to the outer reaches, and then through careful spiritual migration, you have moved inside. When you are building the body, it takes time. You cannot instantly run twenty miles! You work your way toward it. You feed the muscles. You work the body through discipline and routine, and gradually you build your momentum, your strength, your courage, and your focus. This is what must happen for this soul. It must build its energy first, then enter into one of the Golden Cities to connect with a Master Teacher.

I shall take my leave from your dimension, and will come forward in service to the Great and the Mighty ONE. So Be It!

"Thank you."

12

The Fountain of Life

Saint Germain Gives Personal Instruction

GREETINGS IN THAT MIGHTY CHRIST.

I AM Saint Germain, and I request permission to come forward, Dear students.

"Please Dear one, you are most welcome."

We have requested to come forward this day to give you discourse about the upcoming times and changes. Alongside me today is beloved El Morya, Chohan of the First Ray as he has instruction to bring to you; however, before we proceed, I would like to give you a short discourse.

This discourse is in preparation for the times to come, the times ahead. It is a discourse not only on Forgiveness, but a discourse on Transmutation. As I have always said, "Down with death!" Death, you see Dear ones, is a consciousness that is held. It is also a pattern held, and it is also a pattern held in the body and in the Cellular Memory. How do we destroy the consciousness of death and allow the consciousness of life to become the ever-present life force?

It is as simple as electromagnetics; but, it is also as simple as thought, feeling, and action—as we have always taught in these teachings. When you decree a thing through the voice and the power of sound, you bring it into a level of manifestation. When you speak with your voice, the voice you recognize, the words of your language create a quality of consciousness.

That is, the brain has allowed a thought to come forward to pattern the cells of the body. So, when you speak the decrees we have given you and with the word I AM, which commands the God presence into action, you are, in essence, decreeing a thing into motion, into rhythm, into Sattva.

Dear ones, to bring forward the pattern of life, one must constantly attune their speech patterns and life habits toward the *quality* of effervescent life. Avoid speech patterns that accept death as an inevitable ending as in that final fear in doom and gloom.

For more information and study topics on *The Fountain of Life,* see Appendix L, page 241.

Haven't you come to understand that consciousness, indeed, is the quality that can hold either pattern of life or death? Then it is consciousness that is the *key* that holds the final pivotal point and acceleration to the New Dimensions. The New Dimension[s] that we speak of at this moment is the Fourth Dimension of Vibration. This Fourth Dimension of Vibration is indeed the next level that must be developed to understand life eternal. The first Three Dimensions that we speak of are held within the Karmic waves of life and death. The Karmic waves of life and death are where consciousness and death consciousness are programmed—the understanding that death could rule life. However, you have known through these teachings that knowledge rises above superstition. The belief systems that once held you in the trappings of illusions and death are just those, illusions. It is time Dear ones, stalwart followers of this work, chelas, and disciples of the Violet Flame, to come forward now, and decree life unto your being:

I AM the effervescent life flowing through.
I AM the effervescent life transmuting.
I AM the effervescent life of life!

Those who have sought the fountain of youth have now discovered that the fountain of youth lies within the fountain of consciousness! Open your fountain of consciousness—let the waters pour forward into your life, into your energy fields.

This wellspring, this fountain of life that exists within you, will lead you onward to Fourth Dimensional Consciousness. Fourth Dimensional Consciousness is indeed the Consciousness of Vibration. When we enter into your energy fields, we enter and access through the Fourth Dimension. That is why we ask, "Do we have permission to come forward?" For this permission allows us to access *your* Fourth Dimensional [Energy] Fields; to raise them to a higher level of vibration. When one opens the third eye through the pineal gland that exists in the physical body, you are opening an entry, a door, a portal, to the Fourth Dimension.

The Fourth Dimensional Consciousness is where we reside when we come to give discourse. Now is not the time or the dispensation when the Masters—spiritual teachers—will appear in Third Dimensional bodies. For you see Dear ones, the earth, her people, and her transition have allowed the collective consciousness to fall to yet *even* a lower state; a lower state that will not allow our entry at this moment. However, a time will come when we shall appear again, not only in the Fourth Dimension, but in the other dimensions [such as the Third Dimension] as you are now experiencing.

This will come after the great shift of the poles; after the great shift in consciousness. You will rest your weary feet and hands. But for now how shall you persevere throughout these days, these final days, the days of transition? It is important to continue with your spiritual disciplines as I have outlined in this discourse: call a thing into action and call Transmutation into action. This is done through the use of the Violet Flame, and at this time, the Violet Flame is the greatest gift for all of humanity. When you call upon the Violet Flame, it alone has the ability to transmute and change *any* situation at *any* time. Even the wars currently waging in the Middle East could be changed if the focus were placed on Transmutation and the Violet Flame. But there are the Doubting Thomases among you, and that Doubting Thomas has crept into your consciousness and there it resides! You hold the key through your consciousness. Therefore, through your choices you bring forth the manifestation.

Dear hearts, if you wish to change anything in your life, anything that you are currently experiencing, first you must conceptualize it. Also, you must understand it through that will of intention as beloved El Morya has taught. You must choose life over death for there to be regeneration in any situation. You Dear ones, students in this schoolhouse called life, must understand the rules and the laws of which you have been brought here to your own manifestations. Yet, you cry and weep when you find that you are living the result of your own creations! These are your own manifestations, but give conscious awareness to your creations through choosing effervescent life.

The fountain of life is indeed the fountain of youth. How shall I change the present situation? How shall I take my body and regenerate each cell from old age? How do I take worn out perspectives and attitudes, and transmute—change them? Charge them with the Violet Flame through your daily use of decrees and through your daily focus of consciousness. This indeed will raise you above all trial and tribulation. All things that come to you that you wish to change, blaze with the Mighty Violet Flame through your consciousness, and you will see that I have offered you that most refreshing drink!

Humanity is on the brink of Devastation, but humanity is also upon the brink of great evolution and spiritual awakening. During these times, as you ride the wave, or walk the cliff or the precipice, ask, "How can I move forward? How can I move forward without Devastation to myself or to others?"

Call upon the teaching that you have known deep within your heart; the teachings of Grace, Forgiveness, and Transmutation are always there as your eternal and infinite tools. They are indeed the *fountain of life*. Call upon these tools, Dear ones. In this schoolhouse learn to use these tools to bring forth beauty and cooperation for evolution.

Questions?

Question: "In everyone's daily life, your advice, your guidance, and the law is to apply the Violet Flame decree to anything that's challenged and transmuted? In doing this you're stating that this law is a Law of Compassion, a Law of Forgiveness and Understanding. In a Three Dimensional collective world, it seems only that the Law of Balance exists. Are you saying that the higher Law of Transmutation will neutralize this Law of Balance?"

Dear beloveds, it is the higher Laws of Forgiveness and Transmutation that *restore* balance. One cannot walk in balance until they have opened to purification, to Transmutation. These are the tools and the way that one enters; to begin to walk in balance.

Question: "Bearing this in mind, if anyone on this planet wants to create a balance in their economy, their health, their personal relationships, their political relationships, or even with the environment, then the only solution is through the use of this higher law. Is that correct?"

This is so, Dear beloved, and yet humanity, through beliefs and old dialectics has interpreted Forgiveness as *turning the other cheek*. This is simply not so! It is a Law of Purification; a Law of Transmutation. It is the Law of Alchemy that comes forward, transmuting the animal consciousness into the human consciousness; transmuting the base realities into the greater realities; bringing the First, Second, and Third Dimension into an understanding of Fourth Dimension. It is all of these things, Dear hearts, beloved students and chelas, *all* of these things. It is not putting your tail between your legs and groveling for the respect that you are *recognized as* Divine Human Beings! It is indeed that refreshing drink. It is the understanding and the realization that you are whole. It is the understanding and realization that you are Divine. Dear beloveds, Transmutation and purification cleanse the old cobwebs of the mind; the old patterns that no longer create the world in which you wish to live. It allows the new door to open, and shuts forever the door on death and illusion!

Question: "Then in essence, if you are choosing to alter an outcome that seems inevitable by the moment's standards, or the understanding of the moment, it is through the application of the Violet Flame that this outcome can be altered?"

If only you would use the Violet Flame vigilantly, every day, many of the trials and the tribulations in your life would be lifted from you. You would be taken to a greater understanding; a greater understanding would be given to you and seen in all your affairs. As we have always stated before, Dear chelas, place your attention solely upon the work at hand! There has been that individual who has walked as a dark shadow alongside your work and has taken the work of the hierarchy, adulterated it, and used it for personal gain. This, of course, is none of *your* concern, but it is *our* concern. Do not allow your energies to be filtrated or misused by one who is simply manipulating Laws of Fear and Death. Close the door forever on this energy, and allow it never to come amongst what you are doing. Do you understand Dear ones?

Answer: "Yes. However, the personal sense of injustice is great."

How would there be injustice when you hold the key to your own creation? When you hold the key to your own creation? How could injustice exist when you have been given the key of how you, yourself, now can walk in balance? You must call upon the Transmutation, the purification—the Violet Flame. Close the door to death; let the fountain of life resume.

Answer: "As you have instructed, I will follow. It makes perfect sense."

I do hope you realize, Dear beloved, that death and illusion have attracted or attached to you. Now it is time to resume the work that has been given to you. Do not allow your intentions to be diverted away from what has nothing to do with the work and the message brought forward through this body of material and information. As you know, the Great White Lodge does not and will not sponsor information that leads an individual to the trappings of fear or the trappings of illusion. As you see, with this individual, there has been the soulful test of, shall we say, "guru status" as beloved K.H. [Kuthumi] has so eloquently spoken. This is the time of the death of the outer guru and the time of ever-present knowledge *within* the individual. As we have always stated before, Dear ones, Dear hearts, it is towards the individual [one undivided] that we aim our work for and toward, and yes, while there is the Vibration of Unana—the unity of all, the merging of consciousness, the understanding of the mighty and glorious Christ that we all exist of—there is also the *complete sovereign individual* who shall shine forth in these days to come. This is the individual who will understand the HU-man, the God-man, and the work of the Ray Force, individualized within that beam as God-force, a true son, daughter of God. This is the work that we strive for, Dear ones, do you understand?

Answer: "Yes, completely."

Do not let your attention or your energies be diverted into the trappings of hate, judgment, and guilt. For are not all of these a fountain of death? Place your attention on that which brings you life, which moves you forward, not backward, Dear ones! Place your feet on the path and move ahead toward the goal. It is easy to be diverted in this world of duality that you are learning through, so easy to divert your energies at any time. Understand Dear ones, we are here as your elder Brothers and Sisters, and as your guides. We have walked before you and we shall continue to hold the lamp high! A time shall come when you will do this too for those of lesser consciousness. But for now, you must keep your attention on the path, on the task at hand. Do you have further questions?

Answer: "No, you have satisfied all immediate curiosities and desires. Thank you. I'm grateful."

13

The First Golden City

The Traditions of Shamballa

GREETINGS BELOVED CHELAS. I AM SAINT GERMAIN.

Shamballa and greetings beloved students and chelas of the Seventh Ray! As you have requested my presence, I come forward in the service of the Mighty Violet Ray—that Mighty Violet Ray of Mercy, Compassion, and Forgiveness.

Shamballa is a time when we all gather; you have asked questions concerning the celebration of this focus of our thought, our feeling, and our action. You have asked questions about this celebration; and I have come forward today to give discourse on this time, as I have given you information in past discourses regarding the Time of Shamballa. It is of course a time of great feasting; a time of celebration; a time of camaraderie among friends in the service of the ONE. It is the time for the anchoring of energies on the Earth Plane and Planet. It is a celebration of the Rays of Light and Sound; it is a celebration of the creation of humanity, and the work of the Spiritual Hierarchy upon this Earth Plane and Planet.

Yes, Shamballa is our spiritual home and the third retreat located above the Gobi desert now in that Golden City also known as Gobi. Energy steadily arches across to the beloved Star of Gobean where El Morya now holds his focus for that Mighty Blue Ray of Transformation, Harmony, and Peace on the planet. We have always stated that it is in the apexes of the Golden Cities where celebrations, or focuses, should be held for the movement of energy upon the Earth Plane and Planet. And naturally, Gobean would be the first place where one would travel to anchor peace in the hearts of the collective consciousness. For this is one of the activated portals, the first, in fact, of that mighty Galactic Web. That web bursts forth this new creation known as the New Age.

This New Age was prophesied long ago by many other messengers of this Lodge. And you are both sharing in that service of messenger—as a Prophet. It is an important time, the birth of this New Age. We've stated before, the hierarchy has worked for thousands of years to bring this time to the apex of its fruition. One that will not be realized yet for still thousands of more years; however, you are now at *this* time on the verge of revolution—a point of departure. Now a point that steadily, and with the focus of the mighty I AM, moves the energy of the New Age forward. It has grown from the point of 51-55 per cent. Continue in the stalwart plan, Dear ones. Align your focus and your energy with the Master Teacher of

---

For more information and study topics on *The First Golden City*, see Appendix M, page 247.

Gobean—El Morya—for he has come forward to bring the focus of the energies that will bring the supreme completion to the activation of Gobean. Align your energies and loyalty to the Mighty Teacher of the Blue Ray; align your energies, Dear ones, for this is how you now may serve!

Shamballa is a time, yes, of feasting, supping, and celebration among us; but, it also represents many teachings that have been passed on since the birth of humanity. You have asked when it begins, and it begins on that seventeenth of December, a day of the Christ, and the awakening of the Christ Consciousness within each and everyone of you. The seventeen signifies in ancient numerology the birth of the Star of the Magi—the gift of the Sun of Light within. Sons and daughters of light, come forward this day, on the seventeenth, and celebrate the opening of Shamballa!

Shamballa takes place for exactly four weeks—twenty-eight days to be exact. And during these twenty-eight days, a celebration of the four elements is carried forward. Let me explain further for your understanding.

The first week is the opening of the energies, and it is here, during this week, that we celebrate the first primal substance that brought humanity to the earth, and the earth element itself. So it is the earth element that is celebrated in the first seven days. We suggest that the first seven days of your celebrations and festivities are focused upon Earth Healing and Earth Celebrations. Celebrate the birth of Mother Earth! Celebrate and give thanks to Mother Earth—beloved Babajeran—for she has given you your physical bodies from her own body, cloaking the Mighty Spirit I AM with her substance.

Dear ones, Shamballa is the time when we carry forward our celebrations for the Earth Mother. We also carry forward ceremonies and rituals for her healing as celebration and thanks for what she has given each and everyone of us, and for the opportunity to come here for the joy of the experience.

The second week is ruled by the element of air. From the traditions that you well know, air rules all mental movement. Mentalism is conscious thought; however, as a tradition during Shamballa, the second week is celebrated as the week of the Messengers—those who traveled forth in consciousness—to give the message of this Lodge to humanity. This is the week when there are various celebrations of Krishna, Buddha, Christ, and the many other avatars and adepts who have carried forward the focus of this Lodge to those of humanity who are willing to see and to hear. In your Christian traditions, this is the week of the celebration of the birth of Jesus-Sananda, the Christ. If you wish to celebrate, celebrate in the fullness of *all* teachers. Celebrate in the fullness of *all messengers* who have come to ease the pain and the suffering of humanity. The Week of Air is celebrated with thankfulness and gratitude for the world teachers who have gone before you.

The third week is ruled by water, and as you know, water moves emotion. The third week of Shamballa is a celebration of love—Brotherly and Sisterly love. This is the time when feasts are set at many tables in Shamballa. It is also the time of the passage of one [solar] year to the next. It is a time of camaraderie, where family and friends gather. It is a week of feasting and supping together as ONE. On the Earth Plane and Planet this is the most perfect week to perform the Cup Ceremony to understand that you have traveled together as a soul-family—a group of souls focusing on a point of consciousness. All components in a family make this Mighty ONE. Your hand consists of five fingers; however, it is *one* hand. Each finger needs the movement of the other finger to perform its functions. Water movement rules the third week of Shamballa.

The fourth week of Shamballa is ruled by fire. Fire is the Seal of Solomon, placed as a capstone on the other elements. It is the message of spirit, the soul, the Jiva, and the Monad. This is the essence of *all* of life, the song of the soul. The purpose of the fourth week is Spiritual Fire. This is the most perfect time to receive messages, to meditate, to pray, and to purify the body and mind to receive that which is most perfect for your movement into the next year. During this week members of the hierarchy—the Brotherhood and Sisterhoods of Light of this Lodge—meet together and position their most perfect plans for the coming year. As you shall see, this is a week of planning, orchestrating, and understanding the movement of the collective consciousness. It is also a week of supreme service, beginning first through the purification of the individual and then moving into the collective.

You, of course, have had many celebrations during this Time of Shamballa, a time of the death of darkness and the birth of the lighted ones. Carry out many celebrations. Carry out the service of love, as dear Sananda has always instructed you to. We too give gifts to one another during this time. We give four gifts total, one for each week; each gift signifying the earth, air, water, and fire elements, for overall it is a time of sharing and understanding.

Unana becomes our focus—the unity of ONE. After twenty-eight days, two more days are added for the sealing of divinity when we work together as ONE to become a cohesive unit. For in the *unity of all* is that Mighty Light of God that never fails!

Do you have questions?

Question: "The only pertinent questions I have are about the ceremony during the Time of Shamballa. Can you offer a ceremony we can do on this Plane and Planet that will coordinate with your celebrations in other dimensions? This, of course, is totally up to you. It's only a thought that may make students, chelas, and aspirants feel closer to you. It will help build that tradition of unifying the Lodge of the universal world, but I leave it up to you."

There are many symbols used during Shamballa. One symbol for the earth is salt, and we always place a bowl of salt upon our altar to represent the earth substance [element]. This represents the Spiritual Fire in the substance of Mother Earth. The Dove of Peace is the symbol of the messengers, and many doves—Doves of Peace to soothe the ailing hearts of humanity—are released during the second week. Of course you know water is signified by the Cup. It is used in many of your ceremonies, and it is used as we have instructed in each of the ceremonies during Shamballa. Fire is signified by the lighting of the seven candles for each of the seven Rays; it signifies the seven mighty Hermetic Laws that rule all of creation that humanity will experience, learn, and Master on the Earth Plane and Planet. At the beginning of the opening of Shamballa, one candle is lit; one candle represents the Mighty Light of God that never fails! This candle is held in Shamballa as an eternal flame—a fireless light—which is conceived from the heart of *all life*. The fireless light is lit continuously throughout the entire thirty days of celebration. At the closing of the thirtieth day, the light is taken home by a light-bearer, back to the planet of Venus, where it is held in continuous consciousness until the next year of Shamballa.

These are the traditions we share. There are many more ceremonies, some of them from individualized perceptions of the same teachings. Many of them [ceremonies] carry these symbols that represent the eternal and infinite truth that have always ruled those who come to the earth. There are many things that will be occurring in the next year, and these of course, will be set out in the plans to come in the following week. It is during this time that we will formulate a Master Plan for the movement of consciousness in the mighty Galactic Web and the activation of the Golden Cities. Shamballa, as you know, was originally created as an etheric city to hold a perfect consciousness for the evolution of humanity. And now, as we reach this time when more [people] have come and more shall choose, it is important that we continue to focus on the building of all fifty-one etheric Golden Cities, so that the spiritual template is laid in the hearts of all men.

Do you have questions?

Answer: "I have no further questions."

In that case my beloveds, I must return to the celebrations at Shamballa. Know that always I AM here at your request. In service to that Mighty Breath of Light and Action of God, I AM Saint Germain.

14

The Ever-Present Perfection

Saint Germain on Energy Movement

GREETINGS IN THAT MIGHTY CHRIST.

I AM Saint Germain and I stream forth on that Mighty Violet Ray of Mercy and Transmuting Forgiveness. As usual, Dear hearts, I request permission to come forward to bring discourse.

"In the most effervescent life, please come forward Dear one."

Today the topic of our discussion shall be that ever-present perfection of life, the Eight-Sided Cell of Perfection. [Saint Germain diagrams the Eight-Sided Cell of Perfection. For more information see Appendix N.]

As you see on this chalkboard, I have diagramed an Eight-Sided Cell of Perfection, better known as an octagon; each side is in perfect harmony with the center. For you see, each side is always in perfect harmony with the center of its source. This is the premise of *all perfection*. Perfection mirrors more perfection, and therefore perfection is infinite. This is the philosophy and the understanding.

The eight represents the four elements of the earth in duality—two times two. [(2x2)2] For you see, Dear ones, two times two represents eight perfect mirrors of perfection mirroring from the central source of being. All energy movement on the Earth Plane and Planet follows the course of the magnetic poles, the South and North Poles, and the center, of course, is known as the core of the earth. Imagine this Eight-Sided Cell of Perfection superimposed over the planet, with eight perfect mirrors throughout the planet. Now, if you extend this with dimensional vision, you will see many mirrors at the central core—the source of *all perfection*. Perfection mirrors itself back infinitely, creating infinite *absolute perfection*.

As the earth travels through its many sojourns and epochs, we now see times on the Earth Plane and Planet when perfection is less than its complete out-picturing; times when disharmony and discord run rampant on the Earth Plane and Planet. This thought, feeling, and action mirrors disharmony through the perfect source. Why does this happen? Through the qualification of energy through the use of the free will. For you see, Dear hearts, you have

For more information and study topics on *The Ever-Present Perfection*, see Appendix N, page 253.

been given that mighty illuminated mind in which you may choose which path to tread. This again is the choice of a Co-creator.

In this time of your epoch, north is the direction that humanity is facing. This is toward a more darkened perspective on life itself. Facing the south—where more light comes to the planet—is a more enlightened perspective. Those who face south understand the feminine aspects of creation and [have] a more enlightened mind.

Facing east are the scholars; those who have achieved a literal and an intuitive way of viewing life through the scholastic way of viewing the disseminating processes of the mind. To the west are those who sing the song of philosophy; those who understand through the literal and expressive intuition that energy movement comes forward.

This is a brief teaching of the four directions as understood through the teaching of the Eight-Sided Cell of Perfection. The Eight-Sided Cell of Perfection covers the entire planet and is also planted within the heart of your being. This infinite source, the center of the Eight-Sided Cell, is where the Unfed Flame of Love, Wisdom, and Power resides. There was once an epoch, many ages ago, where the Unfed Flame had risen to such a high state of infinite awareness that those who carried this plume about them resonated only perfection and harmony. This group of souls now resides as Cosmic Teachers over this planetary system and have evolved from earth, beloved Babajeran.

Dear hearts, when you begin to understand the energy movement of the Eight-Sided Cell of Perfection you will begin to understand how consciousness moves on the planet. You are currently in the transitory state before a major shift of the poles, not only in consciousness, but in the most literal sense. That is why I have come forward with this teaching, so that you would understand the movements of energy and consciousness, the Mirrors of Perfection.

In most ancient teachings nine movements are taught, nine being the 3x3, the understanding of the Christ energy. There are, indeed, nine movements of perfected energy within the Eight-Sided Cell of Perfection. These nine perfected movements begin always in the central source, the heart. This is the *Temple of Your Being*, and within all Shamanic movement upon the Earth Plane and Planet, the central location is always where the temple resides. This is *infinite space* from which all future holograms of perfection mirror—it is the central source. It is the perfection of *all being* [creation] and it mirrors perfection throughout the rest of the movement within the Eight-Sided Cell of Perfection. Facing, of course, this most central area is the altar, or the Unfed Flame of Infinite Being and Energy. This creates energy through the career, fame, and fortune, which you have chosen as your Divine Path. This is the next perfected movement of expression.

The next expression is the movement toward marriage, or the longing for another with whom to share life. Naturally, this next movement is known as *family*.

Let me diagram these for you again. The first movement exists in the center and is indeed the altar or the Temple. The next movement is toward the Divine Path [Dharma]. These are essentially as ONE. They are also known as *Divine Purpose.*

The second movement from here, or the third in sequence, is indeed marriage. It is the longing for the twin flame, the other half of yourself.

The fourth perfected movement is that of family. For when two become as one, they move in *cosmic purpose*. This also relates to cosmic movement in its totality [macrocosm]. These are the first four movements of energy in the Eight-Sided Cell of Perfection.

Now let us move to the human body. These exact movements are the same within the physical system. They bring about healing for another who may have problems in any one of these areas. They also address the direction or the course of energy movement through the knowledge of the Eight-Sided Cell of Perfection.

Perhaps if one is having trouble in their career—or Divine Purpose—you will note the Ray as it arcs from the central source of the heart, and you will understand how to bring forth such a treatment. The same goes for one who desires to meet their beloved, and to bring forth the fruition of marriage on this plane. And so you see there are numerous applications!

The movement of energy in the microcosm is mirrored with the macrocosm.

Now let us continue. As there are five more directions, each direction matches with the fingers of the hand and the toes of the feet. For you see Dear ones, these are all concerned with manifestations brought forward on the Earth Plane and Planet, the first four manifestations belong to the Divine Heavens—an infinite understanding of being. These last five movements are equally important, as they are the measurement of Cause and Effect. They are the measurement of your planes of duality and your understanding of Hermetic Law.

The fifth direction is *children*. Children bring and represent that great fruition and understanding between the sexes. Children are a generation of the forces of nature; they are made of the energies of male and female—the Yin and Yang—coming together. Children represent the future, and they also represent the path of abundance that a couple or a union shares.

The sixth movement is of benevolent beings of a higher force that assist this family or movement. This is where your spiritual teachers reside. It is through this energy of the sixth movement that your spiritual teachers, contacts, and guides come through at the most auspicious moment to help and assist you, to guide you, and lead you further on the path of evolution.

The seventh direction is the direction of abundance. This is the understanding that not only wealth, but *total* prosperity bring perfection to the incarnation on the Earth Plane and Planet.

This is the best location to grow gardens—outwardly and inwardly—and develop your link to beloved Mother Earth—Babajeran. Are there questions, Dear ones?

Answer: "No, not at this time."

The eighth movement is the direction of occupation. The eighth understanding determines where we toil in this in this world, and it is much different from the career. For instance, one may have the Divine Purpose of a mother. However, her daily occupation may be as caregiver, nurse, or doctor. So the career—or the Divine Purpose—of this woman is that, indeed, of mother, however, her occupation is *much* different. Do you understand this difference?

Answer: "Yes."

The final direction, of which we will concern ourselves, is the direction of outer influence. It is indeed a much misunderstood direction, but it is one that is of vast importance. It is choice! Choices are made to enhance or dehance [weaken]. These are the types of choices made within the lifetime—the embodiment. It is here where one decides to take a higher or a lower way. Which way shall I go? Through the comprehension of *choice,* supreme knowledge is obtained. Understand the *difference* in choices, and knowledge is understood. The final direction is known as the Star of Knowledge. It is through this movement that all chelas and initiates of this work begin to follow, most discriminately. You see, Dear ones, choice creates our future, yet choice remains with us as the past. The Star of Knowledge contains within it the infinity of time. For *it* contains *both* past and future, and we return home to the infinite Temple of Love, Wisdom, and Power! From this direction, infinity is known, and the Eight-Sided Cell of Perfection mirrors to the first direction again, and so on, and so forth.

Each of these directions is a spiritual discipline, and one may incarnate only to perfect but one mirroring. Perhaps they have chosen to be the most perfect parent, and therefore, arc the greater part of energy toward that direction. Another may decide that they shall be a priest, and therefore, mirror or project their energy toward the sixth direction. Another may decide that he or she shall mirror his or her energy into business and into the eighth movement. Does this bring an understanding of perfect energy?

Answer: "Yes."

Within the seventh direction of abundance, you will find a tendency for your money and wealth to grow. So understand too, if one is directed in their incarnation toward continuous prosperity and abundance, often they will choose occupations that are geared toward the flow of money, banking, and economics. Do you understand?

Answer: "Yes."

Each of these teachings is a perfect path, spiritually linked toward the central source. As you see the flow of the energy of this perfection, do you see how disharmony through war and poverty is brought on the earth? Without the understanding of infinite perfection, it is difficult to proceed upon this path of Mastery, for one begins to perceive imbalance.

Yet when one moves to the understanding that all things are in perfect balance at all times, balance is then achieved through the Path of Perfection. It is important always to keep your mind upon the Path of Perfection. Left balances out right; hot balances out cold; and the front balances out the back. Study and assign attributes to each of these Paths of Perfection, and see that balance is present at all times.

Balance is always found in the center point—the heart of all understanding, the infinite understanding of Love, Wisdom, and Power, all brought together through that perfect blend.

All energy moves through light, and indeed through sound. Have you noticed as you open the windows in your house, how the sunlight carries energy that circulates throughout your home? This is also true of sound; one who carries a pleasant voice also carries the benevolence of the Gods. When you play harmonious music, the strings of a harp and the tone of a piano carry a higher vibration and energy. This energy feeds each of the paths of perfection. You have noticed that through light and sound, healing comes forward to a patient. Have you not?

Answer: "Yes, indeed."

This is the same with all of your other activities. Even in your business, bring forward light and bring forward sound. Light and sound moves stagnant and dead energy, energy that needs to be moved out! As one develops a Mastery of the movement of energy through light and sound, one begins to understand the cause *behind* the force that moves. This returns to the center of this understanding, the infinite source—that Unfed Flame. Thought, feeling, and action are *the movers* of light and sound! When they come together in perfect partnership, the movement is even more potent or powerful! This first concept is taught through that process known as *mentalism*. We have always stated before that "as a man thinketh, so he becomes." Have you noted this?

Thought creates. Thought moves light, and thought, indeed, moves sound. Thought entering into perfect union with sound is also known as *feeling*. When one feels the purpose of their thought, again, it's a much more powerful movement. It adds the trinity of action in that same, direct course—thought, feeling, and action move together in perfect partnership through the perfect path of light and sound movements of energy. Do you understand that it is desirable to learn the movement of energy through thought, feeling, and action of light and sound?

Answer: "Yes."

When one begins to Master these components, one truly becomes the Master of all energy movement. I stated earlier in this discourse that there is a slight difference in the direction of energy movement prior to a polar shift; you will notice that your westerly directions are off five to sixteen degrees depending on the flux of the energy fields of the earth. It is important to consider this in all of your calculations. It is also important to understand this for the times to come.

As I stated before, the direction of collective consciousness is now directed more northerly, or toward more male-dominated experiences. This has created in your societies an overextension toward warring and an overextension toward materialism and comfort seeking; and too much harshness, inflexibility, and hardness in the world. After the pole shift, an orientation toward the south will become prevalent. Therefore, this will be known as a Golden Age—the Age of Gold. For Gold is indeed the metal associated with the south. A southern exposure of consciousness will orient toward the feminine; an understanding of unity; and a softness, shall we say, of consciousness.

Do you see the contrast again: hot and cold, soft and hard? Do you see, Dear ones, how the earth is the most perfect, benevolent schoolhouse? It's a perfect mirror of your thoughts, of your feelings, and of your actions. Through this understanding, your world is the total creation of perfection—a total creation of the Eight-Sided Cell of Perfection; each of these paths mirror from within through your thought, your feeling, and your action. All that manifests comes through the perfection of your out-picturing and through the perfection of your conscious attunement; what's in your being is fed through the infinite ONE. Do you have questions?

Answer: "Not at this time."

When one begins to understand the movement of energy, one is able to enter on a path of total Mastery over their created world. For you see, you have come forward to learn how to create your perfect world. Through the creation of an imperfect world, one learns and moves forward to create a perfect world, a perfect experience. Through perfection comes Mastery, and through the spiral of evolution comes increased duty and responsibility. As you have known for some time, in this creation of the new Golden Age which is peaceful and feminine, you are moving forward in your own evolution to become a Master: first a Master of your created worlds, and then a Master directing the created world of form.

The Ascended Masters have been appointed to guard the evolution of humanity at this time so that humanity may move forward in a most constructive and non-destructive manner. We work through the energy of consciousness much like Shamans of energy movement. We, too, work with chi, orgone, light, and sound! These are a few words that you have come to know energy through and by. This energy movement is quite important in the movement of consciousness, for again, as stated in the law, "as a man thinketh, so he becomes." So as humanity thinketh, so it is! The great civilizations that have flourished in other Golden Ages understood the one perfect focus that all carried—the one perfect path from the Eight-Sided

Cell of Perfection. That was the sole focus—unity and harmony of their thoughts, of their feelings, and of their actions together as ONE organism. This, of course, is known as a collective consciousness aimed toward a collective focus.

When we move our energy toward a collective focus there are times when we come together. Sometimes, beloved El Morya or beloved Portia joins alongside me in directing an energy focus toward an entire group of chelas aimed toward collective unity!

We have Started a movement, working through our chelas, to understand this current Time of Transition and the upcoming Time of Change. That is why we have sent the Prophecies of Change. There are those who resonate toward this message. Those are the ones who have come under the direction of the movement of *our* light and sound vehicles [light bodies]; those are the ones who have been sensitized and are aware of the perfect path.

Now, these beloved ones have come together in an understanding through this Divine Focus for the building of the Golden Age—the time *beyond* the changes. In this time you shall move forward as Divine Inheritors, and each path of perfection will be experienced in its totality, allowing you to spiral up the stairs of the Eight-Sided Cell of Perfection toward the infinite union of the ONE.

Do you see how the evolutionary process works through these Eight Paths of Perfection that are aimed toward the unity of the last and final path—complete Mastery over your thoughts, your feelings, and your actions? As this Mastery is attained, another level of understanding is brought forward into a greater service and a greater union with the ONE. At that staging point, the movement of energy becomes even greater. But for now, so that you may keep your focus on the task at hand, it is most important that you first Master your own world, and bring forth the path of perfect harmony. As Kuan Yin has often stated, "perfect harmony with a perfect path."

Do you see, Dear ones, how this movement of energy, once it is Mastered, can instigate the calculation or strategy of your next move? For you have thought for some time, "Where should I move: to the left or to the right, to the front or to the back, do I move up or do I move down? Therefore, you move not at all! This non-movement causes stagnation. Have you noticed that when a pool of water has no movement, the waters become stagnant and rancid? This is what happens when you refuse to move *beyond* what you have indeed Mastered. We have asked you several times to make movement, and yet you find it impossible to move beyond where you have contained yourself, and therefore the energy—the chi, the light, the sound—enacts a series of events that are non-movement. The lack of movement causes disease and problems within your world, and sometimes even a backward motion ensues! Now that you have had this experience, Dear ones, do you see the microcosm as a reflection of the greater macrocosm? Can you understand why the earth will go through its Time of Great Change? Humanity refuses to move forward, and this causes stagnation. Your work is to be a light to those so they may move forward during these times. Do you see now, through the path of the Eight-Sided Cell of Perfection how all must move forward with perfect alignment to the perfect plan?

Answer: "Yes, I understand. Thank you."

15

The Point of Perception

Saint Germain on Conscious Co-creation

GREETINGS BELOVEDS, IN THAT MIGHTY CHRIST.

I AM Saint Germain and I stream forth on that Mighty Transmuting Violet Ray of Mercy and Forgiveness. As usual Dear hearts, I ask permission to come forward.

"Saint Germain, you have permission."

Often you ask within, "What is my purpose here? What is the purpose of life and this existence in the physical?"

Dear ones, the work of Prophecy has been brought forward to show you that you are indeed the Creator of your reality. It is a teaching that scratches only the surface, and only the chela that is willing to go deeper within discovers that he or she is linked to the purpose of all things.

Prophecy is a teaching that begins at the greater reality, and then leads one into the inner-reality. That greater reality is of the world: political systems, social systems, and geophysical systems. Then the student or chela faces the inner being; the inner systems that exist, such as the soul's intention; and the individual's purpose of life in the physical reality.

You have asked many times in your meditations, "Why am I doing this? What is the intention of this work? What is the purpose of my life on earth?" You see, Dear hearts, you are here for one sole purpose, and that *is* your choice. You have all *chosen* to come here! All choose to take physical incarnation. All choose the circumstances of each birth. All chose the time that each incarnates.

When one begins to understand that they are the Creator of their circumstances, their situations, and all things surrounding them, they are placed, shall we say, into a *new* division. For you have begun to understand that thought, feeling, and desire through the expert of your focus creates your reality, it creates your circumstances, and it creates each situation.

For more information and study topics on *The Point of Perception*, see Appendix O, page 271.

You may wonder, "Where does time fit into all of this?" You see time as a nonexistent entity, and a way to identify each circumstance, each situation. Time is relative in this respect, Dear hearts. Time comes forward to *serve* your creation. So then, you move on to understand that there is no past, there is no future, there is only *now*. The time is now! We have always stated this in the introductory teachings of Prophecy. The times that come ahead, which *could* be a time of geophysical, social, political, and economic upheaval, are all those events chosen by the will of the collective consciousness.

Collective consciousness is a higher structure, a higher arching of energy of individual consciousness. You, yourself, as an individual have individual consciousness. This we have studied, Dear hearts, in understanding layers of the auric field and the flame within the heart. However, as we have taught in many other teachings, you are linked to a greater Oneship—the consciousness of Unana, the consciousness of the ONE. This consciousness of the ONE is comprised in its simplest form of *two or more*. However, there can be many more linked into this greater scope of consciousness. This we have called in other teachings as a *unified field of thought*. This is taught in the First Jurisdiction in the teachings of Creatorship as *harmony*.

When harmony is present among *two or more,* there is the potential and the possibility for a unified collective thought. The unified collective thought creates a greater reality, a greater understanding. This greater understanding, which comes forward in the consciousness of Unana, is what is meant by the term *collective consciousness*. Collective consciousness acts on a greater will, greater than the individual; and it serves the plan of the group united in harmony.

You may scratch your head and wonder, "We have created this reality through harmony?" This is indeed so! What you see, you have created. What you are living is what *you* have created. This creation comes forward through harmony. It is very similar to adjusting your television to a bandwidth to receive a television program. In the same manner you adjust your *own receiver* to a bandwidth of new experience.

Let me explain this even further. There are indeed different planes, or unified fields of collective consciousness that you may tune yourself individually. This is how you adjust experience. This is how you can adjust the way that you perceive a situation—a circumstance. When you understand this concept there are many possibilities that exist within a bandwidth of collective consciousness. You will begin to understand the power of your choice and the power of your Creatorship. You are in essence, as consciousness surfing upon the waves of time.

Time again, is perceived by the individual, but you are surfing upon a selection of circumstances and situations, and you are at the controls. You are the Master of this show, the Master of Ceremony of your life! Bearing this in mind, Dear hearts, Dear ones, Dear chelas, you are now ready to move forward. Understand that through your ONE collective reality that you have created exists a multitude of choices and a multitude of experiences that you may now choose from. Have you not noted while driving in traffic that your experience can be one of many? You can be frustrated; you can be peaceful; you can be focused; you can be detached—a multitude of feelings that you can have through the simple act of driving.

Now, let us take this idea to a greater idea, a greater experience.

In your life today are many choices, many possibilities of how you may live out each moment. Each moment—not time—each moment is a situation, a circumstance of how you choose to experience living in a greater collective reality. Do you see that you are surfing the greater reality, choosing your experiences? Choice *does* indeed create!

The creation comes through harmony. This greater harmony that you have come to experience is imbedded, again, in the principle of your choice. As your choices come together, there is indeed the collective reality. Do you see the relationship, Dear one?

Answer: "Yes."

So in laying this framework, this groundwork, I would like to proceed and impart more understanding. As you now see that you have many experiences to choose from, how is it that you may travel among each of these experiences, each of these circumstances, each of these situations? It is through your consciousness. Now let us refer back to the beginning teachings of consciousness. Consciousness creates an electromagnetic pulse. This electromagnetic pulse is the basis of the field of life that exists around you known as the Human Aura. I have explained this in previous teachings, and the Human Aura can be separated into different bodies or fields of light. Each of these fields of light experiences a different circumstance, a different situation. We call these simply the *emotional body*; the *mental body*. These are teachings that I have given in prior discourse, and if you review them, you then will understand this next point.

Much as you are able to adjust your experiences among each situation that you choose, and each circumstance that you choose, how is it that you are able to perceive the difference? Is is through creation, again through thought, that a new body is formed through that mental Point of Perception. This allows the consciousness to travel to each experience. This body of light, as it is called and known by in these teachings, radiates through each of these experiences. Now, there would be those who call this a Simultaneous Experience, but now you understand yourself as a Creator, as the originator, the God-source of these different bodies of light. You see, within yourself is a hierarchy of creation! Many different bodies of light travel through to an experience, a point in time that is perceived, and then the totality of that experience is allowed through circumstance and situation. What enfolds from this unified field of understanding is Simultaneous Embodiment, fields of light springing from the ONE continuous source that precedes, and even from one point again, as one point has sprouted from that source. Again it contains the source within it, and so it is able to sprout again, or perceive a new reality, a new consciousness. Let me diagram this so that you understand with greater clarity.

(Lori: He is now drawing on a chalkboard. And he has drawn out a circle at the top right-hand corner, and from that he has drawn a line down and drawn another circle.)

This, you see, is the Point of Perception from the Source to a new experience. Now, at the point of the Source, ONE has not given up its one perception. Instead, the perception becomes dual, therefore, there are two experiences happening simultaneously.

(Lori: Now he is drawing four more lines from the first.)

And so you see, Dear hearts, as this Point of Perception travels to another sphere and dimension—Point of Perception of understanding—there is now the opportunity, again, for more perception and more understanding. And so you see, it is a web of creation, hierarchal in a sense, but connected and joined. You see, at all times, all is emanating from this Source, the center of this creation, this creation of choice, yet, it is perceiving different circumstances—different situations. Yet they are all linked ideally as ONE. It is indeed a web of consciousness that creates a greater understanding and a greater reality. This is how our consciousness is linked with your consciousness. This is how your consciousness becomes linked into a new reality, a new circumstance, a new situation. Indeed, we are the Creators of time! Therefore, we must become *the Masters* of Time. Do you have questions?

Question: "Do I experience you because I can perceive you?"

This is true. But understand this, dear chela, the perception you have is because of our link *to* each other. Do you understand?

Response: "No."

We are linked together through the perception of consciousness. Now you perceive me as an entity of consciousness to be greater than you, and yet this is not true! We are linked together. We contain the ONE Source. We are equal in this sense. Now again, I may have a Mastery of my creation that you may not, but then again that difference is always as dear Sananda has stated, "the experience." So my challenge to you, Dear hearts, is to understand these lessons in creation, understand these lessons in projecting consciousness. Questions?

Question: "Does a poor person live in poverty because that is all they can perceive?"

This is so. This is my point exactly! Each reality is created through the perception. Now, you can have a simultaneous perception, however, those perceptions may or may not have harmony. That is contingent upon your out-picturing. Now, can poverty and wealth exist simultaneously? Of course they can! Yet, there are those who perceive that you may only be poor or you may only be wealthy, yet we know, as the world has proven, that they exist side by side. Is this not so?

Answer: "True, because poverty may not just be money; you may be wealthy but poor of character, poor of intention."

Well stated, Dear one, yet these are simultaneous experiences. The Master of the creation understands that harmony exists within *each* of these experiences. Harmony, as outlined in the Hermetic Law, is founded upon Laws of Polarity and Laws of Satvva, or Rhythm. For every time there is a season. Now, the Master of the creation begins to understand that there is a rhythm to creation, and there is a rhythm to the Point of Perception. What does this mean in the greater reality? It means that at *any* time perception can be shifted. The focus, or point of perception, can be taken on one experience, and removed, and put on another. This is what is known as shapeshifting—shifting the Point of Perception, becoming what is necessary to fulfill the desire within the heart, the desire of creation.

Now, does the other creation continue? It could. It depends on the amount of energy that is poured into it by the Creator for experience, circumstance, and situation. But as the Point of Perception, the preceptor begins to pour the consciousness forward to another stream in time. Then the energy of thought, feeling, and action is poured to that point. Do you understand?

Answer: "Yes, I do. The thought that comes to me is, I am perceived by you and you are perceived by me. However, I am of the opinion that you have out-pictured me to do what I am doing."

Yet, do you not contain the ONE within you?

Answer: "True, because it is all the same point of purpose."

It is *all* connected to the ONE, and therefore, each point is not less than but equal to! Therefore, if indeed I have out-pictured to you, then could you not return to me?

Answer: "True."

Then could you not out-picture onward into your own creation?

Answer: "True."

That is *your* choice. Therefore, you are equal to. If there is a hierarchy, it is only a hierarchy *of understanding*. Steeped in ignorance and superstition, the teachings to the masses contain no hierarchy—just a desire to control. Yet, there is this understanding, that when one grasps it, they understand that *they* are the center of *their* universe. They are their own Great Central Sun. Inside of each individual is Helios and Vesta, for invested in them is the God Source. Now, Dear hearts, when we speak of Monad or Jiva that is what we speak of. It is the great flame that we are all of.

Now let us get on to the work at hand—creation and Creatorship. As I had mentioned, there are light bodies that exist for traveling among each out-pictured reality. The consciousness perceives itself as whole among each reality or each dimensional leap, for each reality is ideally as ONE. But let us, just for now, say it is between a dimension. Let me explain.

(Lori: He's walking to the board, and he is showing the line that exists between the second circle and one where he has drawn the four circles.)

You see from this perspective . . .

(Lori: He is pointing at the end to one of the four circles.)

Perception from here would say... from this line to this line.

(Lori: Now he's pointing between the circles.)

One would perceive that this is higher than this. One would perceive that this is higher than this.

(Lori: Now he is moving between each of the circles in the diagram.)

But indeed, these are not *higher* realities. Indeed, these are not other dimensions. That is only what *this* experience labels it as *in perception*. These are instead united as ONE. However, the sense of separation is this circle, here, that is on the end, has not yet out-pictured and created another stream of consciousness. Now, how does this circle—the one on the end—which perceives itself on the end, begin to understand its link to all of consciousness? It comes through the creation of additional light bodies. Inasmuch as the Human Aura has been created by the being through the out-picturing of the being linked to it, this [light body] now begins to project another body of light to another reality. This projection comes again through what you have known as thought, feeling, and action.

This projection begins first through the dream world. Many are of the perception that the body requires rest. This, as you know, is entirely untrue. Instead, it is a time allotted in the creative activity to allow the consciousness to create! The consciousness, at this time, is projecting to another point in the ONE. The stream of consciousness projects to what you will now call in your experience, another dimension. However, it is experiencing a projection into a unified ONE. There [the person] projects through thought, and feeling; it desires a new body, a new electromagnetic energy, and a current force from the might ONE—the Monad. This is why at night you may have many experiences, each of them very different, each of them varied within the range and scope of experience, each of them containing a different force or life. This I know you understand, because you have experienced it. Do you awaken some mornings feeling disjointed, feeling as if you have been in many different places all at once?

Answer: "Quite frequently."

Indeed, this is the experience of the projection of consciousness into many different places, into your *own* web of creation. Do you also have an experience when you know that you have been directed to one point and remember this as well?

Answer: "Of course!"

Now what is that? It is but a higher development of that body into a directed stream. It is gaining force and energy. Do you see how the simultaneous existence *of you* is now possible?

Answer: "But it is only perceived through the dream state."

Now, let us work to bring that dream state into a greater understanding and reality. What is the experience of a vision or a lucid dream? It is the development of memory. Memory is brought through the experience of perseverance. It is a repeated pattern that allows the consciousness to be trained, pouring in a continuous stream of the electromagnetic current of thought, feeling, action, and focus. Do you realize that when you meditate during the day that this meditation is only training the memory to work at night? This trains the consciousness as it is detached from physical reality, and from the physical reality that you are currently experiencing.

Throughout the day you identify with your body. You identify with its movements, its needs, its limitations, its desires. This, too, is an out-picturing of consciousness that has preceded you. But now you are working to bring your web of creation into your Mastery of time and space. So you perceive consciousness as being detached from the body as a stream, shall we say, of pure energy. This you experience in meditation through visualization and through out-picturing. This is put in a greater practice at night into your dream state.

Now, I shall go one step further. Questions?

Question: "Consciousness and perception is multi-level?"

Exactly.

Question: "Is the reality we call Three Dimensional reality the point of consciousness and perception where we have persevered and placed the most focus?"

This is correct.

Question: "To alter the reality that we have created by placing the most focus, we choose another reality that we then consciously, actively, and with perseverance and diligence pour focus into?"

And with purpose, Dear heart, with purpose! Now, this purpose is linked to the desire within the heart. The purpose and the desire link us as ONE. For you see, that is where the harmony streams forth to allow the creation to come forward in abundance.

Question: "So it is the desire that I have in my heart for humanity's freedom that is a linked purpose that you and I have?"

This is so, beloved. Now, do you see the greater understanding that you are indeed linked? We are all linked as ONE. And yet each of us serves through our choice and creates through our choice. That is where individual Mastery is achieved, yet we are all linked as ONE. I would like to proceed to a new level of understanding.

Now we are linked as ONE—one understanding. How do you move into a synthesis of understanding and creation? Do you see, Dear one, how you must become like that [intention, desire] which birthed you to continue your link to the ONE?

Answer: "But, what birthed me was the desire of that freedom!"

That is correct.

Answer: "And the understanding of creation."

So this leads us to the next level of understanding. You must become I; I must become you.

Question: "Well, what are the steps to achieve this?"

You must out-picture and become *conscientiously conscious* of your creations. This conscientious consciousness brings to the forefront the *full memory* of your different points of perception, and then it chooses those creations you pour your energy into. These are simultaneous realities or simultaneous experiences from which you can choose. And in the same way that a great force out-pictured my own existence, now the same happens for you! Each of the bodies that you have created into different experiences requires your conscientious memory. It is always best in these beginning steps of understanding your creations to focus on a half a dozen or so—no more than six at a time—six different possible realities that you are pouring your energy into.

Six different realities that you know and understand create through your perception. This allows you to become more aware of your creations at a memory level. Again, know this, it is the development of memory that we are focusing on. When we say, "to awaken," it is to awaken the greater memory—the knowledge of total experience birthed through the field of harmony. Now, let me give you a hypothetical situation so you may understand this with greater clarity.

Currently, there are six different Earth Changes realities that exist. The first reality is a world that is completely destroyed by the asteroid. The second is a world that has seen the shifting of tectonic plates with only one half of the population of the world left. The third world is filled with pollution, global warming, and flooded coastal cities. The fourth is a world that has begun to understand that it has created this situation—this scenario—and is now enacting treaties at a global level to help the pollution of the earth. The fifth is a reality where the world has been destroyed through nuclear destruction, and the sixth is another reality where the need for global peace has become so strong that all are now living under one great treaty and war is no longer! Now, do you see the different realities that are instantly created? As I described each of these realities, could you see them?

Answer: "Absolutely!"

As I describe each of these could you *feel* them?

Answer: "Yes."

Perhaps you may use as a template, for your thought, one of these realities and project into it, and then *begin* that experience. Now do you understand how your life has been created?

Answer: "Yes."

Now, let us turn this around. Do you see that when you have struggles, or cannot achieve a goal, what the problem is?

Question: "You cannot visualize it?"

You have not been able to *perceive*; you have not been able to out-picture; you have not been able to visualize. It is that simple, Dear one.

Now, to create an alternative reality you must be able to receive it. Perceive—Receive. They are related!

To perceive something, one *must* be able to receive it. This again creates the link among circles, as I have diagrammed on the board. To perceive a creation, one must be able to receive it. To aid in the creation of multiple realities, one must be focused; also, one must be able to experience it, to receive it, and to create it into their reality.

Now, how do we bring this into physicality? How do we take an experience that we perceive and are ready to receive? How do we generate it into the physical reality? It is pouring the energy with the *focus of consciousness*. It is that simple. It is the pouring of consciousness *into*. It is the focus, you see.

Do you see how each of the six possible realities *could* become your reality if you poured the focus into them?

Answer: "'Pouring focus in,' is a very foggy statement!"

I see. Let me explain. Remember when you were given the exercise by El Morya to become ONE with the candle?

Answer: "Yes."

That is the point of focus. You poured your intention. You poured your thought, and soon you become ONE with it. Did you not become the heat of the flame in that moment?

Answer: "Yes."

That is the point of consciousness traveling through what you perceive as time to another point in consciousness.

Dear Sananda has brought this teaching forward. For new wine to be poured it must be poured into a new wineskin—there must be a place to pour consciousness into. That place is your Point of Perception. That place is how *you define yourself*, and you pour your focus and intention into it, and become one with it. But, you are still linked to the point of departure, you see, because departure and arrival become as ONE. They are two points linked in immortality. They are deathless. They are filled with the effervescent life.

Now, what you are speaking of, and I shall get to *the point*, is what is known as a *mental block*. Sometimes mental blocks occur. They occur through doubt, lack of trust, lack of faith, lack of understanding, ignorance, and again, superstitions! These, too, are creations where you have poured energy. You have poured more energy into the doubt, into the superstition, into the ignorance and therefore, you see, it too has created a force. Men have the choice to create truth or ignorance. Yet, they are linked to the ONE. Remember, as we spoke, that poverty or wealth can exist simultaneously? Again, it is where you choose to pour your consciousness toward—your desires, your actions, your emotions, and your feelings. See how it works, Dear one? It is as simple as *honing* the consciousness.

Question: "Is it almost picturing yourself in the situation?"

It is. See yourself, feel the forces about you, become aware through your senses—smell it, touch it, see it, hear it! This, I know you can do!

Question: "So, do this as a mental and spiritual exercise?"

This is what out-picturing is!

Response: "In the event of the candle, in stepping into the candle, you step only into the flame, at least from my experience. I'd become the flame, the light, never burning but ever burning, always light."

Much the same as you choose another experience, you see yourself stepping *into that* experience. But, if you are blocking, or stopping the experience from happening because of an old creation, you must first withdraw your energy from the old creation.

Response: "I see."

It is hindering you. This is the parable of the new wineskin. You must create the new body of light to travel through consciousness.

Question: "So the purpose in the Violet Flame Decrees?"

Is to destroy the old wineskin!

Question: "To dissolve the old creations?"

Precisely.

Question: "Now in utilizing that technique to dissolve old creations, if you don't visualize what you are dissolving, can you still dissolve it? Can you dissolve it just by saying your intention is to dissolve this block?"

Yes.

Question: "And that is enough?"

As long you retain the focus, you see. Consider one who comes from an alcoholic pattern or who has engaged in drug abuse—it's a misperception of creation. These subjective bodies, which we have discussed must be dissolved, for they are hindering the creation of the new desire. The universe has responded objectively and without judgment.

Question: "So when the person thinks or feels that they're unworthy?"

Then, they *are* unworthy.

Question: "Truly. And the Violet Flame Decrees, you can just utilize and say out loud, 'I AM now dissolving this sense, feeling, thought of unworthiness?' Use decrees, and it dissolves? Eventually, would you have to stop the decrees so there is no more energy going into the pattern of unworthiness?"

This is so. But it is through the training of the consciousness, for you see the universe will immediately respond without judgment and without hesitation.

Question: "I see. And so it almost sounds like the person who decides they want a new car, and they take a picture of it and tape it on the refrigerator."

It is training *and* ingraining the consciousness again to that Point of Perception. Train the consciousness to perceive the desired result.

Question: "So what has really happened with the world? Is this the creation of destruction, Earth Changes, or catastrophe for civilization? Is this something that collectively everyone hasn't decided they don't want?"

Some have chosen to do so. Some have chosen not to. And then there are those who choose nothing at all, for they are not ready. For everything there is a time and a season.

Question: "So, on the one point of creating a pristine planet."

It is for those who wish to have that experience; and for those who wish to have destruction, they, too, shall have it! Do you see, Dear heart, you are *equal to.*

Question: "It is most interesting. I have wondered whether some people who don't even perceive destruction of the planet or Earth Changes, whether that is ever going to be a reality for them, or will they go through it because collectively there are many who do not perceive it?"

Then, those who do not choose, choose to go along.

Response: "I see."

Let me continue. In the dream state you have created several different bodies that you utilize for different experiences. These bodies stay in their Point of Perception when the consciousness returns to the physical body. These different light bodies are developed for you to put on as a seamless garment—a seamless garment in a point of time that allows yet another creation. As I've always said, "Down with death!" For you see, the aging of your physical body is the aging of your perception in *that* experience. Do you understand?

Question: "While we're on that subject, would it be wise to have a picture of yourself younger?"

If you wish to youthen the body, this is so. Or you may create another simultaneous experience in which you pour energy. Now when the body dies, it is a stream of consciousness leaving and departing to another reality that has been created.

Question: "That's interesting. So you could almost pre-create the new life?"

This is so. Do you remember in the teachings that have been given to you, the dropping of the body?

Answer: "Yes."

It is the dropping of a Point of Perception and moving onward to another Point of Perception. Until the other is developed, how can the other go? It is the development of the new wineskin. Now let us get even further into this.

There may be many bodies that are created from this ONE central source, right now, in this experience; you, *now*, in this physical body. You see, you may be creating up to a dozen, or even thousands of different bodies from this Point of Perception.

Question: "Where is this being created?"

It is created all around you, for the universe responds without judgment.

Question: "As we've discussed earlier, even these bodies you are dissolving, you are creating? And you could step into one of those in another time continuum? I see what you are saying."

Exactly! This is the principle of bi-location. Now, when one becomes aware of the different realities that exist, they become quite focused on its creation and begin to duplicate the same consciousness, the same body, into another field of reality. Therefore, when you begin to understand this principle, and within this, abandon the idea of time, you are able to create the same body elsewhere. You create a different body depending on your choice, depending on the field of circumstances and situations. This is how a Master can be in *many* places at once. It is through the development of consciousness, the Point of Perception!

Response: "If you can perceive it, you can create it."

This is so. In the same way that you became the candle, you can also become crystallized to the Point of Perception through thought, feeling, action, and experience.

Question: "So when you appear to us as a young man, vibrant, virile, and energetic, it is your choice of creation that you appear to us in?"

This is so. You too, may create various realities you live in! You may have full life in many realities, many different realities existing simultaneously from this point now in time. When the consciousness decides to move on, that is, destroy the physical body through death, and it moves to a new reality or to several newly created realities. That is indeed the choice of the Creator. But there are those who have not yet Mastered or created the body into which they would move! There are those who have not yet perfected this technique, and they move on into a realm where they are cared for by the person who sponsored them, who out-pictured them. Do you understand? They return to what out-pictured them, for you see, they are linked as ONE, as ONE creation, and so you see, the force of the consciousness is contingent upon the force of all.

Question: "So, in the event that I was to leave my body today, I would come back to you?"

This is so. And there you receive instruction that would fit to the unified field of harmony, into the greater plan Divine.

Response: "Interesting. It is truly my desire, though, to sustain this body for a period of time as an example to the consciousness here."

And if you wish to sustain the physical, you may do so. But I also encourage you to create other light bodies which shall indeed create physical bodies so that you may travel between. There you have the fullness of Mastery. There you have the fullness of experience.

Question: "Interestingly enough, I have often wondered why so many people on the street will wave to me no matter where I would be in the world!"

It is as I have taught you today as simultaneous reality, a simultaneous experience. Therefore, there is no such thing as "time," as you have perceived it in the past, but there *is time* as you perceive today.

Question: "Time is not a line. It's a web?"

It is indeed that, but it is the structure that we pour our consciousness into.

Question: "So time exists as a medium for focus to create space?"

It is a point of understanding, and that is *all* it is. It is no different than a mathematical system that is given to reference quantity. It is as much as that. And now, Dear one, I shall give you *time* to reflect upon this and shall return for discourse at a later point in time.

Response: "Thank you. At your earliest convenience, please return. I thank you again."

So be it.

Spiritual Lineage of the Violet Flame

The teachings of the Violet Flame, as taught in the work of I AM America, come through the Goddess of Compassion and Mercy Kuan Yin. She holds the feminine aspects of the flame, which are Compassion, Mercy, Forgiveness, and Peace. Her work with the Violet Flame is well documented in the history of Ascended Master teachings, and it is said that the altar of the etheric Temple of Mercy holds the flame in a Lotus Cup. She became Saint Germain's teacher of the Sacred Fire in the inner realms, and he carried the masculine aspect of the flame into human activity through Purification, Alchemy, and Transmutation. One of the best means to attract the beneficent activities of the Violet Flame is through the use of decrees and invocation. However, you can meditate on the flame, visualize the flame, and receive its transmuting energies like "the light of a thousand suns," radiant and vibrant as the first day that the Elohim Arcturus and Diana drew it forth from our solar sun at the creation of the earth. Whatever form, each time you use the Violet Flame these two Master Teachers hold you in the loving arms of its action and power.

The following is an invocation for the Violet Flame to be used at sunrise or sunset. It is utilized while experiencing the visible change of night to day, and day to night. In fact, if you observe the horizon at these times, you will witness light transitioning from pinks to blues, and then a subtle violet strip adorning the sky. We have used this invocation for years in varying scenes and circumstances, overlooking lakes, rivers, mountaintops, deserts, and prairies; in huddled traffic and busy streets; with groups of students or sitting with a friend, but more commonly alone in our home or office, with a glint of soft light streaming from a window. The result is always the same: a calm, centering force of stillness. We call it the Space.

Invocation of the Violet Flame for Sunrise and Sunset
I invoke the Violet Flame to come forth in the name of I AM that I AM,
To the Creative Force of all the realms of all the Universes, the Alpha, the Omega, the Beginning, and the End,
To the Great Cosmic Beings and Torch Bearers of all the realms of all the Universes,
And the Brotherhoods and Sisterhoods of Breath, Sound, and Light, who honor this Violet Flame that comes forth from the Ray of Divine Love—the Pink Ray, and the Ray of Divine Will—the Blue Ray of all Eternal Truths.

I invoke the Violet Flame to come forth in the name of I AM that I AM!
Mighty Violet Flame, stream forth from the Heart of the Central Logos, the Mighty Great Central Sun! Stream in, through, and around me.

(Then insert other prayers and/or decrees for the Violet Flame.)

Glossary

Absolute Harmony: Order and peace permeate throughout

Absolute Perfection: State of completion and purity without lack, blemish, or fault

Adept: An unascended Master of thought, feeling, and action (physical plane), and an initiate of the Great White Brotherhood

Age of Cooperation: The age humanity is currently being prepared to enter; it occurs simultaneously with the Time of Change.

Age of Peace: The time period prophesied to exist after the Earth Changes.

Aggregate Body of Light: The sum or mass of our individual energy bodies

Alchemy: The process of Transmutation

Alignment: Convergence or adjustment

Apex: The center, especially the top of a Golden City Vortex.

Aryan: Active intelligence

Ascended Masters: Once an ordinary human, an Ascended Master has undergone a spiritual transformation over many lifetimes. He or she has Mastered the lower planes—mental, emotional, and physical—to unite with his or her God-Self or I AM Presence. An Ascended Master is freed from the wheel of Karma. He or she moves forward in spiritual evolution beyond this planet; however, an Ascended Master remains attentive to the spiritual well-being of humanity, inspiring and serving the earth's spiritual growth and evolution.

Ascension: A process of Mastering thoughts, feelings, and actions that balance positive and negative Karmas. It allows entry to a higher state of consciousness and frees a person from the need to reincarnate on the lower earthly planes or lokas of experience. Ascension is the process of spiritual liberation, also known as moksha.

Aura: The subtle energy field of luminous light that surrounds the human body

GLOSSARY

Avatar: When an Ascended Master takes on a physical body to bring blessings to the world, he or she is known as an avatar. This perfected physical manifestation usually casts no shadow or leaves no footprints. Masters rarely appear to the general public and can become invisible if necessary.

Babajeran: A name for the Earth Mother that means, "grandmother rejoicing."

Balance: "Put into proper order."

Belt of Golden Light: This etheric Golden Belt of high-frequency energy has been in place since the early 1950s. It holds back catastrophic Earth Changes until humanity has a better chance to evolve. The belt also plays a significant role in mankind's spiritual growth.

Bi-location: The ability to be in more than one place at one time in the physical dimension.

Cellular Awakening: A spiritual initiation activated by Master Teachers Saint Germain and Kuthumi. Through this process the physical body is accelerated at the cellular level, preparing consciousness to recognize and receive instruction from the Fourth Dimension.

Ceremony: Intentionally using the language of symbols to initiate or activate consciousness and subtle energies

Chakra(s): Sanskrit for wheel. Seven spinning wheels of human-bioenergy centers stacked from the base of the spine to the top of the head.

Chela: Disciple

Chi: Energy

Chohan: Another word for Lord

Christ, the: The highest energy or frequency attainable on earth. The Christ is a step-down transformer of the I AM energies, which enlighten, heal, and transform all human conditions of degradation and death.

Circle of Known: A measurement of all known knowledge is contained in the circle; the unknown falls outside the circle.

Co-creation: Creating with the God-Source

Collective Consciousness: The higher interactive structure of consciousness as *two or more*

Conscience: The internal recognition of right and wrong in regard to one's actions and motives

Consciousness: Awakening to one's own existence, sensations and cognitions.

Cosmic Teacher: A teacher of the Ascended Masters

Cosmic Wave Motion: Belts of energy that weave a pattern throughout the universe; they originate from the sun.

Cup: A symbol of neutrality and grace

Dark Government: The dysfunctional aspect of leadership that knowingly or unknowingly creates tyrannies of fear, control, destruction of life, and the suppression of human rights.

Dead Zone: A consciousness of slumber and unawareness

Desire: Of the source

Deva: Shining one or being of light

Dharma: Purpose

Dis-ease: Lack of harmony

Disembodied Spirit: A person or thought-form that survives the death of the body but maintains consciousness.

Divine Cloak: A heavenly, protective Veil of Energy.

Divine Mother: The Mother Goddess or feminine aspect of God

Divine Spark: A Gnostic principle that God is contained in the human body. The Divine Spark is encouraged to grow and reunite with the I AM Presence.

Divinity: Derived from the Sanskrit word *Deva*, this notion is the transcendent power of light or God.

Dove: A symbol of peace and renewal

Duality: An understanding that the world is divided into two perceptible categories

Eabra: The seventh Canadian Golden City located in the Yukon and Northwest Territories. Its qualities are joy, balance, and equality; its Ray force is violet; and its Master Teacher is Portia.

Earth Changes: A prophesied Time of Change on the earth, including geophysical, political, and social changes alongside the opportunity for spiritual and personal transformation.

Earth Plane: The dual aspect of life on earth

Earth's Grids: Geometrical patterns that cover the earth and follow symmetrical links to sacred geometry and crystalline shapes.

Eastern Door: The east side of a Golden City gateway, also known as the *Blue Door*

Eight-Sided Cell of Perfection: An atomic cell located in the human heart. It is associated with all aspects of perfection, and contains and maintains a visceral connection with the Godhead.

Eighth Energy Body: A new light body that develops to assist the growth of Unity Consciousness.

El Morya: Ascended Master of the Blue Ray, associated with the development of the will.

Elemental: A nature-being

Elohim: Creative beings of love and light that helped manifest the divine idea of our solar system. Seven Elohim (the Seven Rays) exist here. They organize and draw forward Archangels, the Four Elements, Devas, Seraphim, Cherubim, Angels, Nature Guardians, and the Elementals. The Silent Watcher—the Great Mystery—gives them direction.

Emotional Body: A subtle body of light that exists alongside the physical body. It comprises desires, emotions, and feelings.

Energy Field Balancing: Healing modality which energizes, heals, and stabilizes the light bodies comprising the Human Aura.

Energy Fields: Distinct and definable layers of energy that exist around all forms of physical life: mineral, plant, animal, and human.

Feminine: Esoteric philosophy considers the Mother Creative principle as the highest expression of being. Femininity is akin to the Goddess; it comprises one half of God whose gender is neutral. Feminine energy represents love, beauty, seduction, sensitivity, and refinement—the characteristics of the Goddess Venus. On the dark side, it reflects vanity, superficiality, fickleness, and exhaustion. Femininity is the intuition, a nurturing force which, above all, produces the first creative spark in our Sun of Truth; the female essence serves as the inspiration and aspiration for life's goodness and purity—a devotion to truth.

Fifth Dimension: A spiritual dimension of cause, associated with thoughts, visions, and aspirations. This is the dimension of the Ascended Masters and the Archetypes of Evolution, the city of Shamballa, and the templates of all Golden Cities.

Fourth Dimension: A dimension of vibration associated with telepathy, psychic ability, and the dream world. This is the dimension of the Elemental Kingdom and the development of the super senses.

Free Energy: A continuous, abundant state of energy that heals and restores the spirit, mind, and physical body. Many of the spiritual teachings of Saint Germain are based on the use of this universal substance. Free energy creates health and joy in the path of Mastery, adeptship, and immortality.

Freedom Flame: An energy field that covers the entire American continent; it holds within it the principles of sovereignty, free will, and choice.

Freedom Star: The earth's future prophesied name

Freedom Star Map: The I AM America Map of prophesied worldwide Earth Changes.

Galactic Web: A large, planet-encircling grid created by the consciousness of all things on earth—humans, animals, plants, and minerals. Magnetic Vortices, namely the Golden Cities, appear at certain intersections.

Geometric Language: The symbols of sacred geometry

Geo-Sensitive: A person who is sensitive to and can read the earth's energies.

Gobean: The first United States Golden City located in the states of Arizona and New Mexico. Its qualities are cooperation, harmony, and peace; its Ray force is blue; and its Master Teacher is El Morya.

Golden City Vortex: According to the prophecies, these large Vortex areas are havens of safety and spiritual growth during the Time of Change.

Golden Flame: An energy field of spiritual enlightenment. The teachings of the Golden Flame are said to originate from the Pleiades.

Grace: Neutrality, calmness, peacefulness

Great White Brotherhood and Sisterhood (Lodge): This fraternity of ascended and unascended men and women is dedicated to the universal uplifting of humanity. Its main objective includes the preservation of the lost spirit, and the teachings of the ancient religions and philosophies of the world. Its Mission: to reawaken the dormant ethical and spiritual spark among the masses. In addition to fulfilling spiritual aims, the Great White Lodge has pledged to protect mankind against the systematic assaults—which inhibit self-knowledge and personal growth—on individual and group freedoms.

Grey Man: An archetype of an ordinary man, who easily fades into the background and blends into the crowd. He is often used to carry out the secret Missions of the dark government.

Guru: Another name for teacher

Harmony: The first virtue of the Twelve Jurisdictions based on the principle of agreement.

Helios and Vesta: The God and Goddess of our physical sun

Hermetic Law: Philosophical beliefs and principles based on the writings of Hermes Trismegistus, the Greek sage who is analogous to the Egyptian God Thoth.

Hilarion: Ascended Master of the Green Ray and associated with the attainment of personal truth and the development of faith.

Hitaka: "So be it."

HU-man: The God-Man

I AM: The presence of God

I AM America Map: The Ascended Masters' Map of prophesied Earth Changes for the United States

I AM Presence: The individualized presence of God

I AM Race: A new race of man destined to serve as the nucleus of the planet's future Utopian society. It will inherit the work and the development of fellowship among the nations of the world.

Individualized: A state of wholeness and cannot be divided

Jiva: The immortal essence of a living thing that survives death

Karma: Laws of Cause and Effect

Klehma: The fifth United States Golden City located primarily in the states of Colorado and Kansas. Its qualities are continuity, balance, and harmony; its Ray force is white; and its Master Teacher is Serapis Bey.

Kuan Yin: The Bodhisattva of Compassion and teacher of Saint Germain. She is associated with all the Rays and the principle of femininity.

Kuthumi: An Ascended Master of the Pink, Ruby, and Gold Rays. He is a gentle and patient teacher who works closely with the Nature Kingdoms.

Laws of Attraction and Repulsion: Like charges repel; unlike charges attract.

Laws of Cause and Effect: For every action there is another event, which is the consequence or result of the first.

Law of Correspondence: "As above, so below."

Law of Death and Rebirth: Reincarnation

Law of Love: "If you live love, you will create love."

Law of Opposites: Every action has an equal and opposite action

Law of Polarities: Everything in the universe can pursue two opposite paths, each with its own essence. Following this logic, all pairs exist in a spectrum comprising an infinite number of points among ends. Diametric termini are identical in nature but different in degree; they contain the possibility of the other in its essence. Everything encompasses its opposite; therefore, the macrocosm embraces the microcosm.

Law of Rhythm: Everything ebbs and flows; rises and falls. The swing of the pendulum is universal. The measure of the momentum to the right is equal to the swing of the left.

Law of Synchronicity: Nothing is happenstance: "There is no mistake ever, ever, ever!"

Laws of Octaves: The relationship of planets, colors, and musical notes are based on the Law of Octaves, also known as the Law of Seven.

Lei-lines: Lines of energy that exist among geographical places, ancient monuments, megaliths, and strategic points. These energy lines contain electrical or magnetic points.

Lemuria: An ancient civilization that existed before Atlantis, largely in the South Pacific North America, Asia, and Australia

Light: "Love in action."

Light Body: A body of subtle energy surrounding the human body. It survives death, and develops and evolves over lifetimes. Also known as the aura, the light body divides into layers of light energy. These strata are referred to as *light bodies* or layers of the field of the aura.

Lighted Stance: A state of light the body acquires during Ascension.

Lords of Venus: A group of Ascended Masters who came to serve humanity. They once resided on the planet Venus.

Lotus: An Eastern symbol of the maternal creative mystery—the feminine. The lotus signifies the unfolding of spiritual understanding, and the opening and development of the chakras. It also represents the growth of man through three periods of human consciousness—ignorance, endeavor, and understanding. This idea is mirrored in nature, too. In Oriental philosophy the lotus manifests in three elements, earth, water, and air. Thus, man exists on the material, intellectual, and spiritual planes. In Western culture, the symbology of the rose is similar to the lotus.

Love: "Light in action."

Maltese Cross: The Maltese Cross, a symbol often used by Saint Germain, represents the Eight-Sided Cell of Perfection, and the human virtues of honesty, faith, contrition, humility, justice, mercy, sincerity, and the endurance of persecution.

Malton: The second United States Golden City located in the states of Illinois and Indiana. Its qualities are fruition and attainment; its Ray force is ruby and Gold; and its Master Teacher is Kuthumi.

Mantle of Consciousness: Ascending to or attaining a new level of conscious awareness that produces tremendous change

Masculine Energy: The Father creative principle. In esoteric literature, this is referred to as the Monad.

Master Teacher: A spiritual teacher from a specific lineage of teachers—gurus. The teacher transmits and emits the energy from that collective lineage.

Mastery: Possessing the consummate skill of command and self-realization over thought, feeling, and action.

Mental Body: A subtle light body of the Human Aura comprising thoughts

Mind: The aspects of consciousness manifested as thought, perceptions, true memory, will, and imagination.

Mirroring: "As (when looking in) water, face reflects face, so does one's heart find reflection in another's." Proverbs 27:19

Monad: Dynamic will, or purpose and life, as revealed through human demonstration. It is also understood as the Father creative principle.

Mother Mary: Ascended Goddess of the Feminine who was originally of the angelic evolution. She is associated with the Green Ray of healing, truth, and science, and the Pink Ray of love.

New Age: Prophesied by Utopian Francis Bacon, the New Age would herald a United Brotherhood of the Earth. This Brotherhood/Sisterhood would be built as Solomon's Temple, and supported by the four pillars of history, science, philosophy, and religion. These four teachings would synergize the consciousness of humanity to Universal Fellowship and Peace.

Northern Door: The north side of a Golden City gateway, also known as the *Black Door*

Om Manaya Pitaya or Om Manaaya Patiya: This Ascended Master statement has several meanings. Two spiritual translations are: "I AM the Light of God," and "I AM the Seer of the Lord." The Sanskrit translation means: "Amen, honored Lord."

Omni-presence: Present everywhere

Omniscience: Infinite knowledge

ONE: Indivisible, whole, harmonious Unity

Oneship: A combination of many, which comprises the whole, and when divided contains both feminine and masculine characteristics.

Open Ears, Open Eyes: The ability to see and hear spiritual truths

Open Heart: Evolved love of openness, sharing, and Brotherhood

Out-picturing: To envision in the mind and project to the outer world

Perceive: To observe, feel, sense, and have awareness of.

Pillar of Light: A tube of protective light, impenetrable to anything not of light that surrounds the subtle light bodies and the physical body.

Point of Perception: A certain position of understanding that allows for immediate or intuitive recognition

Portia: The Goddess of Justice and Opportunity. She represents Divine Justice on earth. Her action is balance, expressed as the scales. Harmony holds balance. Some say her electronic pattern, a mandala, is the Maltese Cross.

Prana: Vital, life-sustaining energy

Prediction: A forecast or conjecture of an upcoming circumstance or event

Prophecy: A spiritual teaching given simultaneously with a warning. It's designed to change, alter, lessen, or mitigate the prophesied warning. This caveat may be literal or metaphoric; the outcome of these events are contingent on the choices and the consciousness of those willing to apply the teachings.

Ray: A force containing a purpose, which divides its efforts into two measurable and perceptible powers, light and sound.

Re-embodiment: Reincarnation

Refreshing Drink: A metaphor for the Universal Supply of Life

Ring of Fire: A geographical area, which encircles the basin of the Pacific Ocean, prone to volcanic eruptions and earthquakes.

Rose: The Western symbol of the maternal creative mystery—the feminine. It represents the chakra as a spiritual Vortex; a garland of roses typifies the seven chakras and their unfolding and attainment. In Eastern culture the symbology of the lotus is similar to the rose.

Rosicrucian: An ancient mystery school with its teachings rooted in the study of Western esoteric teachings. Also known as the *Rose Cross*, its foundation is the study of Alchemy through Hermetic-Christian traditions.

Saint Germain: Ascended Master of the Seventh Ray, Saint Germain is known for his work with the Violet Flame of Mercy, Transmutation, Alchemy, and Forgiveness. He is the sponsor of the Americas and the I AM America material. Many other teachers and Masters affiliated with the Great White Brotherhood help his endeavors.

Sananda: The name used by Master Jesus in his ascended state of consciousness. Sananda means joy and bliss, and his teachings focus on revealing the savior and heavenly kingdom within.

Sanat Kumara: One of the original Lords of Venus who founded the Great White Brotherhood at Shamballa. He is also known as *Lord of the World*. The bible refers to him as *Ancient of Days*.

Sattva: Harmonious response to vibration; pure and spiritual in effect.

Seamless Garment: The Ascended Masters wear garments without seams. This clothing is not tailored by hand but perfected through the thought and manifestation process.

Serapis Bey: An Ascended Master from Venus who works on the White Ray. He is the great disciplinarian—essential for Ascension; and works closely with all unascended humanity who remain focused for its attainment.

Seventh Manu: Highly evolved lifestreams that embody on earth between 1981 to 3650. Their goal is to anchor freedom and the qualities of the Seventh Ray to the conscious activity on this planet. They are prophesied as the generation of peace and grace for the Golden Age. South America is their forecasted home, though small groups will incarnate other areas of the globe.

Seventh Moon: A storied Earth Changes legend that recounts a large-asteroid impact on earth. It occurred near the present-day Yucatan Peninsula, forming the Gulf of Mexico.

Shalahah: The fourth United States Golden City located primarily in the states of Montana and Idaho. Its qualities are abundance, prosperity, and healing; its Ray force is green; and its Master Teacher is Sananda.

Shaman: An intermediary between the natural world and the spirit world. Indigenous Shaman place a strong emphasis on their environments; nature spirits and animals play important roles and act as omens, messengers, and spirit guides.

Shamballa: Venusian volunteers, who arrived 900 years before their leader Sanat Kumara, built the earth's first Golden City. Known as the City of White, located in the present-day Gobi Desert, its purpose was to hold conscious light for the earth and to sustain her evolutionary place in the solar system.

Simultaneous Realities or Experiences: A transmigratory experience based on a non-linear perspective of time. It holds all the possibilities of past, present, and future events. Simultaneous realities maintain the capacity for multiple experiences and outcomes. Each reality exists side by side. A person could consciously open himself or herself to these scenarios to gain insight and self-knowledge.

Six-Map Scenario: A series of six maps of the United States. The Ascended Masters prophesied this schematic to illustrate choice, consciousness, and their relationship to Earth Changes.

Soletata: The feminine

Soul: The self-aware immortal essence unique to every living being

Soul Mate: Two people who have known each other in the journey of lifetimes through many different types of relationships, e.g. lovers, friends, parents, children, Brothers, Sisters, and so on. Attracted by this affinity, the souls—before entering physical bodies—plan the specific and important roles they will play to each other in their lifetime together.

Source and destination: The teaching of a fundamental process that moves conscious energy from one point to another.

Southern Door: The south side of a Golden City gateway, also known as the *Red Door.*

Spiritual Awakening: Conscious awareness of personal experiences and existence beyond the physical, material world. Consequently, an internalization of one's true nature and relationship to life is revealed, freeing one of the lesser self (ego) and engendering contact with the higher (Christ) self and the I AM.

Spiritual Hierarchy: A fellowship of Ascended Masters and their disciples. This group helps humanity through the mental plane with meditation, decrees, and prayer.

Spiritual Migration: The process of moving to and living in certain geophysical areas to purposely integrate and assimilate earth's sacred energies for spiritual growth and evolution.

Sponsorship: To support and engender spiritual growth and evolution

Star: The apex, or center of each Golden City.

Star Seed Consciousness: The Star Seed is a family or soul group whose members have evolved to Fifth-Dimensional awareness. Star Seeds can also contain members who have not yet evolved to this level and are still incarnating on earth.

Subjective Energy Body: This type of energy is similar to a *thought-form,* which causes behavioral changes when triggered. They are created through intense emotions, addictive behaviors, and the use of addictive substances, and often contain elements of lower consciousness.

Terra: Earth

Third Eye: The inner eye, referring to the ajna (brow) chakra.

Thought, Feeling, and Action: In Ascended Master teachings and tradition, thought, feeling, and action are the cornerstones of the creation process. Thought represents the mental (causal) body and the Yellow Ray. Feeling represents the emotional (astral) body and the Pink Ray. Action represents the physical body and the Blue Ray.

Time Compaction: An anomaly produced as we enter into the prophesied Time of Change. Our perception of time compresses; time seems to speed by. The unfolding of events accelerates, and situations are jammed into a short period of time. This experience of time will become more prevalent as we get closer to the period of cataclysmic Earth Changes.

Time of Change: The period of time currently underway. Tremendous changes in our society, cultures, and politics in tandem with individual and collective spiritual awakenings and transformations will abound. These events occur simultaneously with the possibilities of massive global warming, climactic changes, and seismic and volcanic activity—Earth Changes. The Time of Change guides the earth to a new time, the Golden Age.

Time of Transition: A twelve-year period when humanity experienced tremendous spiritual and intellectual growth, ushering in personal and global changes. In the year 2000 a new era, called the *Time of Testing,* got underway. It's a seven-year span of time when economies and societies encountered instability and insecurity. These years are also defined by the spiritual growth of humanity; Brotherly love and compassion play a key role in the development of the earth's civilizations as mankind moves toward the *Age of Cooperation.*

Transfiguration: Changes encountered during the Ascension Process

Transmutation: Alchemy and the transformation of a lower energy into a higher energy, nature, or form

True State Economy: An economy based solely on the trading of metals, natural resources, and goods.

Twelve Jurisdictions: Twelve laws (virtues) for the New Times that guide consciousness to Co-create the Golden Age. They are Harmony, Abundance, Clarity, Love, Service, Illumination, Cooperation, Charity, Desire, Faith, Stillness, Creation/Creativity.

Unana: Unity Consciousness

Unfed Flame: The three-fold flame of divinity that exists in the heart and becomes larger as it evolves. The three flames represent Love (pink); Wisdom (yellow); and Power (blue).

Universal Laws: Laws that apply to the entire universe; considered a fundamental basis of nature and reality.

Vibrational Toning: A process of spiritual Transmutation that affects the physical body

Violet Flame: The Violet Flame is the practice of balancing Karmas of the past through Transmutation, Forgiveness, and mercy. The result is an opening of the Spiritual Heart and the development of bhakti—unconditional love and compassion. It came into existence when the Lords of Venus first transmitted the Violet Flame, also knows as Violet Fire, at the end of Lemuria to clear the earth's etheric and psychic realms, and the lower physical atmosphere of negative forces and energies. This paved the way for the Atlanteans, who used it during religious ceremonies and as a visible marker of temples. The Violet Flame also induces Alchemy. Violet light emits the shortest wavelength and the highest frequency in the spectrum, so it induces a point of transition to the next octave of light.

Violet Ray: The Seventh Ray is primarily associated with Freedom and Ordered Service alongside Transmutation, Alchemy, Mercy, Compassion, and Forgiveness. It is served by the Archangel Zadkiel, the Elohim Arcturus, the Ascended Master Saint Germain and Goddess Portia.

Vortex: A Vortex is a polarized motion body that creates its own magnetic field, aligning molecular structures with phenomenal accuracy. Vortices are often formed where lei-lines (energy meridians of the earth) cross. They are often called power spots as the natural electromagnetic field of the earth is immensely strong in this type of location.

Wahanee: The third United States Golden City located primarily in the states of South Carolina and Georgia. Its qualities are justice, liberty, and freedom; its Ray force is violet; and its Master Teacher is Saint Germain.

Western Door: The west side of a Golden City gateway, also known as the *Yellow Door.*

Will: Choice

APPENDIX A

Topics and Terms for Earth Healing

The Law of Harmony
Where Attention Goes, Energy Flows
Agreement Formation
The Golden City of Klehma
Karma is Relanguaged
Group Gatherings to Hold Collective Consciousness

Prophecies of Peace:

A series of spiritual laws and teachings designed to lead humanity and the earth into a New Time of enlightened thinking and harmonious living. Prophecies of Peace given in this lesson are:

1. After the Time of Change we will experience a Time of Peace on earth.

2. We are moving beyond the Third Dimension in conscious experience, and onward to Fourth and Fifth Dimensional understanding.

3. The human chakra system is changing alongside the energy systems of Mother Earth.

4. The New Times will bring many changes in our governments and societal structures.

5. The family unit will change significantly in the New Times, and children are conceived and birthed in a different way. The higher spiritual energies produce children conceived first through thought and higher consciousness.

6. Many lifestreams, which do not have as high of a Karmic burden as those of the past, are coming to earth. These new souls raise the consciousness of the earth and are blessed with *Dharma.*

7. A portion of the new souls that incarnate on earth are known as the *Seventh Manu.* These special children are conceived and sponsored through the process of conscious

thought. Others are born in the Golden City Vortices. They play a tremendous role in raising the overall Vibration of the earth.

The Law of Harmony:

The First Jurisdiction. The Twelve Jurisdictions are an integral part of the Prophecies of Peace and are specific teachings of spiritual practices. When applied, these spiritual laws move consciousness beyond fear-based thinking and into Co-creative-based experience. Harmony is based on the spiritual teachings of cooperation, agreement, and balance. "All energy, in order to be sustained for creation, must be maintained in balance—balance is the continuous cycle of harmony." [To learn more about *The Twelve Jurisdictions* see *New World Atlas, Volume One*.]

Earth Changes Prophecies; The Cascade Mountains:

These revelations identify massive geological changes worldwide, however, the most profound calamity occurs in the Pacific Northwest. According to the original I AM America Earth Changes Prophecies, the Cascade Range—spanning from Northern California to British Columbia—experiences far-reaching volcanic and seismic activity. A mega-shaking earthquake in Oregon and Washington drowns the cities of Seattle and Portland. The resulting flood creates the Bay of Harmony; the Pacific Ocean's new coastline laps the communities of Spokane, Washington and Lewiston, Idaho. Meanwhile, much of the Cascade Range, including Mount Rainier in northern Washington and Mount Hood of northern Oregon, becomes a tropical archipelago known as the Islands of Fortune. [For more information regarding the United States Earth Changes Prophecies see the *I AM America Map*.]

Vortex:

The existence of Vortices is the foundation of the I AM America Prophecies—that's why the understanding of this concept is paramount to grasping the teaching of the Ascended Masters. The Vortex is a polarized motion body, meaning it creates its own electromagnetic field. It's characterized by a concentration of energy and, in some cases, psychic gravity. Rock formations act as energizing points for the earth's electromagnetic energies.

Vortices often form at the intersection lei lines (the earth's energy meridians), also known as "power spots." Think of it as the geographic equivalent of the longitudinal and the latitudinal coordinates that circle the globe. The convergence of meridian lines can warp time and energy, and align molecular structure with phenomenal accuracy. Vortices and lei lines also embrace animate characteristics: the yin and yang; female and male.

Although all Vortices embody electromagnetic properties, they fall into two general categories: electric and magnetic. Electrical Vortices, the yin or the feminine, tend to open the central nervous system and stimulate neural passages. Magnetic Vortices, however, identify with spiritual or ethereal energies, and the yang or the masculine essence. These Vortices encourage deep meditation and physical rejuvenation. A person's psychic awareness—along with his or her telepathy and the frequency of lucid dreaming—may intensify in these areas.

Many Vortices are highly sacred places where dimensions interplay like cracks between worlds. For instance, the geomancy—or divination of earth material—of the Sedona Vortices is well documented. These formations serve as hallowed highways, ferrying spiritual energies to the material realm. Here, the healing of physical, emotional, and spiritual maladies is optimal.

The Five Golden City Vortices of the United States:

Gobean: Arizona and New Mexico; Blue Ray; Master Teacher, El Morya.
Qualities:Transformation, Harmony, Peace

Malton: Illinois and Indiana; Ruby and Gold Ray; Master Teacher, Kuthumi.
Qualities: Fruition (fructification), Attainment

Wahanee: Georgia and South Carolina; Violet Ray; Master Teacher, Saint Germain
Qualities: Justice, Liberty, Freedom

Shalahah: Montana and Idaho; Green Ray; Master Teacher, Sananda.
Qualities: Abundance, Prosperity, Healing

Klehma: Colorado, Kansas, Nebraska; White Ray; Master Teacher, Serapis Bey.
Qualities: Continuity, Balance, Harmony

According to the Master Teachers, a Golden City Vortex works on the principle of electromagnetism, but the surrounding geology is also key to understanding this natural phenomenon. Research is proving that Vortices seem to appear near fault lines and that they may be channeling energies of the inner earth. (i.e. Gobean Vortex: Mongollon Rim; Malton Vortex: New Madrid Fault line; Shalahah Vortex: A rediscovered ancient fault line near the Snake River and Hells Canyon.) Basalt pillars and ancient lava deposits with their high iron content are also natural conductors of electromagnetic energies. It is a proven scientific fact that igneous rocks are more strongly magnetized than sedimentary rocks. The presence of basalt and rocks with high iron content is visibly apparent at Mount Baldy, Arizona (the apex of the Gobean Golden City Vortex) and throughout the Gobean Vortex. This is also true of the Golden City Vortex of Shalahah. Water is also a key element and may play a role in the disbursement of Vortex energies. Underneath the Gobean Vortex is the largest aquifer in the Southwest; three huge fresh water lakes, Coeur d'Alene and Pend'Orielle in Idaho, and Flathead Lake in Montana are located in the Shalahah Vortex. [For more information about the United States Golden Cities, see the *I AM America United States Golden City Map.*]

Golden City Vortex:

A Golden City Vortex—based on the Ascended Masters' I AM America material—are prophesied areas of safety and spiritual energies during the Times of Changes. Covering an expanse of land and air space, these sacred energy sites span more than 400 kilometers (250 miles) in diameter, with a vertical height of 355 kilometers (200 miles). Golden City Vortices, more importantly, reach beyond terrestrial significance and into the ethereal realm. This system of safe harbors acts as a group or universal mind within our galaxy, connecting information seamlessly and instantly with other beings. The Master Teachers coin this phenomenon the *Galactic Web.*

Fifty-one Golden City Vortices are stationed throughout the world, and each carries a different meaning, a combination of Ray Forces, and a Divine Purpose. Some are older than others; some Vortices are new; and some shift locations. The activation of Golden City Vortices occur in patterns—that's the crux of the numbering system. The Master Teachers call the earth *Beloved Babajeran.* [See following definition]

Although the Masters, as a group, oversee all Golden Cities, each stewards his or her own Vortex. A Golden City Vortex works on the principles of electromagnetism and geology. Vortices tend to appear near fault lines, possibly serving as conduits of inner-earth movement to terra firma. The Gobean Vortex near the fissure-filled Mogollon Rim of Arizona; the Malton Vortex of the Midwest, adjacent to the New Madrid fault line; and the Shalahah Vortex of Idaho, an ancient cleft near the Snake River and Hells Canyon, lend credibility to this theory.

Geology has a profound effect on the potency of a Vortex. Not surprising, the five Golden City Vortices rest on areas of highly magnetic geologic formations. The iron-rich content of basalt pillars and ancient-lava deposit serve as natural conductors of electromagnetic energy; igneous rocks, according to geologic data, create more magnetic pull than sedimentary rocks. That's why Gobean exudes so much energy. Landmarks—such as Mount Baldy in Arizona, the apex of the Southwestern Vortex, and the Golden City Vortex of Shalahah—are filled with basalt and iron-rich rocks.

Water also drives the disbursement of Vortex energies. The Gobean Vortex sits atop the largest aquifer in the Southwest. Shalahah, too, surrounded by three, huge freshwater lakes near Coeur d'Alene and Pend'Oreille, Idaho, and Flathead Lake in Montana, draws power from water.

Visitors to Golden Cities experience spiritual and psychic development—they feel a heightened sense of balance, harmony, and peace. Natural places of meditation, connection with spirit guides, and contact with past-life experiences, Vortices can instantly align the human energy field (aura). During your first stay in a Vortex, you may sleep more while your body adjusts to powerful energies. As you acclimate, you'll undergo a rejuvenation of the body and the spirit. After the shock subsides, many Vortex-seeking pilgrims will engage in prayer and group ceremonies with friends and spiritual mentors, awakening deep connections among fellow humans.

Babajeran:

A term the Master Teachers often use when referring to the Earth Mother. Babajeran means, "the grandmother cries with joy." The term "baba" is, among other languages, Bulgarian, for grandmother. "Jeran" comes from the Israeli word, "jaron," which means, "cry of rejoicing."

The Inner Marriage:

A process achieved through the spiritual integration of the masculine and feminine aspects of self, uniting dualistic qualities into greater balance and harmony for expression of self-Mastery.

Holo-Leaping:

The process of consciousness traveling among dimensions. Very often a person can view alternative realities in this state of perception. As this ability develops, a reported a sense of *timelessness* and *deja-vu* is common.

The Seventh Manu:

The word *Manu* comes from the Hindu word "to think," an apt root for this highly evolved society of young souls prophesied to incarnate the earth during the New Times. But the idea of *Manu* is expansive; its significance reaches far beyond the context of the I AM America Prophecies.

Manu refers to a root race or a group of souls inhabiting a vast time period (era or epoch) on earth. The concept of Manu is found among Native American tribes, too. The Hopis describe this term as *worlds* e.g. fourth world, fifth world. Manu is also a mythical, cosmic being who oversees the souls during their incarnation processes throughout the duration of that specific time period. Some consider Manu a type of spiritual office, not unlike a "World Teacher." For example, one evolved-cosmic being will serve as Manu for one world cycle, and when it ends, it moves on in the evolutionary process. A different entity serves as Manu for the next group. Each group of souls has a different energy and purpose. Seventh Manu children will possess advanced capabilities—astute intellect, vast spiritual knowledge, and keen psychic abilities. Forerunners of the Seventh Manu will pave the way for this metaphysically venerated population. Carrying less Karmic burden than those of the past, these forbearers of every-increasing enlightenment promote a sense of higher consciousness. As Dharma flourishes, the Seventh Manu, sponsored by the Beloved Mother Mary, proliferates.

The majority of this Seventh-Manu generation will settle in an area of Brazil known as the Swaddling Cloth. [You can view the geo-physical perimeters of the Swaddling Cloth on the *I AM America Freedom Star World Map.*] Others will be born in the Golden City Vortices.

The Seventh Manu will play a large role in raising the consciousness and the Vibration of the earth. Saint Germain first prophesied the appearance of the Seventh Manu in a Trance-Mission on May 1, 1993. [This transcript can be read in *New World Atlas, Volume Two.*]

The Lords of Venus:

The Lords of Venus comprise a group of Ascended Masters—former residents of the planet Venus—who came to serve humanity millions of years ago. Esoteric scholars say this ancient coterie of metaphysical sages existed in the nebula known as Pleiades before settling on Venus to adjust their energy frequencies for their work on earth. Their spiritual teachings and principles center on the practice of bhakti, a type of selfless love that manifests as compassion for others. The summoning of the Violet Flame (a form of Karma yoga) purifies the consciousness to higher states of understanding, awareness, and empathy.

APPENDIX B

Topics and Terms for Love's Service

The Energy of the Christ
The Unfed Flame
The Violet Flame
Subtle Energies and the Integration of Spiritual Energies

Prophecies of Peace:

1. The first great change occurs as the individual hearts of many are opened to understanding the ONE.

2. The understanding of the ONE moves every individual into the collective consciousness. Our communities and societies will reflect this spiritual movement.

3. The understanding of the ONE can change the outer world and the extent of the prophesied Earth Changes.

4. The Golden Cities are activated in a two-year sequence pattern. [See Activations and Subtle Energies, Appendix B.]

5. As contact with the ONE becomes more prevalent in each individual, a Transmutation process occurs in the physical body. As the physical body accepts the new energy, *Vibrational Toning* occurs.

6. Vibrational Toning is a three-fold process that takes approximately four to five years. These processes are described as:

   a. Physical fire (inflammation), which affects the lymphatic system and the joints. Increased water and aromatherapy of violets, jasmine, and cinnamon can relieve stress.

   b. Changes in the electrical field (a light body) occur; the presence of Gold light shapes the Human Aura. Spending ten minutes a day in thought and prayer on the Violet Flame can integrate and further transmit the new energies and light frequencies.

c. The magnetism of this light-field causes many changes, and the Ascended Masters suggest following diets that contain organic fruits and vegetables. To further increase light absorption, they suggest using chakra breathing techniques, and limit or eliminate flesh-foods—meats, chicken, fish, and shellfish.

7. The energies within activated Golden Cities accelerate, and begin to attract many new inhabitants who wish to grow and learn spiritually.

The Unfed Flame:

According to the Masters, this Unfed Flame is a Flame of Divinity and of spiritual consciousness. The Masters refer to this phenomenon in other terms: the Threefold Flame, Monad, and Jiva. The Unfed Flame urges humanity to evolve beyond its present state of spiritual consciousness through Co-creative thought, feeling, and action. Relying upon a higher, spiritual consciousness, the Lords of Venus—servants of humanity and onetime denizens of the planet Venus—rooted Love, Wisdom, Power, and the Unfed Flame in the human heart. These divine tenets empower humans to achieve a higher sense of consciousness, thereby assuring humanity a type of spiritual immortality.

The grafting of the sublime Unfed Flame to the carnal human heart occurred from afar. Ancestral helpers on Venus directed a collective and everlasting energy force toward humanity on earth. The Venusian and ever-youthful lord named Sanat Kumara, the overseer of Shamballa, spearheaded this Mission. With an etheric Silver cord, he connected the Unfed Flame to every life stream incarnation on earth. When this flame of spiritual consciousness began to develop among individuals, Sanat Kumara led a group of higher beings to earth where they established the first Golden City, later known as Shamballa. This spiritual center possessed unrivaled opulence; streets paved with Gold passed jewel-encrusted Temples and Schools of Higher Wisdom and Knowledge. [For more information on Shamballa see the taped Trance-Mission: *Three Shamballa Messages* and Appendix M.]

In addition to its metaphysical influence on the human body, the Unfed Flame serves as a portal to a being of greater spiritual consciousness—the I AM Presence—to which we are indelibly connected. [See Appendix L, the I AM Presence.]

Meanwhile, these legends appear in other doctrines. Vedic Cosmology—Hindu-based metaphysics—mirrors a similar creation story. According to the sacred Sanskrit text of Hindu philosophy, the Bhagavad-Gita, fourteen planetary systems exist in the intangible universe. The highest is Satyaloka where residents grasp advanced spiritual knowledge. Sanat Kumara and Sananda—who in Vedic culture is referred to as Sanandana Kumara—are two of the four sons of Brahma and inhabit in the second-tier planetary system of Tapaloka. Earth, known as Bhurloka, falls seventh in line.

Each planetary system creates a unique experience for its dwellers—the sentience of the space-time continuum and the manifestation of the physical being differentiate higher from lower beings. Residents of enlightened strata perceive time durations in millennia, have no sense of fear, and do not confront disease or the aging of the body. In the lower planetary systems, residents experience shorter life spans, marked fear, widespread disease, and increased apprehension.

The Violet Flame:

Simply stated, the Violet Flame stabilizes past Karmas through Transmutation, Forgiveness, and Mercy. This leads to the opening of the spiritual heart and the development of bhakti—the unconditional love and compassion for others. Our Co-creative ability is activated through the Ascended Master's gift of the Unfed Flame in adjunct with the practice of the Law of Love, and the Power of Intention. But the Violet Flame, capable of engendering our greatest spiritual growth and evolution, is spiritual velocity pure and simple.

Invoking the flame's force often produces feelings of peace, tranquility, and inner harmony—its ability to lift the low-vibrating energy fields of blame, despair, and fear into Forgiveness and Understanding, paves the path to love.

The history of the Violet Flame reaches back thousands of years before the Time of Christ. According to Ascended Master legend, the Lords of Venus transmitted the Violet Flame as a spiritual consciousness during the final days of the pre-Atlantis civilization Lemuria. As one society perished and another bloomed, the power of the Violet Flame shifted, opening the way for Atlantean religiosity. This transfer of power initiated a clearing of the earth's etheric and psychic realms, and purged the lower physical atmosphere of negative forces and energies. Recorded narratives of Atlantis claim that Seven Temples of Purification sat atop visible materializations of the Violet Flame. The archangels Zadkiel and Amethyst, representing Freedom, Forgiveness and Joy, presided over an Atlantean Brotherhood known as the Order of Zadkiel, also associated with Saint Germain. These Violet Flame Temples still exist today in the celestial realm over Cuba.

The Violet Flame benefits humans and divinities equally. During spiritual visualizations, meditations, prayers, decrees, and mantras, many disciples seek the Violet Flame for serenity and wisdom. Meanwhile, the Ascended Masters always use it in inner retreats—even Saint Germain taps into its power to perfect and apply its force with chelas and students

The Violet Flame, rooted in Alchemic powers, is sometimes identified as a higher energy of Saturn and the Blue Ray, a force leavened with justice, love, and wisdom. Ascended-Master lore explains the Violet Flame's ability to release a person from temporal concerns: Saturn's detachment from emotions and low-lying energies sever worldly connections. That's why the scientific properties of violet light are so important in metaphysical terms. The shortness of its wavelength and the high Vibration of its frequency induce a point of transition to the next octave of light and into a keener consciousness.

While its primary focus balances negative personal and planetary Karmas, Saint Germain says, "If you are having trouble utilizing that law, it is as simple as taking a few seconds and visualizing that Violet Flame streaming forth from your feet and extending to the top of your head. You'll feel it first as an electrical shock throughout your system, as it stimulates each of the centers of light upon the physical body. This is the assistance and the gift from the Lords of Venus so you would someday understand the ONE that is contained within each and every one of you."

Activations & Subtle Energies:

Golden City Vortices are activated in two-year periods during the New Times. Located in Arizona, Gobean, the first for the Time of Change, developed in the late 1970s and continued its growth into the early 1980s. Once the new energies began to flourish on earth, the Ascended Masters, Archangels, and Elohim, in 1994, initiated a sequential, two-year awakening of the remaining Golden Cities throughout the world.

1. Malton: 1994 (United States)
2. Wahanee: 1996 (United States)
3. Shalahah: 1998 (United States)
4. Klehma: 2000 (United States)
5. Pashachino: 2002 (Canada)
6. Eabra: 2004 (Canada)
7. Jeafray: 2006 (Canada)
8. Uverno: 2008 (Canada)
9. Yuthor: 2010 (Greenland)
10. Stienta: 2012 (Iceland)

Once a Golden City matures, humans can tap into Vortex energies for healing, growth, evolution, development, and transformation: personal, planetary and spiritual recovery form the foundation of humanity's Ascension to a higher consciousness.

Golden City Vortices are considered safe places where ongoing spiritual growth and advancement bloom. In these sacred harbors, energy finds asylum from exploitation. Saint Germain says, "These gateways or Vortex areas are protected areas for interaction with spiritual energy." [For more information see: *New World Atlas, Volume One.*]

Activated Golden City Vortices function at the Third, Fourth, and Fifth Dimensions in their attributes and release of beneficial energies. Golden City Third-Dimensional energies create harmonious connections to Mother Earth. Humans who physically assimilate to Golden City Vortex energies receive the gifts of longevity (slower aging); greater healing abilities (health and well-being); and physical regeneration (cell replication).

The Golden City Fourth-Dimensional energies affect human light bodies (the aura). Connections to the invisible kingdoms develop; one cultivates the ability to see gnomes, fairies, and Elementals. In this dimension, a person tunes into his or her telepathic and psychic abilities (the development of the super senses), and experiences lucid dreaming (dimensional awareness), honing preternatural skills and talents—natural functions in human spiritual evolution.

Fifth-Dimensional Golden City energies operate within the realm of the Ascended Masters; Shamballa; advanced spiritual teachers; archetypes of evolution; and the templates of all Golden Cities. At this level, our spiritual evolution initiates a profound relationship with the Master Teacher and the Ray Force that serves a particular Golden City Vortex. Experiences of Unana, the ONE, and the collective consciousness are common. At this dimension, all beings live in spiritually perfected communities. The body takes on an ageless, perfected state—one without disease or fear. [For more information regarding Golden Cities throughout the World see *Freedom Star Book.*]

Monad:

Monad means dynamic will, or purpose and life, as it is revealed through human demonstration. The Monad is often referred to as the Lord of ceaseless devotion, knowledge, and intelligent activity. H. P. Blavatsky writes of the Monad in the Secret Doctrine:

> "For the Monad, or Jiva, per se, cannot be called even Spirit; it is a Ray, a breath of the Absolute, or the ABSOLUTENESS rather; and the Absolute Homogeneity, having no relations with the conditioned and relative finiteness, is unconscious on our plane. Therefore, besides the material which will be needed for its future human form, the Monad requires (a) a spiritual model, or prototype for that material to shape itself into; and (b) an intelligent consciousness, to guide its evolution and progress, neither of which is possessed by the homogeneous Monad, or by senseless though living matter. The Adam of dust requires the Soul of Life to be breathed into him... therefore when the hour strikes for purusha (spirit) to mount on Prakriti's (substance) shoulders for the formation of the Perfect Man... the Celestial Ancestors (entities from preceding worlds) step in on this our plane, and incarnate in the physical or animal man, as the Pitris (solar angel, I AM Presence) had stepped in before them for the formation of the latter... the Pitris shoot out from their ethereal bodies still more ethereal and shadowy similitudes of themselves, or what we should now call 'doubles'... in their own likeness. This furnishes the Monad with its first dwelling, and blind matter with a model around and upon which to build henceforth."

Aryan:

Dark and ignorant elements of society have sullied the meaning of 'Aryan' to describe a genetically superior race, one that dominates and destroys all others. This semantic contrivance is intended to confuse humanity of the true nature and Mission of the Rays, and the intention of their services. Esoteric teachings tell us humanity, regardless of race, color or creed, is ONE race; Aryan is this race—we are ONE race.

APPENDIX B

Throughout the evolution of light and consciousness on this planet, humanity has embraced a physical incarnation of one of three distinct races: the Lemurian, the Atlantean, and the Aryan. According to the teachings of the Ray(ces), only one lineage, without exception, can embody and inhabit the earth at one time. Each culture assumes a distinctive composite of Ray forces, which determines the physical and emotional vehicles of its members. The presence of certain Ray(ce) combinations is primarily psychological and affects the shared outer mind of humanity. This collective mentality carries the Divine Plan forward through the Divine Mind. The three best known Ray(ce) combinations are:

1. *The Lemurian*: The contintent of Lemuria, also known as Mu in other ideologies, was located somewhere between India and Australia. Some prophecies say it existed no more than 20,000 years ago; others suggest it dates back millions of years before Christ. This Eden-like civilization met its end when the warm waters of the South Pacific Ocean swallowed its landmass during a cataclysmic event. Many metaphysical scholars believe Lemurian survivors live inside Mount Shasta and on the African island of Madagascar.

Lemurians thrived during the first wave of consciousness. According to esoteric teachings, Lemurians triumphed over animal consciousness and rooted the flame of divine humanity in the human heart. Their primitive physical vehicles—clumsy bodies, exposed pineal glands, and one-eyed vision—required absolute mindfulness to hold form and sustain body functions. The result: animal consciousness dominated the physically and spiritually feeble Lemurians. Some say this ancient race developed Hatha Yoga to hone and coordinate external movements and internal mechanisms. Over time, genetics trained the heart to circulate blood, the lungs to respirate air, and the stomach to digest food. Consciousness shifted from the corporeal to the incorporeal, thus establishing the foundation of an involuntary nervous system and the basis for our present-day level of conscious absolution, the Age of Spiritual Freedom. The Rays of modern times liberated our conscious minds, giving it independence and expression. Meanwhile, the extinction of the dinosaurs paved the way for new Rays of consciousness and a new race of humanity.

2. *The Atlantean*: The existence of Atlantis—the lost continent—still stumps the keenest minds of scientific and metaphysical communities. Even the great Greek philosophers pondered its rise and fall. According to legend, Atlantis emerges as a civilization about 400,000 years ago; its demise abuts the beginning of recorded history. Ancient lore places Atlantis in the Atlantic Ocean or near the Straits of Gibraltar; other texts say it once flourished near present-day Cuba.

A group of Atlanteans escaped the sinking of Atlantis and found refuge in America. They became the I AM Race of souls; their active intelligence continues to develop—their purpose, to foster Brotherly love among all nations.

Atlantean cognizance emerges from animalistic instinct into HU-man behavior. The emotional body of this race resembles modern-day mankind. Blessed with pointed intuition, this go-between group bridges the gap between consciousness and intelligence. It introduces the first social order of religion, which, through a chosen code of behavior, disciplines the emotions and the emotional light body. This enlightenment reveals a religious purpose, connecting the emotional body to the intelligent choice (conscience) and preparing humanity for social order.

3. *The Aryan*: Metaphysicians allegorically associate seven divisions of the Aryan to the seven apocalyptic churches of St. John's vision in the Book of Revelations: Ephesus, India; Smyrna, Persia; Pergamos, Chaldean-Egyptian-Semitic; Thyatira, Greece-Latin-Roman; Sardis, Teuton-Anglo-Saxon; Philadelphia, Slavic; Laodicea, Manichaean (Persian Gnostic Teachings). According to the Master teachers of the I AM America teachings, the Aryan race traces its ancient roots to Africa including the primeval Egyptian city of Meroe, Ethiopia and the majestic, sacred Mount Meru, Tanzania. The word *Aryan* denotes active intelligence; in Sanskrit it means nobility. Scholars say the destiny of this contemporary race—Aryan—is linked with Lemurian civilization; it carries the Divine Plan forward through the qualification of active intelligence. That's why this dynamic, modern race continues to develop the cognitive ability to apply intelligent emotions, thoughts, and actions in its decision-making process.

Consciousness:

It is important to note the difference between the two words and their meanings: *conscience and conscious.* Conscience is the internal recognition of right and wrong in regard one's actions and motives. Conscious(ness) means 'the awakening to one's own existence, sensations, and cognitions.'

APPENDIX C

Topics and Terms for Changing of the Guard

Sensing Changes in Energy
Karma: Cause and Effect
Ascended Masters Adjust Energy
Sanctus Germanus, the Holy Brother
The United States of Europe
Governments and the Right to Vote
Guidance on Diet, Food, and Pesticides
Erasing Death Consciousness
The Dark Government

Karma:

Karma means actions, both bad and good. It comes from the Sanskrit word, *kri,* which means to act. This term also describes the consequences of past actions, including the activities and the circumstances of former lives.

Shamballa and the development of the Mystery Schools:

In Sanskrit it means a place of peace, tranquility, and happiness. To the Buddhists, Shamballa is an Eden, a Shangri-La tucked away in the mountains of Tibet. The Ascended Masters consider Shamballa a mystical and venerated city, a metaphysical paragon that exudes untarnished energy, absolute beauty, and spiritual perfection. But, earth could not sustain its perfection and purity. Shamballa thrice experienced cataclysmic Earth Changes, the final initiated by the Lords of Venus. And until humanity embraces a higher spiritual consciousness, Shamballa will continue to exist in the ether. Its true purpose forever smolders in the embers of this city. Open to eternal speculation and distortion, Shamballa will always reside in the spiritual virtue of the Fifth Dimension.

According to Ascended-Master legend, the Venusian Lord Sanat Kumara sparked, literally, Shamballa's destruction. He surrounded the city with piles of sandalwood logs and set it afire. And though only ashes remained of this once glorious Golden City, the Lords of Venus established an etheric template, relocating the magnificent Temples and Schools of Higher Knowledge. Entry is exclusive and limited to those "whose eyes and ears were open." That is, those evolved and spiritually developed souls who perceive and understand the Fourth and Fifth Dimensions. The Lords of Venus, however, remained accessible and helpful to Third-Dimension members of humanity. They established hidden and secret schools of knowledge throughout the earth: centers that encourage spiritual growth until individual contact with higher-dimensional schools is obtained.

These groups and organizations include Lodges, mystery schools, and Brotherhoods. Brahmanist, Eleusian, Samothracian, Isis, Orphism, Cabeiri, Egyptian, Druidic, Delphinian, Dionysiac, Hermetic, Rosicrucian, and Free-Masonry Lodges are among this cryptic and storied fellowship. The members of these secret societies understand the brittle underpinnings of their work. And though they strive to help humanity achieve a higher level of consciousness, organized and forceful resistance often stymies their progress. That's why they close ranks, to operate freely, detached from persecution, harassment, and discrimination, within the safety of their vows of secrecy, ancient knowledge, and road-tested wisdom. Well aware of the duality and vibratory nature of the earth experience, these secret organizations train special emissaries to roam the world and counter resistance. The Master Teacher Saint Germain is one of these great ambassadors. These remarkable personages, forming an order quite different from society, guide humanity through critical periods of history.

Saint Germain, the Holy Brother:

The Lord of the Seventh Ray and the Master of the Violet Flame, Saint Germain lived numerous noteworthy lifetimes, dating back thousands of years, before incarnating as the Comte de Saint Germain during Renaissance Europe. In his own Trance-Mission, *Changing the Guard*, he illustrates his life as the Englishman Sir Francis Bacon, the sixteenth-century philosopher, essayist, and Utopian who greatly influenced the philosophy of inductive science. His most profound and well-known work on the restoration of humanity, the *Instauratio Magna* (Great Restoration), defined him as an icon of the Elizabethan era. Research also shows his co-authoring of many Shakespearean sonnets.

According to Esoteric historians, Queen Elizabeth I of England—The Virgin Queen—was his biological mother. Before Bacon's birth, the queen married Earl of Leicester, quieting ideas of illegitimacy. Elizabeth's lady in waiting, Lady Ann Bacon, wife of the Lord High Chancellor of England, adopted him following the stillbirth of her baby. Bacon was, therefore, the true heir to the crown and England's rightful king.[1] But his cousin James I of Scotland succeeded the throne. Sir Bacon described this turn of events in his book, *Novum Organo*, published in 1620: "It is an immense ocean that surrounds the island of Truth." And Saint Germain often reminds us to this day "there are no mistakes, ever, ever, ever."

Bacon's philosophies also helped define the principles of Free Masonry and democracy. As an adept leader of the Rosicrucians (a secret society of that time), he set out to reveal the obsolescence and oppression of European monarchies.

Eventually, Bacon's destiny morphed. He shed his physical form and sought the greatest gift of all: immortality. And that's what placed him in the most extraordinary circumstances throughout history. Even his death (or lack of) evokes controversy. Some say Bacon faked his demise in 1626—the coffin contained the carcass of a dog.

According to the author, ADK Luk, Saint Germain ascended on May 1, 1684 in Transylvania at the Rakoczy mansion. He was 123 years old. Some say Saint Germain spent the lost years—from 1626 to 1684—in Tibet. During this time he took (or may have been given) the name Kajaeshra. Interpreted as *God's helper of life and wisdom,* it was possibly a secret name and rarely used. Kaja has several interpretations: in Greek it means *pure;* Balinese, *toward the mountain;* early Latin (Estonian), *echo;* Hopi, *wise child;* Polish, *of the Gods;* and Hebrew, *life.* The second part of the name—Eshra (Ezra)—translates into *help or aid.*

Indeed, Bacon's work would impact centuries to follow. During his time in Tibet, tucked away in silent monasteries, Germain designed a society that eventually created a United Brotherhood of the Earth: Solomon's Temple of the Future. It's a metaphor used to describe the raising of consciousness as the greater work of democracy. Author Marie Bauer Hall studied the life of Francis Bacon. In her book, *Foundations Unearthed,* she described the legendary edifice: "This great temple was to be supported by the four mighty pillars of history, science, philosophy, and religion, which were to bear the lofty dome of Universal Fellowship and Peace."[2]

But Germain embraced an even deeper passion: the people and nation of America, christening it *New Atlantis.* He envisioned this land—present-day United States, Canada, Mexico, and South America—as part of the United Democracies of Europe and the People of the World. America, this growing society, held his hope for a future guided by a Democratic Brotherhood.

The Comte de Saint Germain emerged years later in the courts of pre-revolutionary France—his appearance, intelligence, and worldliness baffled members of the Court of Versailles. This gentleman carried the essence of eternal youth: he was a skilled artist and musician; he spoke fluent German, English, French, Italian, Portuguese, Spanish, Greek, Latin, Sanskrit, Arabic, and Chinese; and he was a proficient chemist. Meanwhile, literary, philosophic, and political aristocracy of the time sought his company. French philosophers Jean-Jacque Rousseau and Voltaire; the Italian adventurer Giacomo Casanova; and the Earl of Chatham and statesman Sir Robert Walpole of Britain were among his friends.

In courts throughout Europe, he dazzled royalty with his Mastery of Alchemy, removing flaws from gems and turning lead into Gold. And the extent of Germain's ken reached well into the theosophical realm. A guru of yogic and tantric disciplines, he possessed highly developed telepathic and psychic abilities. This preternatural knowledge led to the development of a cartographic Prophecy—the Map of Changes. This uncanny blueprint, now in the hands of the scion of Russian aristocracy, detailed an imminent restructuring of the political and social boundaries of Europe.[3]

But few grasped Germain's true purpose during this Time of historic critical mass: not even the king and queen of France could comprehend his tragic forewarnings. The Great White Brotherhood—a fellowship of enlightened luminaries—sent the astute diplomat Saint Germain to orchestrate the development of the United States of Europe. Not only a harbinger of European diplomacy, he made his presence in America during the germinal days of this country. Esoteric scholars say he urged the signing of the Declaration of Independence in a moment of collective fear—a fear of treason and ultimately death. Urging the forefathers to proceed, a shadowed figure in the back of the room shouted: *Sign that document!*

To this day, the ironclad identity of this person remains a mystery, though some mystics believe it was Saint Germain. Nevertheless, his avid support spurred the flurry of signatures, sealing the fate of America—and the beginning of Sir Francis Bacon's democratic experiment.

The Comte de Saint Germain never could shape a congealed Europe, but he did form a lasting and profound relationship with America. Germain's present-day participation in U.S. politics reaches the Oval Office. Some theosophical mystics say Germain visits the president of the United States the day after the leader's inauguration; others suggest he's the fabled patriot Uncle Sam.

According to the I AM America Prophecies, Saint Germain says that the people of America have a unique destiny in the New Times. America contains within it a unique anagram:

A M E R I C A = I A M R A C E.

The I AM Race of people is a unique group of souls who lived in America as Atlanteans. But their destiny has evolved since those ancient times. Instead of sinking on a continent destroyed by the misuse of technology and spiritual knowledge, their active intelligence continues to develop in modern times. Their service is focused on the Brotherly love of all nations. In the I AM America Earth Changes Prophecies Saint Germain states, "America will be the first to go through the changes, and then give aid to the rest of the World."

Interpretations of this Prophecy explain why American is possibly the chosen land—the first society to experience dimensional change. Members of this regenerated, enlightened society will share and teach the benefits of this new understanding with the rest of humanity.

Saint Germain identifies with the qualities of Brotherhood and freedom. He is the sponsor of humanity and serves as a conduit of Violet Light—a force some claim is powerful enough to propel one into Ascension. When Saint Germain accepts a chela, the Master appears in physical form. Sometimes, he playfully disguises himself, leaving clues of his identity, most often purple clothing.

Today the essence of Saint Germain—that eternal, eloquent diplomat—fills the world. His presence assures humanity of an alternate path to evolution and growth. In Changing the Guard he illustrates this point: "We have spent our time adjusting that Collective Consciousness for the days and the times that are coming. We also would like to remind you that we cannot, at any time, readjust the Karma of mankind. For what mankind has created, mankind must now receive. This is the Law of Cause and Effect. But we work with those causes to readjust that plan of the best and highest good." Perhaps our present Karma is indeed predestined, but how we work through Karmas is engendered in our free will and choice.

Emergent Evolution:

When the spiritual growth of an evolving life reaches a certain stage of conscious awareness, the soul forces itself into contact with higher streams of divine expression and consciousness. The union of these two states of consciousness produces a new evolutionary being as an aspect of the manifestation of evolving life. This process is known as Emergent Evolution.

The Seventh Moon:

Many Native American creation stories recount an ancient Earth Changes legend involving mass destruction and reincarnation. According to lore, an asteroid collided with earth in the Yucatan Peninsula; the impact formed the present-day Gulf of Mexico. The Masters refer to this astral body as the Seventh Moon: "It contained a Vibration of the Heart of this planet." Some mystics call it the *Star of Renewal* and its energy force—shakti—can create wealth and substance. Coincidentally, the seventh Vedic Moon Sign is Punarvasu (Punar-Vasu). She is the ruling deity of the Seventh Moon—the Mother Goddess Aditi, an Earth Goddess of abundance who tends the ground, preparing the soil and the seeds to bear healthy fruit.[4] Punarvasu is also affiliated with the concretization of the will and the ability of the soul to move beyond human limitation.

Earth Changes Prophecies:

The Ring of Fire: The 40,000 kilometer Ring of Fire is a band of seismic and volcanic activity along the seams of continental-plate movement in the Pacific Ocean. The eastern section rises from South America through Mexico, hitting land in Southern California where two continental plates grinding against one another create the San Andreas fault. It then reaches into northern California and the Pacific Northwest, forming the Cascade Range of mountains. Continuing its movement into Alaska, it runs along the Aleutian and Kuril archipelagos, dropping south to Japan, the Philippines, Java and New Zealand.

In the I AM America Earth Changes Prophecies, Ascended Master Kuthumi adjusts and oversees the energies of the Ring of Fire. According to the Earth Changes Prophecies, once the Ring of Fire is activated, the more than 400 volcanoes along its perimeter will erupt. An ensuing period of global ash-induced darkness marked by constant precipitation lasts between two and four years.

Polar and Dimensional Shifts: The I AM America Earth Changes Prophecies describe three polar shifts within a short period of time. The catalyst: global warming. The first begins when excess equatorial water addles the earth's spin. As a result, continents begin to sink. When the proportion of land to ocean changes, the initial shift takes its maiden voyage east. The second shift repositions the pole in Greenland. The earth's magnetism then heads south to the Hudson Strait at the lower end of Baffin Island, about 2,660 kilometers north of New York City; this marks the final fluctuation. The poles in transit raise the vibration on earth, affecting human energy systems: families, societies, and governments. This is the beginning of the Golden Age.

[Editor's Note: according to the Master Teachers, we do not have to wait for an Earth Change to entice the Golden Age. We can begin today. Through our developed awareness of subtle energy changes, spiritual growth, and the use of the Golden Cities, changes can occur without mass destruction. The choice is ours—a change of heart can change the world!]

Changes in Air and Water: During the prophesied Earth Changes, much of the world's water and air supplies become polluted. Aquifers drain, and rivers and streams change direction. To overcome this problem, the Masters provide breathing techniques to ready the body and strengthen the lungs for the New Times. They also give Free Energy methods of recharging water with higher frequencies. And as light (prana) increases on earth, remarkable new energies that embrace the globe, mitigate the body's need for food.

Prophecies of Change:

1. According to the Masters' prophecies, a bartering system will replace the exchange of paper money after the Time of Change. They recommend investing in *tradable resources*, e.g. Gold, Silver, land, and other natural resources and commodities.

2. The Master Teachers suggest that the escalation of crime serves as one of many signs that signal the onset of the Time of Change. Saint Germain says, "When insanity becomes sane, the Times of Change will be coming."

3. In addition to societal and economic changes, the human body will experience adjustments in its systems and energy centers (chakras). Upheavals on earth, say the Master Teachers, affect human DNA coding at the molecular level. This change prepares the body for the New Dimensions.

APPENDIX C

[1] Marie Bauer Hall, *Foundations Unearthed,* originally issued as *Francis Bacon's Great Virginia Vault,* Fourth Edition (Los Angeles: Veritas Press), page 9.

[2] Ibid., page 13.

[3] K. Paul Johnson, *The Masters Revealed: Madame Blavatsky and the Myth of the Great White Lodge (Suny Series in Western Esoteric Traditions)* (Albany, NY: State University of New York Press), page 19.

[4] Dennis Harness, *The Nakshatras: The Lunar Mansions of Vedic Astrology,* First Edition (Twin Lakes, WI: Lotus Press), page 27.

APPENDIX D

Topics and Terms for The Fourth Dimension

Clairaudient Frequencies
Awareness of Vibration
Reincarnation
Journey in Ascension
Preparation of the Golden City Vortices
Golden Cities and the Fourth Dimension
The Role of Mind
Alchemy and the Law of Change
Kingdoms of Creation
The purpose of domestic animals and pets

Time of Transition:

This twelve-year era of spiritual change marks a turning point in the momentum of the earth's energy. It begins with the implementation of a benevolent plan: one that activates the Law of Love while encouraging divine awareness among humanity. Beginning in 1988 and ending in 2000, (however some I AM America prophecies suggest a longer duration) the beloved Ascended Masters, Archangels, and Elohim flood the earth with light (the Rays) to restore mankind's spiritual growth and acuity. Many people know and understand this period as the Spiritual Awakening. During this short but intense interval of Transformation, the proliferation of alternative self-help and healing groups spawns a renewed zeal for other forms of faith. And as the spirituality of the global community gels, the human consciousness—like a river changing course—flows from secular concerns to spiritual viewpoints. The Time of Transition, as a result, fosters an understanding and an experience of Unity among spiritual thoughts, customs, and cultures. And though this divine age ended nearly a decade ago, humanity can still tap into the readily available spiritual infusion of energy to initiate the dawning of human consciousness for the New Dimensions.

Fourth Dimension:

This dimension of light and sound frequencies houses the invisible kingdoms of nature Devas, gnomes, fairies, and Elementals. These arcane beings, however, are not alone. Certain Akashic records—encoded libraries of Universal Knowledge—also inhabit the non-physical planes of the Fourth Dimension. To communicate with this intangible realm, one must cultivate his or her super-senses: clairaudience, sight; clairvoyance, vision; clairsentience, feeling; clairalience, scent; and clairgustance, taste. This state of conscious awareness increases telepathic ability, lucid dreaming, and other forms of dimensional perceptibility.

Hermetic Principle:

To grasp the language of the Ascended Masters is to understand the essence of the Hermetic Principles. This mystical ideology, arguably the bedrock of esoteric doctrine, has experienced a renaissance over the past few years. Inspired by the publication of neo-mystical books such as the ever-popular *The Secret,* age-old occult maxims now provide mainstream spiritual fodder for novice practitioners of Hermetic mysteries. And though its new-age undertones find favor with contemporary audiences, Hermetic Law dates back thousands of years to the seminal days of Vedic, Egyptian, and Greek cultures—its roots sink deep into the secret societies of the Rosicrucians and the Free Masons.

Hermeticism is a how-it-all-works compendium of religious and philosophical beliefs sired by Hermes Trismegistus. The true identity of this ancient enigma stands on faulty ground—even the most learned esoteric scholars can't agree on Trismegistus's origin. Some say this patriarch of Hermeticism is the Greek God Hermes; others claim he's Thoth, the Egyptian deity, son of Isis and Nephthys. And in Jewish, Christian, and Islamic lore, he's the biblical mystic Enoch, the progeny of Cain.

The bible of Hermeticism, so to speak, is *The Kybalion: A Study of The Hermetic Philosophy of Ancient Egypt and Greece.* An anonymous source known as the Three Initiates penned the Kybalion in the early twentieth century. The text outlines the seven interconnected axioms of Hermetic Principles: (1) the Law of Mentalism; (2) the Law of Correspondence; (3) the Law of Vibration; (4) the Law of Polarity; (5) the Law of Rhythm; (6) the Laws of Cause and Effect; and (7) the Law of Gender.

The Seven Hermetic Principles:

1. *The Law of Mentalism: The all is mind; the universe is mental.* According to this law, perception creates your reality of God and the universe—God is an everlasting consciousness, and all reality is an expression of that consciousness. The Law of Mentalism touches the intangible. To understanding this law is to understand nothing: the universe lacks definability. It is an infinite, indescribable construct of the mind.

2. *The Law of Correspondence: As above, so below; as below, so above.* On a transpersonal level, the Law of Correspondence tells us our inner world defines our outer world and vice versa: this universal tenet forms the foundation of our everyday thoughts, attitudes, and beliefs. For instance, if your insides are chaotic and miserable; if you lack confidence and self-esteem; if you're full of anger, resentment, and negativity, you'll experience a tumultuous outer reality. The grasping of this fundamental precept is the key to comprehending

the Laws of Cause and Effect (Karma) and the Law of Attraction. The Law of Correspondence is also described as *mental equivalent.* "But we know now that any outward act is but the sequel to a thought, and that the type of thought which we allow to become habitual will sooner or later find expression on the Plane of action." [1]

3. *The Law of Vibration: Nothing rests; everything moves; everything vibrates.* Closely related to the Law of Attraction, this third Hermetic Principle states that all entities in the universe, including humans, emotions, and spirituality, are in constant motion and perpetual transformation. This translucent friction, which recalibrates energy, creates a synergy among all things in nature. For instance, if your mental waves wealth, it will come to you.

4. *The Law of Polarity: Everything is dual; everything has poles; everything has its pair of opposites; like and unlike are the same; opposites are identical in nature, but different in degree; extremes meet; all truths are but half-truths; all paradoxes may be reconciled.* Everything has an antithesis; opposites, yet mutable, are just two extremes of the same thing—darkness becomes light; cold becomes hot; hate becomes love.

5. *The Law of Rhythm: Everything flows, out and in; everything has its tides; all things rise and fall; the pendulum-swing manifests in everything; the measure of the swing to the right is the measure of the swing to the left; rhythm compensates.* The Law of Rhythm creates the hidden unifying force in the universe: is the catalyst of natural timing and consistency. The right rhythm creates harmony; the left, disharmony. An action produces a reaction—the ebb and flow of the tides, the waxing and waning of the moon, and the rising and setting of the sun.

6. *The Laws of Cause and Effect: Every cause has its effect; every effect has its cause; everything happens according to law; chance is but a name for law not recognized; there are many planes of causation, but nothing escapes the law.* This sixth Hermetic Law—the notion of Karma—states: "But we know now that any outward act is but the sequel to a thought, and that the type of thought which we allow to become habitual will sooner or later find expression on the Plane of action." Nothing in the universe occurs by accident: everything happens for a reason.

7. *The Law of Gender: Gender is in everything; everything has its masculine and feminine principles; gender manifests on all planes.* All forms of nature—animate and inanimate—possess the duality of gender. This final Hermetic Principle says all things in the universe, even energy, exhibit masculine and feminine traits.

[From *The Kybalion: A Study of the Hermetic Philosophy of Ancient Egypt and Greece,* written anonymously by the Three Initiates, Chicago, 1940.]

APPENDIX D

Prophecies of Change:

Appearance of the Ascended Masters: After the Earth Changes, according to the I AM America Prophecies, Ascended Masters will inhabit the Golden City Vortices in physical form for twenty years. As human consciousness moves into the Golden Age, their work will focus on teaching and healing. During these two decades, the earth slips into the New Times, and the appearance of the Ascended Masters throughout the world is not entirely contingent on the Earth Changes. It relies on the spiritual development of humanity and the overall vibratory level of the earth.

[1] Emmet Fox, *The Sermon on the Mount* (New York: Harper & Row, Publishers), page 68.

APPENDIX E

Topics and Terms for The Work of a Master

Nuclear War
Asteroid
Collective Consciousness
Control of the Masses through Money, Power, and Greed
The Nature of Fear
The Power of Harmony
Auric Vision
Color and Aromatherapy

Spiritual Guidance for Living in the Current Times:

1. *The Law of Consciousness* rules these times; seek harmony and balance in your relationships with others and the world around you: these are the first two tenets of the Twelve Jurisdictions. According to Master Sananda, "All energy, in order to be sustained for creation, must be maintained in balance. Balance is the continuous cycle of harmony." And yet, this new paradigm adds another element: alignment. It's the course of action or thought that joins others who pursue the same cause. Strive to unite your efforts, your actions, and your thoughts with your fellow humans; always keep your spiritual symmetry in check, and make adjustments as you stray off course. This constant assessment of your personal parallelism includes a mental process (alignment), and a physical outcome (harmony). An imbalance of these tendencies creates dysfunction and weakness in your fields of energy. If left unchecked, spiritual growth wanes or stops altogether.

2. *Children:* In general, the incarnation of today's children is extremely evolved. The Master Teachers suggest "respecting and honoring their divinity ... come to that understanding that you all live together as ONE family, and then seek resolution through the Laws of Cooperation." By following this lead, parents, teachers, and other adults can help eschew interpersonal conflicts and emotional damage, leading to a child's natural Mastery of Unity Consciousness and the ONE.

3. *Finances:* Harmony bears the fruits of wealth and money. And yet, it's just a matter of alignment. As the Master Teachers say, "Instruct all those who work with you during this time to increase their harmony, and therefore their abundance." To overcome financial insolvency, practice and understand the Laws of Harmony and Abundance.

4. *Conflict with Friends or Family Members:* Spiritual growth and self-Mastery are oftentimes not accepted or understood by close family members or loved ones. The Master Teachers understand this challenge; their guidance mirrors the teachings of the Bible, a verse from Matthew 10:39 "he who has lost his life for my sake shall find it." That is, in some instances, to continue our growth, a new and spirited life may emerge. And when it comes to those who resist your efforts, practice compassion and apply the Law of Love (loving hands = actions; loving heart = emotions) And remember, sometimes to "back away is an act of courage and strength."

Ascended Master:

An Ascended Master is a highly developed spiritual being who has ascended the human physical manifestation beyond the Third Dimension. At one time the members of this cosmically elite fellowship, known as the Great White Lodge or Brotherhood, were men and women tied to a corporeal existence like any other human on earth.

But a higher destiny set these souls apart from ordinary individuals. Over thousands of years, these souls encountered innumerable diverse lifetimes and an arduous yet prolific process of incarnation after incarnation. This boundless experience of trials, tragedy, knowledge, and wisdom culminated in an uncanny spiritual maturity beyond that of a normal human being. They came to understand and acknowledge in their hearts, an undeniable, great truth—divinity. The recognition of this inherent divinity drives human consciousness beyond Third Dimensional perception; it instigates the Mastery of thought, feeling, action, and experience.

A command of the Third Dimension breaks the elusive bond to the Wheel of Karma, freeing the Spiritual Master from the need to reincarnate in an earthbound physical body. Now the individual has attained the role of Ascended Master who dedicates his or her immortal existence to the universal spiritual enrichment of humanity. Many members of this fellowship, though not physically tied to earth, remain close to terra firma and its people. Master Teachers seek others, who, although embody a physical attachment to earth, embrace an innate desire to evolve beyond the Third Dimension.

The Great White Brotherhood or Lodge earns its name from an all-encompassing philosophy of humanity. White refers to white light, which embraces all colors, races, creeds, and genders. The Brotherhood's primary goal focuses on the preservation of the teachings and the spirit of the ancient religions and philosophies of the world. They pledge to protect mankind from growth-inhibiting assaults on individual and group freedoms, self-knowledge, and personal choice. Of paramount importance is their Mission to reawaken the dormant ethical and spiritual spark that is fast disappearing among the masses.

APPENDIX E

The fellowship of the Masters welcomes new members with the following invocation:

An Invitation

"I close by extending an invitation to all of you to join with us. The need is great among humanity today. There is still needless suffering fueled by the fires of ignorance and deception. Quietly listen and you will hear the call in your heart. We are not a religious group or sect; however, we are a service group of elder Brothers and Sisters who have been known throughout mankind's history as the Great White Lodge. Through the medium of consciousness we have merged our efforts and energies aimed towards the unity of all of life.

Our goal is simple, and our work is hard. It is never promised to be easy, however, the reward immeasurable. Come, through prayer and meditation if you feel the urge of the Mission within.

A new cycle awaits humanity. It is a cycle filled with growth, learning, and life. Painfully and lovingly, sometimes this growth is achieved through disease, poverty, and destruction. However, within your heart lies the gentle revolution that can redirect the course of such events.

This is a revolution armed with the power of service, charity, and love. If you should turn your back now, know that timelessly we await.

Let us join in wisdom to extinguish ignorance and inequity.

Let us join in love to extinguish suffering.

Let us join in service to extinguish greed and avarice.

Let us join in charity to extinguish poverty.

Let us join in harmony to extinguish disease.

As our ears are opened and our eyes begin to see, let us join as ONE LIGHT, in our hearts and minds. May this light of wisdom serve all. May this light of truth and justice prevail. May the law be written in hearts and joined through harmony, Brotherhood, and love.

Timelessly and agelessly, the unknown poet sings, *'O, let not the flame die out! Cherished age after age in its dark cavern - in its holy temples cherished. Fed by pure ministers of love - let not the flame die out.'*" [1]

APPENDIX E

The Ascended Masters' Role in Assisting Humanity and the Earth:

The Ascended Masters are also dedicated to helping humanity through unavoidable and seemingly catastrophic events. They accomplish this on a supra-physical level by adjusting and fine-tuning energy fields, which in turn influence physical creations and events on earth. This concept is not entirely new; we learned of these actions in previous lessons.

The Ascended Masters prophesied that earth would experience a cycle of geophysical change; accordingly, Saint Germain spun an etheric Golden Belt of high-frequency energy around this planet in the early 1950s. Its power deters catastrophic Earth Changes until humanity evolves a deeper consciousness; the belt also plays a significant role in humanity's spiritual growth.

"We have known for sometime that humanity has stood on the precipice of nuclear war and cataclysmic Earth Changes . . . did you know that earlier in this century your planet was barely missed by an asteroid?" asks Saint Germain. "It was only by the work of the Hierarchy that this event did not occur," he adds.

Great Central Sun:

According to ancient Vedic rishis, or sages, our solar system rotates around a larger sun. The Master Teachers often refer to this as the Great Central Sun; the Hindus know it as the Galactic Center.

The sun's emanation of Rays regulates life and time in solar systems throughout the universe. A Ray is an energy that contains a purpose; and it guides the following two measurable and perceptible powers: light and sound. The Ray system stewards the principles of Karma and Dharma. Karma comes from the Sanskrit word "to act." Simply stated Karma means "actions—both good and bad." The Law of Cause and Effect "as you sow, so shall you reap" motivates Karmic actions, including the manifestations of past lives. Karma, unlike the conventional Western understanding of the word, is not a punishing force or act.

Dharma or "purpose" balances all actions. More significantly, Dharma denotes a "way of life." This spiritual axiom places a person's lifetime duty, work, and proper action in his or her charge. As Karma and Dharma chart the course of each lifetime, humans experience lessons that we pass, fail, spoil, incomplete, perfect, achieve, and ultimately Master.

Energy Field Balancing:

These are a series of lessons and techniques that move energy through the human energy field—auras and chakras. Energy-field balancing activates personal harmony, symmetry, and healing. The Master Teachers say we can develop these abilities beyond the scope of individual practice; and humanity, through a collective effort, can facilitate Earth Healing: the elimination of landfills, diseased forests, and polluted waters.

Mass Ascension:

According to the I AM America Prophecies, Ascended Masters appear in physical form in the Golden City Vortices during and after the twenty-year period. At that time, Mass Ascensions occur in the Golden Cities, at the Star or center locations of these Vortices, and in select locations around the world, which are hosted by the energies of Babajeran—Mother Earth. [Editor's Note: A model of this type of location is Ascension Valley located in the Shalahah Vortex.]

The energies of the Fourth Dimension, the point of Ascension or light body development, initiates a substantial portion of the world's population. As spiritual advancement and evolution flows, this light body exceeds the physical body, taking permanent residence in the Fifth Dimension. Simultaneously, a separate group of souls, according to the prophecies, experience a Third Dimensional incarnation on earth. The incoming group of Fifth Dimensional Ascended Masters becomes their Master Teachers.

Cellular Awakening:

This spiritual initiation, activated by Master Teachers Saint Germain and Kuthumi, prepares the consciousness to recognize and receive instruction from the Fourth Dimension. Cellular Awakening stimulates seven subtle adjustments on the cellular level, preparing the physical body for an intense spiritual experience. These acclimatizations include:

The Quickening: An acceleration of cells throughout the body creating a union with the I AM Presence.

Higher Metabolism: This physical change activates the Eight-Sided Cell of Perfection, which is located in the heart. According to the Master Teachers, a person can inspire this phenomenon by fasting for twenty-four hours on citrus juices containing a portion of orange, lemon, tangerine, and grapefruit.

Attunement to the Galactic Beam: Also known as the Eighth or Golden Ray, this process prepares the physical body to receive the beneficial results of the Violet Flame. The Galactic Beam emits a high-frequency energy. The earth receives this power from the Great Central Sun. According to the Master Teachers, frequent saltwater baths with two cups of salt and three to four drops atomidine (iodine supplement) will augment this process. [Atomidine is available from the Heritage Store: www.heritagestore.com]

Violet Flame: This powerful universal force disintegrates etheric genetic coding through daily meditation, visualization, and decrees. Saint Germain says that kindling the Violet Flame during the Cellular Awakening affects the water balance of the physical body, including circulation, the lymphatic system, and the emotional body.

Diet: During Cellular Awakening the Master Teachers say to avoid or reduce all animal products from the diet.

Step-down Transformer: The processes instigated through the Cellular Awakening rapidly advance human light bodies. Synchronized with an Ascended Master's will, the awakened cells of light and love evolve the skills of a Step-Down Transformer to efficiently transmit and distribute currents of Ascended Master energy—referred to as an Ascended Master Current (A.M. Current). This metaphysical form of intentional inductive coupling creates an ethereal power grid that can be used for all types of healing.

A.M. Currents release beneficially charged and sometimes spine-tingling rushes of energy throughout the human system. This energy current is often accompanied by an audible high-pitched ring and a visible translucent glow of white or Gold light. Step-down Transformers report sensations of time slowing down and a body-warming flush as hands, feet, and chakras conduct the high frequency energy.

According to the Master Teachers tuning your body and your consciousness as a Step-down Transformer resembles a high quality quartz crystal, emitting effulgent Rays of Light and energy from many directions.

Surprisingly, an A.M. Current is calming and soothing. Since the Vibration of fear is effectively extinguished in its wake, the curative and peaceful frequency influences all who come within contact. Transfers of Step-down energies create a remnant force field that is later detectable, and the frequency can change significantly in strength or weakness dependant on the purpose for the release of the AM Current.

Master Teachers often train students to purposely hold and direct Step-down energies of healing love and light on behalf of earth and humanity. Primarily, Step-down Transformers work solely in private to perfect their craft and skill. When accomplished Step-down Transformers gather in groups the spiritual voltage significantly intensifies. These larger batteries of energy are often circuited into the collective consciousness to bring about positive political change, societal healing, and restorative balance to Mother Earth.

APPENDIX E

The Awakening Prayer: Ascended Masters Saint Germain and Kuthumi offered this prayer to more than 200 people at the 1990 Global Sciences Congress in Denver, Colorado. Group and individual meditation of the Awakening Prayer encourage a heightened spiritual consciousness and Cellular Awakening.

Great Light of Divine Wisdom,
Stream forth to my being,
And through your right use
Let me serve mankind and the planet.
Love, from the Heart of God.
Radiate my being with the presence of the Christ
That I walk the path of truth.
Great Source of Creation.
Empower my being,
My Brother,
My Sister,
And my planet with perfection
As we collectively awaken as one cell.
I call forth the Cellular Awakening.
Let wisdom, love, and power stream forth to this cell,
This cell that we all share.
Great Spark of Creation awaken the Divine Plan of Perfection.
So we may share the ONE perfected cell,
I AM.

[1] Lori Toye, *New World Atlas: Earth Changes for a Planet in Transition, Volume Three* (Payson, AZ: I AM America Seventh Ray Publishing International), page 74.

APPENDIX F

Topics and Terms for No Need for Change?

The Purpose of Prophecy
One World Government
The Alien Government
A World without a Need for Earth Change
Sound and DNA
Living in the Age of Peace
The Divine Feminine
Discipline and Freedom
Earth's Intergalactic Heritage
Cooperation, Not Competition

Shamballa Message:

The ethereal retreat of Shamballa opens its Golden gates once a year. Some say this spiritual event happens between December 17 and January 17. During the Time of Shamballa, earthbound ascended beings, archangels, and Elohim, as well as the inhabitants of other planets and solar systems, gather to establish a plan—a schematic for the spiritual and evolutionary elevation of earth and humanity—for the upcoming year. Throughout these thirty-two days of celebration, divine participants hold meetings, ceremonies, and planning sessions. Communication with earthly students via Ascended Master participation is of particular concern. In dream states or through the oral tradition, pupils receive messages. These parcels of information include divinations about the hierarchy's forthcoming plans; prophesied and pending events; and possible catastrophes averted or lessened through intentional thoughts, meditation, and efforts by individuals and the power of communal prayers on earth.

True State Economy:

A time will come when the world's economy implodes and paper money becomes obsolete, even prohibited. Only then will a new economic paradigm emerge—one that relies on the trading of precious metals, natural resources, and tangible goods. The nascent economy, resembling a Natural Economy, is based on what it produces. This structure eliminates the need to transfer goods, resources, and services via traditional currency.

Republic:

A republic, in simple terms, is a political body led by an elected official, such as a president or consul, rather than a sovereign leader. It follows some type of charter (e.g. the Constitution), which directs the government to elect representatives who will advance national interests and support the right of self-determination. Though the terms *republic* and *democracy,* a system where majority rules, are often used synonymously, the general idea of these political philosophies differ in principle. A republic, in theory, serves the common good of its citizens whom are subject to the rule of law. America in its current state is a republic—consider the Pledge of Allegiance: "I pledge allegiance to the Flag of the United States of America, and to the Republic, for which it stands ..."

Open Society:

Developed by philosopher Henri Bergson, an open society supports the human rights and the political freedoms of its citizens. In theory, an open society is just that: open. The government avoids keeping secrets from the public; rather, it places emphasis on tolerance, transparency, flexibility, and personal responsibility. In his book, *The Open Society and Its Enemies,* Austrian-born illuminato Sir Karl Popper defined an open society as one that allows its populace to throw out the leaders peacefully and without bloodshed. Compare this notion to a closed society—an unpredictable supremacy defined by violent revolutions and riotous coups d'etat.

Devas and Elementals:

Deva, meaning *shining one or being of light,* is a Sanskrit word that describes a God, deity, or spirit. Helena Blavatsky, co-founder of the Theosophical Society, introduced these celestial beings, or angels, to the western world in the nineteenth century. She described them as progressed entities from previous incarnations that would remain dormant until humanity attained a higher level of spiritual consciousness. Devas represent moral values and work directly with nature kingdoms.[1]

Elementals, on the other hand, are an invisible, subhuman group of creatures that act as counterparts to visible nature on terra firma. Medieval alchemist and occultist Paracelsus coined the term for these Elemental spirits. He divided them into the following four categories: gnomes (earth); undines (water); sylphs (air); and salamanders (fire).

1. *Gnomes:* The term comes from the Greek word "genomus" or "earth dweller." These subterranean spirits work closely with the earth, giving them immense power over rocks, flora, gemstones, and precious minerals; they are often guardians of hidden treasures. Some gnomes gather in families while others remain indigenous to the substances they

serve or guard. Members of this group include elves, brownies, dryads, and the little people of the woods.[2]

2. *Undines:* These fairylike pixies, the deification of femininity, synchronize with the earth element, water. Their essence is so closely tied to aquatic milieus that they possess the power to control the course and function of water. Undines, imbued with extraordinary beauty, symmetry, and grace, inhabit riparian environments—rivers, streams, lakes, waterfalls, and swamps. According to mythical lore, these lithe spirits, also known as naiads, water sprites, sea maids, and mermaids, assume male or female identities. Sioux legend says water deities, or wak'teexi in the native tongue, often incarnate as human beings: a telltale blue birthmark on the body will bare their original identities.[3]

3. *Sylphs:* The most evolved of the four Elementals, sylphs—often synonymous with fairies and cherubs—are beautiful, lively, diaphanous, yet mortal demigods. They represent the vaporous element of air and the expression of the female essence. Omnipresent, sylphs float in the clouds and in the ether, though their true home lies in mountaintop hamlets. There, they erect sacred sanctuaries for the Gods. This spritely covey, blessed with millennium-passing longevity and highly developed senses of sight, hearing, and smell, are particularly receptive to the voices of the Gods—that's why theosophical scholars believe the ancients used sylphs as oracles. Guided by Paralda, the king of air, and a communal of female sylphs known as sylphides, sylphs occasionally assume a petite human form. They are intelligent, mutable, and loyal to humans.[4]

4. *Salamanders:* Salamanders represent the invisible Elemental spirit of fire and the embodiment of the male divinity; without their existence, warmth wouldn't exist. Working through the blood stream, body temperature, and the liver, salamanders produce heat in humans and animals. Some theosophical scholars say this class of Elementals occupies balmy southern regions.

The mystical salamander encompasses much more than its amphibious counterparts. According to esoteric teachings, these fabled creatures manifest distinctly different forms. At approximately twelve inches in length, the lizard like salamander is physically tantamount to its terrestrial Urodela cousin. But, unlike earthly species, ethereal salamanders thrive in fire and slither through flames. Lore describes another group of salamanders as a race of giant creatures that wear flowing robes, don protective armor, and emit a fiery, incandescent glow. According to Medieval tradition, the third coterie of these entities are descendents of the great salamander Oromasis—son of the enigmatic Greek, Zarathustra.

But the Acthnici, ruled by the Elemental king Djinn, are the most powerful and feared faction of salamanders. They travel as indistinct globes of light, especially over water. Voyagers and sailors often experience Acthnici at sea as glowing forks of flame on the masts and the riggings of ships. They call this phenomenon St. Elmo's Fire. Scholars and other savants encourage others to avoid these salamanders. The price of knowing them, they say, outweigh the benefits.[5]

New Age of Utopia:

The following concepts form the foundation of a perfect society as outlined by Saint Germain in the teaching, *No Need for Change?*:

1. Lasting and committed marriages
2. Stable families
3. Inflation-free economies
4. Organic agricultural
5. Charity rather than welfare
6. Abolishment of useless taxation
7. Crime-free societies
8. Obsolescence of police forces
9. Open libraries and schools
10. Multilingual societies
11. Holistic health care
12. Eradicate nuclear power and weapons
13. Increased interaction with Nature Kingdoms

Age of Peace:

This Prophecy describes an era when humanity will experience the New Age of Utopia—a Time of higher consciousness free of cataclysmic geological and global changes. This is when peace reigns—its fills the human heart, and infuses families, communities, and our daily affairs with harmony and love.

Soletata:

[Pronounced So-lee'-tah-tah] Soletata is the conscious expression of the divine feminine, not in the sense of modern feminism or to the exclusion of males; rather, this carnal wisdom celebrates the nurturing spirit of women. It supports masculine energy, and represents conception and birth to all mankind, including Nature Kingdoms.

With an open heart and hearth, the divine spiritual power of Soletata unites the Christ energies within (child and mother), and recognizes the father as the *divine spark*. Soletata illustrates the quintessence of motherhood—the maternal role purified to domestic simplicity: the raising of children; the tending of household duties; the baking of bread; the cultivating of gardens; and the hanging of laundry in the wind.

The teachings of Soletata fall in the hands Mother Mary, the divine mother of Western culture; and Kuan Yin, the divine mother of the East. Together, they personify the higher consciousness of Soletata, or compassionate love.

Esoteric Taoist traditions magnify the significance of Soletata. These edifications tell us that the unification of the masculine and the feminine energies creates a tremendous opportunity for profound spiritual development and internal Alchemy. Physically, this phenomenon opens the body's channels or meridians, allowing a subtle yet harmonious integration of the human form and the promotion of healing. In advanced teachings, Unity Consciousness—Unana—awakens the body's feminine currents. Spiritual imitation is achieved by recognizing and using the energies of the Divine Feminine: Soletata.[6]

Age of Reason:

According to Western philosophy, the Age of Reason begins in the seventeenth century with the work of philosopher, Renë Descartes. It represents the unification of knowledge and the end of the medieval paradigm. A new mentality, one that establishes intellectual systems such as metaphysics, philosophy, ethics, politics, and physical science, settles in. This is the Time of Sir Francis Bacon, who later ascended as Saint Germain.

Sacred and Servile Planets:

The universe comprises the following divisions of material planets: sacred and servile. Those who inhabit sacred planets experience higher energies and frequencies, eliminating the need for a physical body, although these beings may express themselves in a physical form, too. They elude the futile afflictions of mankind: they don't suffer from fear, aging, or death. Their bodies easily drift from the spiritual to the subtle—these are the Devas, the demigods, the angels, the spiritual teachers, the great saints, the sages, and the mystics. Despite their evolved consciousness, these altruistic spirits empathize with the plight and the welfare of the denizens of grosser, material worlds. They send emissaries who bring spiritual knowledge and aid in various times and circumstances. Sacred planets represent purity of thought, and exemplify Blue, Yellow, and Pink Ray forces, and will remain intact after the destruction of material worlds.

Life on servile planets experiences an imperiled existence. Fraught with death, old age, illness, and anxiety, these worlds—especially those of lower orders such as earth—commit its inhabitants to a metaphysical vacuum. And though some servile populations possess mystic acumen, great wealth, artistic refinement, and the ability to control gravity, time, and space, these mortals lack true spiritual development. This life is a race against time, the ultimate equalizer, and inevitable death. Those who inhabit lower servile planets help incarnating souls rectify and remediate the most horrifying acts during their human lifetime on earth. "Although life here seems like it goes on for an eternity, in actual fact the duration of one's 'Karmic sentence.' Here may be only seconds or moments," writes author, Howard Beckman.[7] Servile planets express blended thoughts coupled with Green and Violet Rays.[8]

Iamblicus:

A Syrian philosopher who was known as "the divine," and an authority on Neo-Platonism.

APPENDIX F

[1] Orin Bridges, *Photographing Beings of Light: Images of Nature and Beyond* (Highland City, FL: Rainbow Press, Inc.), page 57.

[2] Manly Hall, *The Secret Teachings of All Ages, Diamond Jubilee Edition* (Los Angeles: Philosophical Research Society, Inc.), pages 106-107.

[3] Richard Dieterle, *Waterspirits (Wak'teexi)* (http://www.hotcakencyclopedia.com/ho.Waterspirits.html), (2005).

[4] Manly Hall, *The Secret Teachings of All Ages, Diamond Jubilee Edition* (Los Angeles: Philosophical Research Society, Inc.), pages 107-108.

[5] Ibid., page 106-107.

[6] Lori Toye, *New World Atlas: Earth Changes for a Planet in Transition, Volume Two* (Payson, AZ: I AM America Seventh Ray Publishing International), pages 71-73.

[7] Howard Beckman, *Vedic Cosmology: The Planets of the Material Universe, ACVA Journal* (7.2): 34-39.

[8] Lori Toye, *New World Atlas: Earth Changes for a Planet in Transition, Volume Three* (Payson, AZ: I AM America Seventh Ray Publishing International), page 28.

APPENDIX G

Topics and Terms for Weaving the New Web

Golden City Activations
Earth's Grids
United States Golden Cities and Master Teachers
Sacrifice, Labor, and Discipline
The New Light Body
Earth's Birth into Freedom Star
Dimensional Leaps in Consciousness
Golden City Apex—the Star
Circumventing Certain Earth Changes
The Karmic History of America
Planetary Ascension
The Age of Thought-Vibration
The Galactic Web

Spiritual Prophecies:

Northern Doors of Golden Cities contain a spiritual energy, or substance, that allows one to connect with, understand, and acknowledge their soul families.

Prophecies of Change:

1. During the Time of Change new species of plants and animals will evolve and be discovered.

2. HU-mans will evolve a new light body known as the *eighth body of consciousness.* This light body allows the physical body to transfigure and ready for the new dimensions.

3. The establishment of the light body produces more visible light around certain people. This is known as the *lighted stance.*

4. Our perceptions of time change; humanity abandons conventional timekeeping systems. Earth experiences the phenomenon of *time compaction*: an anomaly that slow down time, and crowds and compacts events, one upon the other. Cosmic Wave Motions, a cosmological tidal system of energy on earth, creates a new light body known as *Freedom Star.*

5. A new galaxy is discovered; it is called *Unana.*

6. Earth, as the Freedom Star, travels through a crack in the universe described as a black hole. When the Freedom Star (earth) reaches the other side, it enters a new consciousness, a new time, a new galaxy—Unana—and a new beginning.

7. Many will perceive this time as hopeless and desperate; however, with hard work and discipline, a leap in consciousness is possible. The Golden Cities augment the opportunity for an elevation in consciousness.

8. Ascended Masters are prophesied to manifest in Golden City Star apexes. This incarnation will occur within a twenty-mile radius of the apex; their physical appearance will further activate their spiritual teachings.

9. Activated Golden Cities can circumvent certain Earth Changes.

10. America—now known as the United States, Canada, Mexico, and Central and South America embrace the principle of world freedom. As this spiritual ideal evolves and grows, it touches many hearts.

11. Many Americans, who were once Atlanteans, reincarnate alongside former Lemurians to help earth enter the new dimension and its new light body as the Freedom Star.

12. Planetary Ascension does not require physical Ascension; however, many humans will access the new earth energies and physically ascend. The Golden City Vortices synergistically assist the physical, emotional, mental, and spiritual light bodies in this process.

13. The Golden Age is birthed through thought-vibration.

Golden Belt:

See Appendix E, "The Ascended Masters' Roles in Assisting Humanity and the Earth."

APPENDIX G

Golden City Activation Sequence:

See Appendix B, "Activations and Subtle Energies."

Golden City Activation:

A full comprehension of the word "activate" is key to understanding this spiritual phenomenon. The following dictionary definitions describe its usage: "to make active;" "to make more active;" "to hasten reactions by various means"; and "to place in active status." So, the term *Golden City Activation* includes several meanings and applications to illustrate the four types of Golden City activations.

1. Ascended Master Activation: *Made Active*

The Spiritual Hierarchy first conceptualized the idea of the Golden Cities by the perfect out-picturing of these spiritual centers. Certain Master Teachers, Archangels, and Elohim—in cooperation with Mother Earth Babajeran—sponsor specific Golden Cities. Their task: to gather the energies of each divine municipality. The grid structure of earth—in tandem with the focus of the appropriate Ray—is held in immaculate concept by each steward and coalesces the energies of each Golden City. And as consciousness increases, members of mankind seek its Fifth Dimension power as spiritual retreats.

2. Geophysical Activation: *More Active*

The interaction of Mother Earth and the Golden Cities—Fifth Dimensional structures—produces Third and Fourth Dimensional characteristics. This phenomenon creates a more active activation. The significance of Third Dimensional activation lies in its ability to generate a Vortex at the intersection of lei-lines. When eight of these invisible coordinates crisscross, a Vortex emerges, including the formation of Golden City Vortices. Vortices move in a clockwise/counterclockwise motion. Geophysically activated Golden Cities have a profound effect on humans: they experience longevity, greater healing abilities, and physical regeneration. In the Fourth Dimension, Nature Kingdoms begin to interact with Vortex energies; human visitors experience telepathic and psychic abilities, and lucid dreaming. [Lei-lines are magnetic lines of detectable energy. For more information see Appendix A, "Vortex," and "Golden City Vortex."]

3. Ceremonial Activation: *To Hasten Reactions by Various Means*

Ceremonial activations, inspired by humans who seek an intense result from a Golden City, occur on an emotional-astral level in areas throughout these sacred Vortices. Similar to pujas or yagyas—known in Hindu as sacrifices—fire or water-driven ceremonies neutralize difficult Karmas and enhance beneficial human qualities.

4. Great Central Sun Activation: *To Place in Active Status*

Produced by a greater timing or origin, this type of activation relies on the energies that emanate from the Great Central Sun or Galactic Center (our universe rotates around a larger sun). Some theosophical scholars say power from the Galactic Center sends subtle energies to our solar system via the planetary fire triplicity: Jupiter, Mars, and the Sun. [For more information see Appendix E, Great Central Sun.]

Earth's Grid:

Ivan T. Sanderson, an early-century Scottish naturalist, first postulated the existence of an earth grid. He discussed a network of twelve, evenly spaced global Vortices, such as the Bermuda Triangle and the Oregon Vortex, which exist near the tropics of Capricorn and Cancer, and the North and South Poles. Here, enigmatic episodes—warped time and space, unexplained disappearances, mechanical malfunctions, and peculiar weather conditions—are the norm.

In the early 1970s, three Muscovite scientists—Nikolai Goncharov, Vyacheslav Morozov, and Valery Makarov—advanced Sanderson's findings. Published in the Soviet science journal, *Khimiya i Zhizn*, their article "Is the Earth a Large Crystal?" described the planet as a "matrix of cosmic energy." According to Russians, earth is a complex life form—a giant sphere of crystal that exhibits crystal-like properties. Images from space lend credence to this theory. Researchers discovered a mosaic of crystalline structures underneath the earth's surface. These grid-like delineations follow fault lines, UFO sightings, and the boundaries of tectonic plates, the centers of ancient civilizations, and the migratory paths of animals. The trio found distinct, faceted patterns: a series of seven crystalline structures comprising the five Platonic solids and two biologically important crystals, rhombic triacontahedron and rhombic dodecahedron. Each face of the crystal produces a grid map, yielding different results and phenomena.

But the secrets of the earth's true makeup reach far beyond present-day theory. Ancient cultures realized our planet's role as a sphere and as a group of crystals. A creation story of the Sioux describes the powers of the earth elements: "In the beginning, all was hoops within hoops, within hoops. These hoops were orbital paths: earth around the sun, the sun's around the center of the Milky Way, and the electron's around the nucleus. Everything at every scale had the same essential spherical shape and orbital path."[1] The conclusion of this Siouan narrative asks humanity to embrace the sixteen hoops, composed of the fifteen edges of earth's crystal group and the sixteenth orbital path.

The Golden City Grid is actually a mathematical equation based on one additional hoop: this creates sixteen facets on the crystal; the seventeenth forms the final orbital hoop. The number seventeen is noteworthy in other historical and theosophical applications, too.

Linked to the Star of the Magi and the birth of the Christ Consciousness, seventeen is a hallmark of ancient Chaldean numerology. This culture believes it is the eight-pointed Star of Venus—an image of love, peace, and immortality. The numerical value of seventeen also shows up in divination practices: the Tarot Star, according to tradition, symbolizes the divine power of nature.[2]

Starseed Consciousness:

Starseeds describe a family or group of Fifth Dimensional entities, such as Master Teachers, specifically Sanat Kumara and Lady Master Venus; Saint Germain and Portia; and Mother Mary and Sananda. These spirits bridge the gap between the Great White Brotherhood and other divine fellowships, and earthbound souls. Their goal: to help humanity usher in the Planetary Awakening during the great changes. But some Starseeds, who exist in lower dimensions, continue to incarnate in a physical form. According to mystical teachings, when a soul group reaches Starseed status, twenty-two soul members attain Mastery over the physical plane—thought, feeling, and action.[3]

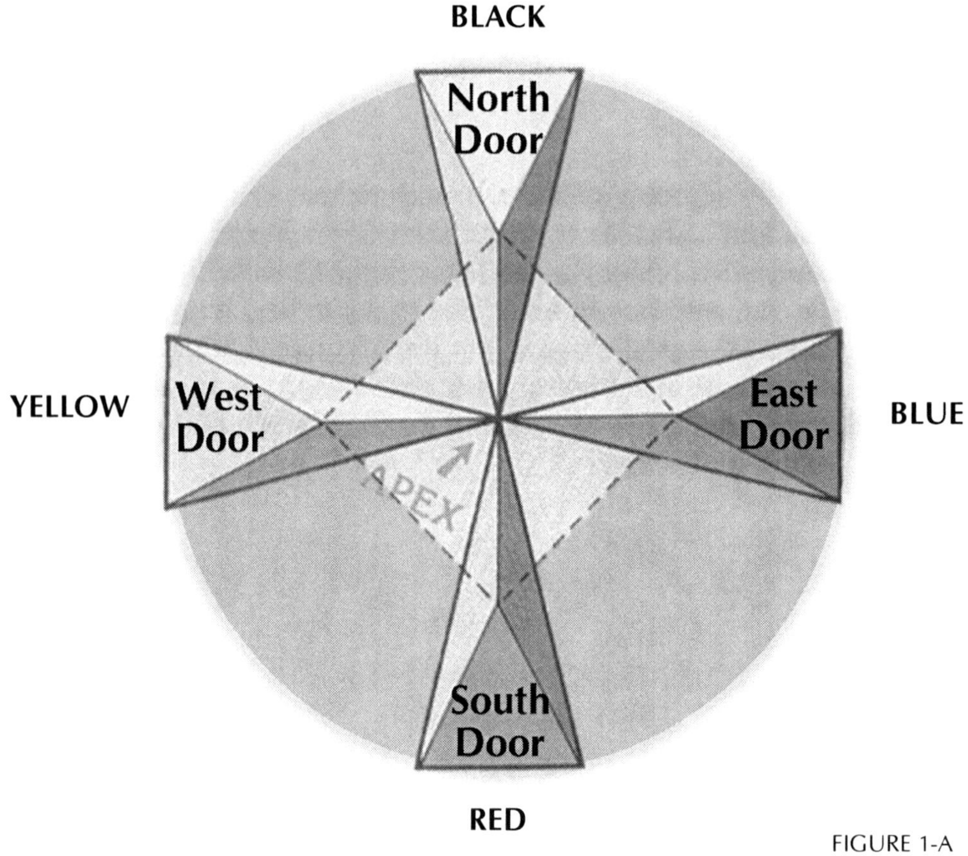

FIGURE 1-A
Doors of the Golden Cities

Doors (gateways) of the Golden Cities:

The four doors of the Golden Cities signify the four directions, and each represents certain attributes and characteristics. They also represent four spiritual pathways or spiritual initiations.

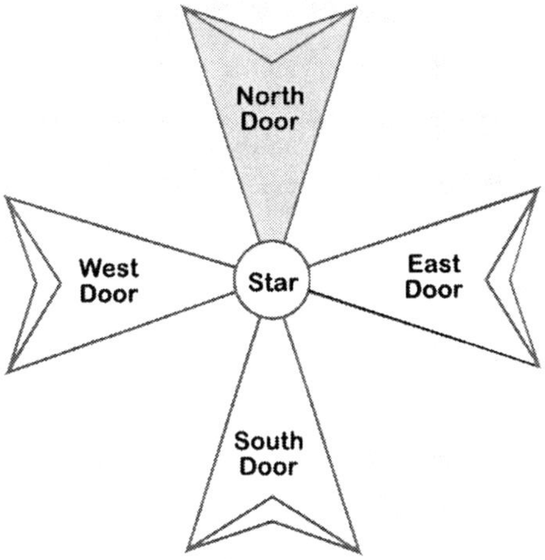

FIGURE 1-B
Northern Door Golden City

The Black Door

Direction: North
Esoteric Planet: Earth, Saturn, Mercury
Qualities:

1. Discipline and Labor
2. Physical Abundance
3. Worldly Benefits
4. Transmutation and Forgiveness

Attributes: The Northern Doors represent discipline and hard work. Spiritually, they denote self-control achieved through Transmutation and Forgiveness. Some say the Northern Doors manifest abundant consciousness and gratified wishes. The prophecies of the New Times foretell bountiful and prolific crops; this doorway is best for commercial and business endeavors.

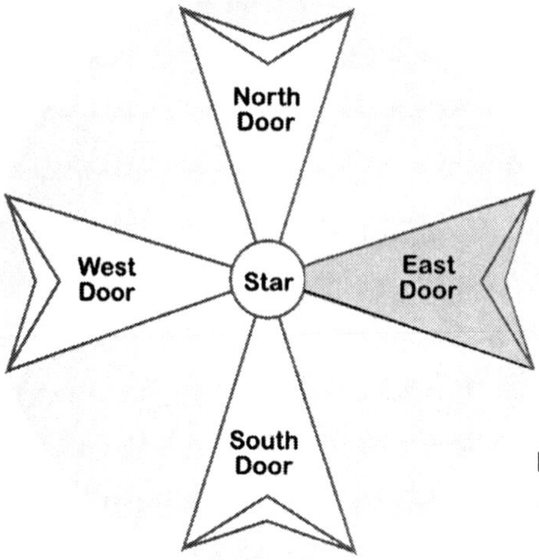

FIGURE 1-C
Eastern Door
Golden City

The Blue Door

Direction: East
Esoteric Planet: Moon
Qualities:

1. Purification and Sacrifice
2. Alchemy
3. Often referred to as, "the Elixir of Life"
4. Friends, Family, Helpful Acquaintances

Attributes: According the Master Teachers, time spent in contemplation at this doorway can resolve relationship and family problems. Prophecies of the New Times say the Eastern Doors of Golden City Vortices are perfect locations for communities, group activities, residential homes, and schools for children.

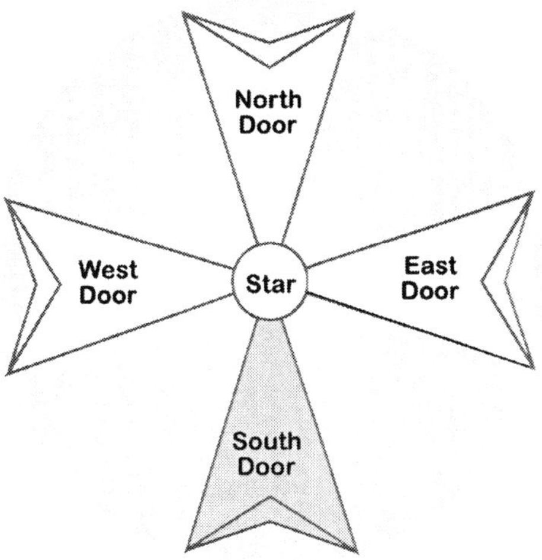

FIGURE 1-D
Southern Door
Golden City

The Red Door

Direction: South
Esoteric Planet: Mars, Jupiter
Qualities:

1. "The Healing of the Nations"
2. Enlightened Love
3. Nonjudgment
4. Faith and Courage

Attributes: The energies of the Southern Door induce physical, emotional, and spiritual regenerations; and miracle healings are commonplace. That's why this doorway is a great place for hospitals, clinics, retreats, and spas.

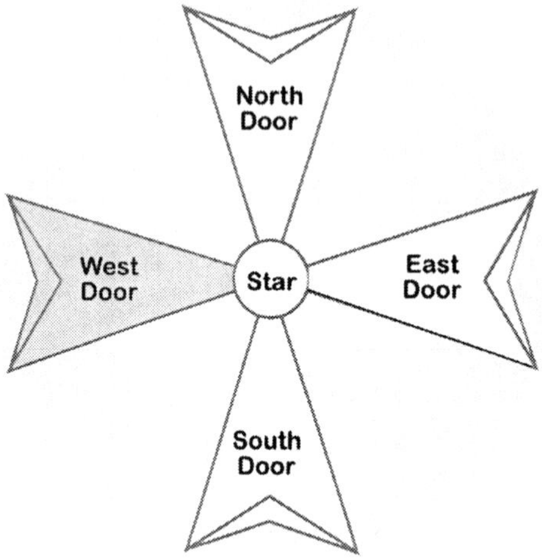

FIGURE 1-E
Western Door
Golden City

The Yellow Door

Direction: West
Esoteric Planet: Sun
Qualities:

1. Wisdom
2. "The Philosopher's Stone"
3. Adeptship and Conclusion

Attributes: The Western Door terminates the four pathways and acts as a portal to the "Star of Knowledge." Here, Golden City inhabitants will find universities and schools of higher, spiritual learning. The Master Teachers say the energies of this doorway create the hub of civic activity: Golden City government, including its administrative structure and capitol will reside here.

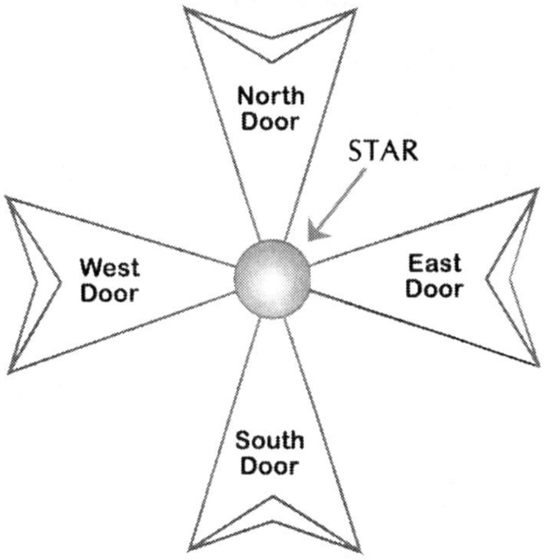

FIGURE 1-D
Star, Golden City

The Star

Direction: Center
Esoteric Planet: Venus
Qualities:

1. Self-Knowledge
2. Empowerment
3. Ascension

Attributes: The "Star" also known as the "Star of Self-Knowledge" punctuates the center of every Golden City. This area, the most powerful of the Vortex, produces self-knowledge and self-empowerment. The energies of the four doorways coalesce here—that's why it's identified as the absence of color, white. Its power reaches beyond the boundaries of the Golden City. Forty miles in diameter, a Star's healing qualities extend as far as sixty miles. Here, spiritual growth in the New Times happens: the Star's energies encourage self-renunciation, meditation, and spiritual liberation. During the Time of Change, the purity and beneficence of a Star's power will attract the Ascended Masters, who will then manifest in physical form. And the city's inhabitants will flock here to absorb spiritual teaching, miracle healings, and Ascensions.

Eighth Energetic Body:

This new light body develops to encourage the growth of Unity Consciousness. It does not, however, belong to the seven energy layers of the Human Aura. Instead, this glow provides an ethereal buffer, a large ball of Golden light, cushioning the body with five to ten feet of Aquamarine luminescence.

Golden City Structure

Golden City Structure, Perspective: Golden Cities are 400 kilometers or 248.5 miles high.

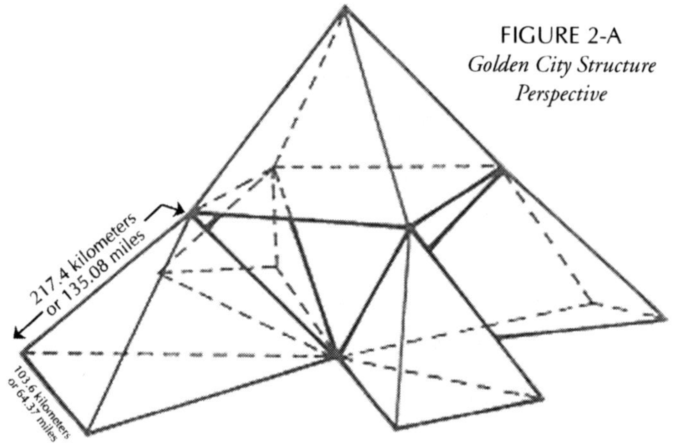

FIGURE 2-A
Golden City Structure Perspective

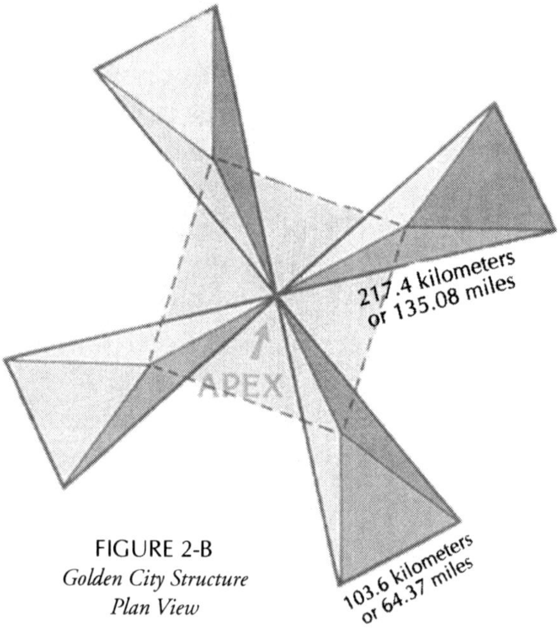

FIGURE 2-B
Golden City Structure Plan View

Golden City Structure, Plan View: Golden Cities are 434.8 kilometers or 270 miles across.[4]

Adjutant Points of Gobean Northern Door:

1. First Point: Masculine Energy Located on the Hopi Indian reservation near Keams Canyon and First Mesa, Arizona. Take Highway 264 to Clenga Canyon Road; bear north for approximately two miles. You will see the mesa from this point.
2. Second Point: Feminine Energy Located near Red Lake on the Navajo Indian Reservation in New Mexico, on Hwy 12 near Canyon De Chelly. Travel up an abandoned road (east) to Squirrel Picnic Ground, at the base of Chuska Peak. [5]

FIGURE 3-A

Adjutant Points
Gobean Northern Door

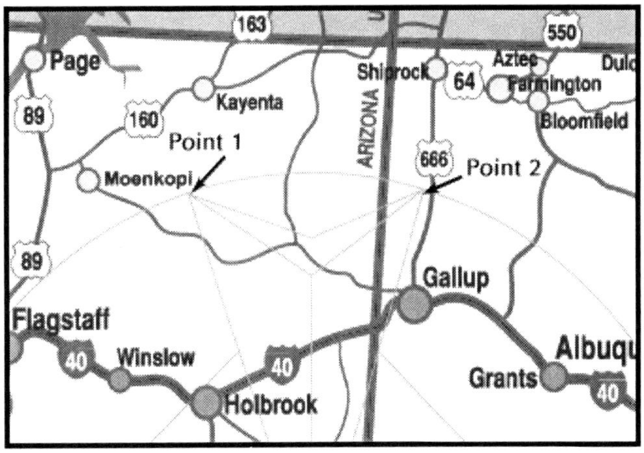

Time Compaction:

This phenomenon warps time as earth enters into the prophesied Time of Change. Our perception of time compresses; it moves at lightning speed; events are squeezed into moments. This experience of time becomes more common as civilizations nears cataclysmic Earth Changes.

Cosmic Wave Motion:

Cosmic wave motions will play a significant force in the universe, especially during the Time of Change on earth. These interstellar belts of energy resemble the ebb and flow of tides. Originating from the sun, cosmic waves drift to certain points in the universe, then recede. And just as the momentum of shoreline ripples collide with the ingoing and outgoing surf, the undulations of the cosmos assume a similar motion, creating an infinite and dynamic flooding of the universe. Cosmic wave motions affect the earth's inhabitants, particularly the human and animal nervous systems. But, these waves produce positive results, too. They trigger an evolution in consciousness, and initiate a greater understanding of unity and compassion.[6]

According to the I AM America prophecies, the movement of these empyreal swells influences the planets of the solar system, controls time, and subsequently governs evolution. During the Time of Change on earth, the "jumbling and tumbling"[7] of cosmic wave belts causes the deceleration or compaction of time. Saturn and Neptune, however, toss a lifesaver to earth, helping the green planet, and ultimately humanity, adjust to the tempestuous eddies.

***Galactic Web*:**

See Appendix B, "Golden City Vortex."

Law of Opposites:

Sir Isaac Newton's third Law of Motion, "Every action has an equal and opposite reaction." When this is understood according to Hermetic insight, everything has a pair of opposites, (e.g. hot and cold), and their difference is separated only by degrees.

[1] Aumear True, *EarthStar A Treasure Map Rediscovered*, Brochure (Ashland, OR: Rosetta Publishing), pages 1-2.

[2] Lori Toye, *Freedom Star: Prophecies that Heal Earth* (Payson, AZ: I AM America Seventh Ray Publishing), page 18.

[3] Lori Toye, A Starseed, 1991.

[4] Lori Toye, *I AM America Map of Earth Changes*, [I AM America Map]. Scale: From Rand McNally Cosmopolitan Series, reduction is 53%. Payson, AZ, I AM America Seventh Ray Publishing, International, 1989.

[5] Lori Toye, *I AM America: United States Golden Cities*. Scale not given. Payson, AZ: I AM America Seventh Ray Publishing, International, 1998.

[6] Lori Toye, *I AM America Six Map Scenario: Detailed Prophecies of Earth Change Progressions to the I AM America Map,* [6-Map Scenario]. Scale not given. Payson, AZ: I AM America Seventh Ray Publishing, International, 1997.

[7] Ibid.

APPENDIX H

Topics and Terms for Golden City Classes

Golden Cities form the New Consciousness
Intention and Aligning the Will
The Role of Golden Cities and the Spiritual Awakening
Holding Consciousness in a Geophysical Location
Learning Assists the Out-Picturing Process
Light is Love in Action
On Soul Mates
Prophecy is a Philosophy and Spiritual Teaching
Altering Outcomes

Spiritual Prophecies

1. The Golden Cities are templates to understand Global Ascension.

2. Each Golden City assists the Spiritual Awakening of humanity.

3. The Golden Cities hold the first seeds of consciousness that awaken the world to the New Times as "a new way of being."

4. At Golden City lei-line intersections, the creation and co-creation processes are heightened.

5. The teachings of the Native Americans create a spiritual bridge between the Eastern and Western worlds.

6. The teachings of Christ Consciousness as "super-consciousness" will begin a new cycle for humanity.

7. "We cannot alter the cycle; however, we can alter outcomes of cycles."

8. The Earth Changes are the completion of a cycle. The Ascended Masters courageously advise, "Do not fear the times ahead of you!" This closure is an opportunity for humanity to embrace critical spiritual growth and evolution.

9. Living the "Law of Love" alongside trust, faith, and hope can create positive change.

Earth Changes Prophecies:

1. The duration of the Time of Change may be as short as six years or as long as 1,000.

2. The cleansing and purification of the earth represent the expunging of various systems. This process of transformation occurs at many levels, outwardly and within. Prophecies say the following systems will undergo tremendous changes:
    a. The Deva Kingdom
    b. The Elemental Kingdom
    c. The Nature Spirits
    d. The Vegetable and Flower Kingdoms
    e. The Mineral Kingdom
    f. The Animal Kingdom
    g. The inner self of every person on earth

Golden City Roles During the Prophecies of Change:

1. The Golden City of Malton: After the Earth Changes, the Golden City of Malton will embody one of the highest vibrational frequencies of harmony on the earth. The cooperation of all Kingdoms of Creation, primarily the Deva and Elemental Kingdoms, promote this city's heightened tranquility and amity. According to the prophecies, bountiful and lavish gardens will flourish in this Golden City of the future.

2. The Golden City of Klehma: In the Golden City of Klehma, many people will begin to understand the wisdom of Ascension and its application for the New Times.

3. The Golden City of Shalahah: During the most tumultuous Earth Changes, the energies of the Golden City of Shalahah hold hope for the future and provide healing power for mankind.

The Great Reason:

According to theosophical thought, the Monad itself is not self-conscious. In fact, it embarks on an evolutionary pilgrimage to acquire and obtain self-conscious intelligence—the human mind. Man's destiny lies in the beauty and cooperation of infinity. This is referred to as the *Great Reason*.

The HU-man:

Hu is an ancient name for God. When Hu is combined with 'man,' it elevates humanity to the divine: the God-man. According to the Master Teachers, HU (pronounced 'hue'), when used as a mantra, invokes the Violet Flame throughout the aura. The mantra's lulling tone activates the Eight-Sided Cell of Perfection and the perfected God-source within.

Seamless Garment:

The idea of the *Seamless Garment* symbolizes perfection and immortality, or what's known as the *Electronic Body*. This is the regalia of the Ascended Masters; not woven by hand, but fashioned by the perfected thought and manifestation process. It is the essence of eternal youth and beauty; it is unbound by limitations; and it exists in a consciousness free of space, time, age, and place. The term also refers to the Ascension Process or a symbol of Oneness—unity.

The Map of Rings:

The Ascended Masters refer to a sketch of the Earth's Grid as the "Map of Rings" or the "Many-Ringed Map." It illustrates the relationship among the elements, the Elementals, and the Elemental life forces on earth; overlapping geomantic bands that often intersect at sacred sites and power points around the globe; and the planet's major lei-lines. [For more information see Appendix G, "Earth's Grid."]

El Morya:

El Morya incarnated from a long line of historical notables, including the fabled King Arthur of England; the Renaissance scholar Sir Thomas Moore, author of *Utopia*; the patron saint of Ireland, Saint Patrick; and a Rajput prince. El Morya is even linked to the Hebrew patriarch Abraham. But in spite of his illustrious lifetimes, El Morya is best known as Melchior, one of the Magi who followed the Star of Bethlehem to the Christ infant.

El Morya first revealed himself to the founder of the Theosophical Society Helena Petrovna Blavatasky—also known as Madame Blavatsky or H. P. B.—during her childhood in London; that mid-nineteenth century meeting forged a lifelong connection with her Master and other members of the Spiritual Hierarchy. Some esoteric scholars recount different, more dramatic scenarios of their initial introduction. Blavatsky herself claimed El Morya rescued her from a suicide attempt on Waterloo Bridge.[1] The gracious Master dissuaded her from plunging into the waters of the Thames River. Others say the two met in Hyde Park or on a London street. According to Blavatsky, El Morya appeared under a secret political cover as the Sikh prince

Maharaja Ranbir Singh of Kashmir, who served as a physically incarnated prototype of Master M. Singh and died in 1885.

Metaphysical scholars credit Blavatsky's work as the impetus for present-day theosophical philosophy and the conception of the Great White Brotherhood. Devoted disciples learned of the Hindu teacher from Blavatsky's childhood visions, and later on in a series of correspondences known as the *Mahatma Letters*, which contained spiritual guidelines for humanity. El Morya's presence in H.P.B.'s life enriched her spiritual knowledge, and she shared this transformation in a prolific body of texts and writings, namely *Isis Unveiled* and *The Secret Doctrine*. During a visit with Madame Blavatsky, A.P. Sinnett, an English newspaper editor, found the first of these letters among the branches of a tree. Over the years, the true meaning and authorship of the Mahatma Letters, reportedly co-authored by fellow Mahatma Kuthumi, have spurned controversy; some say Blavatsky herself forged the messages.

Master M. is associated with the Blue Ray of power, faith, and good will; the Golden City of Gobean; and the planet Mercury. A strict disciplinarian, El Morya dedicates his work to the development of the will. He assists many disciples in discovering personal truths, exploring self-development, and honing the practice of the esoteric discipline. El Morya passes this wisdom to his numerous chelas and students. The Maha Chohan—El Morya's guru, Lord of the Seven Rays and the Steward of Earth and its evolutions—educated him during his earthly incarnations in India, Egypt, and Tibet. Declining the Ascension a number of times, it is said that El Morya finally accepted this divine passage in 1888, ascending with his beloved pet dog and horse. (Esoteric symbols of friendship and healing.)

Kuthumi:

In the late nineteenth century, Ascended Master Kuthumi—also known as Koot Hoomi or K.H.—collaborated with Helena Blavatsky and El Morya to introduce humanity to the spiritual teachings of theosophy. And like Master M., K.H. is dedicated to advancing the spiritual fitness of mankind to a higher consciousness. Thus, Kuthumi approached his interaction with humans in the same manner as his mahatma contemporary: he veiled his identity behind the Indian dignitaries of the time, in this case, Thakar Singh Sandhawalia, leader of the Singh Sabha movement. Founded in the early 1870s, this Indian independence campaign emerged as a grassroots effort to maintain the purity of Sikhism, otherwise eroded by Christian Missionaries. Sandhanwalia, Ranbir Singh—one of El Morya's aliases—and H.P.B joined forces to spread theosophy throughout India.

Kuthumi and El Morya shared a close relationship through the ages. Both trained by the Ascended Master Maha Chohan, the spiritual duo, as two of the wise men, paid homage to the baby Jesus: K.H. as Balthazar and Master M. as Melchior. Kuthumi also shows up as Sir Percival at the round table of King Arthur (aka El Morya). But his incarnation history isn't limited to associations with his spiritual Brother. Kuthumi's past lifetimes include the Greek philosopher Pythagoras; Thutmose III, the warrior pharaoh of the eighteenth dynasty; Shah Jahan, the emperor of India and builder of the Taj Mahal; and founder of the Franciscans, Saint Francis of Assisi.

Highly educated and extremely private, Kuthumi, a Cambridge University alumni, spent 200 years in seclusion in the Himalayan Mountains before ascending in 1889. He is a gentle Master affiliated with the Golden City Malton, and the Gold and Ruby Rays of ministration and service to humanity. In one of his earliest letters to A.P. Sinnett, Kuthumi calls the holy Golden Temple of the Sikhs his home, although he's seldom there, preferring the solitude of Tibet.[3]

Author Alice Bailey, who continued to work with the Masters after Blavatsky's death in 1891, writes about a visit from K.H.: "Master Koot Hoomi, [is] a Master who is very close to the Christ." In 1895, Kuthumi told the fifteen-year-old Bailey that she would travel the world "doing your Master's work all the time" and that "I would have to give up being such an unpleasant little girl and must try and get some measure of self-control. My future usefulness to him and to the world was dependent upon how I handled myself and the changes I could manage to make." [4]

A.D.K. Luk writes of Kuthumi:

> "He was such a lover of nature that he would watch a certain phase for hours, or would stay a whole day with a flower to see it open into full bloom, and perhaps watch it close again at night. He was one of the few who represented the heart of the Nature Kingdom. He was able to read through the Elemental Kingdom and accelerate his consciousness to a point where he was of assistance in that realm. Birds and animals were drawn to him to be in his radiance which was about him; drawn by his constant attention and adoration to his Source." [5]

Serapis Bey:

The lore of Serapis Bey is heavily linked to the story of Helena Blavatsky, Master M., K.H., and the founding of the Theosophical Society. According to lore, Serapis Bey incarnated as Paolos Metamon, an Egyptian magician. Metamon and Blavatsky connected in the mid-1850s during her wanderlust years in the Middle East. H.P.B soon became his pupil. He introduced her to the secret world of the occult and possibly served as her first Master. But many esoteric scholars disagree; they say the Ascended Master of the Fourth Ray is rooted in the Greco-Egyptian mysteries, and appropriately so. Before his Ascension in 400 B.C., Serapis Bey embodied as a high priest at the Ascension Temple of Atlantis more than 11,000 years ago. Other myths put the Master—carrying the Flame of Ascension to Egypt by boat—at the banks of the Nile River near Luxor before the demise of Atlantis and the Earth Changes of Dvapara Yuga.[6] He also incarnated as the Egyptian pharaohs Akhenaton IV and Amenophis III; the heroic King Leonidas of Sparta; and Phidias, the great architect of the Parthenon, the temple of the Goddess Athena, and the colossal statue of Zeus.

A tireless and strict disciplinarian, Serapis Bey, the Master Teacher of Ascension, identifies and prepares souls for Ascension. He accomplishes this by the destruction of the lower self, the state of animal-man, that is captivated by worldly ignorance. And when the corporeal attachments dissolve, the Real Self emerges, a step essential to the attainment of Ascension. The Ancient Egyptians followed a similar practice in their Temples of Serapis. Priests carried out initiatory rites involving rigorous and severe rituals; symbolic illusions of the lower world through which the soul of man wanders for the truth. Those who survived the ordeal were ushered into the presence of Serapis—an awe-inspiring figure, illumined in unseen lights. Serapis became known as the Adversary or the Trier who tested the souls of those seeking union with the Immortals, the Ascension.[7] Serapis Bey serves on the Fourth Ray—it is associated with the absence of color, white; harmony through conflict; and the path of beauty.

The number seven plays a significant role in the worship of this Ascended Master. It begins with his name—*Serapis*—which contains seven letters. During worship, disciples chant hymns comprising seven vowels, the seven primary sounds. And when expressed in imagery, Serapis wears a crown of seven Rays, symbolizing the seven divine intelligences represented through solar light. Meanwhile, the word "serapis" has many associations: it is the ancient term for sun; in Hebrew it means "to blaze out"; and it is the soul, enmeshed with the form during physical life, which escapes from the body at death.

FIGURE 4-A
Sananda

Sananda painting, printed with permission, © 1990, Avedis Dermakelian.

Lord Sananda:

During his paradigm-altering incarnation more than 2,000 years ago, Lord Sananda, also known as Sananda Kumara, embodied the Christ Consciousness, as Jesus, son of God. Some esoteric scholars say he's one of the four sons of Brahma—Sanaka, Sanatana, Sanat-Kumara, and Sanandana—his namesake. According to Vedic lore, the foursome possess eternally liberated souls and live in Tapaloka, the dimension of the great sages. Before manifesting in physical form, Jesus belonged to the Angelic Kingdom. His name was Micah—the Great Angel of Unity. Micah is the son of Archangel Michael who led the Israelites out of Egypt.[8] [For more information on the life story of Jesus' life, I recommend reading, *Twelve World Teachers,* by Manly P. Hall.]

Sananda Kumara revealed his identity to the learned scholar and channel Sister Thedra. Her Master first contacted her in the early 1960s and instructed her to move to Peru, specifically, to a hidden monastery in the Andes mountains. There, undergoing an intense spiritual training, she kept in constant contact with Sananda, and he shared with her prophecies of the coming Earth Changes. After leaving the abbey, Sister Thedra moved to Mt. Shasta, California where she founded the Association of Sananda and Sanat Kumara. She died in 1992.

Sananda posed for a photograph on June 1, 1961 in Chichen Itza, Yucatan. He told Sister Thedra that though the image is valid, he is not limited by form of any kind; therefore, he may take on any appearance necessary. [See *Freedom Star, Prophecies that Heal Earth*].

Golden Cities and Ancient Cultures:

Every Golden City holds specific Akashic Records of ancient civilizations and cultures. These Fifth Dimensional libraries include:

Gobean—Ancient Egypt, aligns to Giza.

Malton—Druid; aligns energy with the great Vortex above Glastonbury.

Wahanee—Ancient African tribal peoples and the Ancient Civilization of the Sahara Desert. Aligns with the Golden City Eabra, located in Alaska and Canada.

Shalahah—Vedic culture and the Ancient Civilization Magadha of Eastern India.

Klehma—the Native American culture and the civilizations of North and South America. This Golden City will bridge the spiritual teachings and the traditions of the East and West.

Soul Mates:

Some people experience an unexplained bond with another person—this is called a soul mate. These spirits have known each other in past lifetimes as lovers, friends, parents, children, siblings, or any other type of close relationship; and before they enter into physical bodies, they agree on specific and important roles to achieve during their life on earth. And the functions are endless. The Master Teachers often refer to these objectives as a *Mission.* The term soul mate denotes the essence of harmony and compatibility; however, in many cases this is far from the truth. Soul mates can be the best of friends during their ethereal existences and mortal foes on earth. The key point of a soul mate is the notion of desired results—the agreements made before an incarnation.

Ray Force Entering Golden City

FIGURE 5-A
Great Central Sun
and the Seven Rays

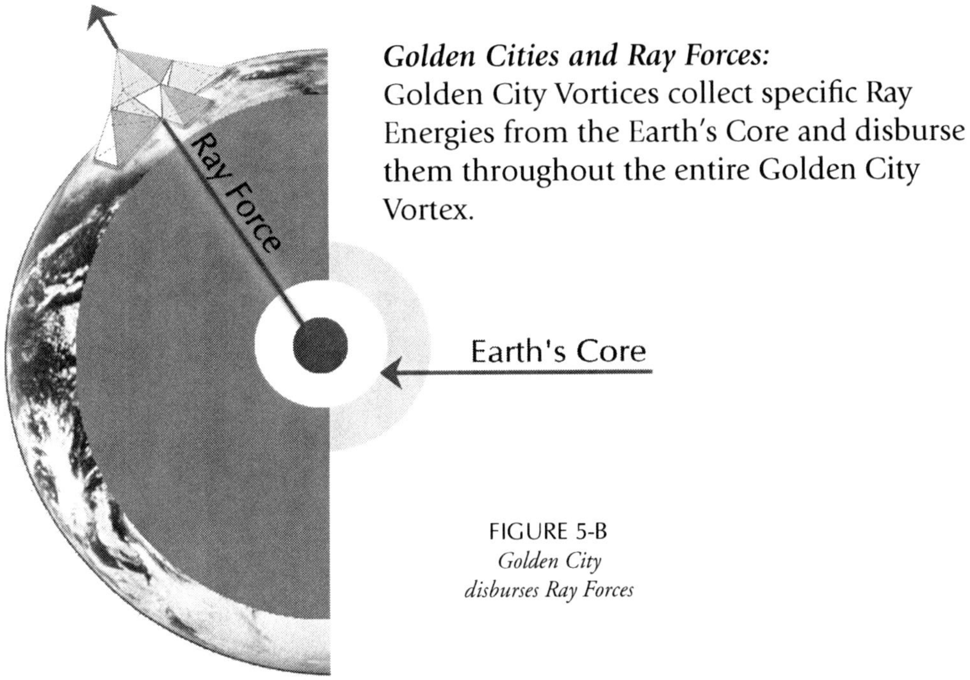
Golden Cities and Ray Forces:
Golden City Vortices collect specific Ray Energies from the Earth's Core and disburse them throughout the entire Golden City Vortex.
Ray Force
Earth's Core

FIGURE 5-B
Golden City
disburses Ray Forces

APPENDIX H

[1] Papastavro, Tellis S., *The Gnosis and the Law* (Tucson, AZ: Group Avatar), page 53.

[2] Johnson, K. Paul, *The Masters Revealed: Madame Blavatsky and the Myth of the Great White Lodge (Suny Series in Western Esoteric Traditions)* (Albany, NY: State University of New York Press), page 41.

[3] Ibid., page 154.

[4] Bailey, Alice A., *Unfinished Autobiography* (New York: Lucis Publishing Company), page 36.

[5] Luk, A. D. K., *Law of Life, Book II* (Pueblo, CO: ADK Luk Publications), page 275.

[6] Ibid., pages 277-279.

[7] Manly Hall, *The Secret Teachings of All Ages, Diamond Jubilee Edition* (Los Angeles: Philosophical Research Society), pages 26-27.

[8] Papastavro, Tellis S., *The Gnosis and the Law* (Tucson, AZ: Group Avatar), page 358.

APPENDIX I

Topics and Terms for Vibrational Shifting

Dimensional Acceleration
Insanity During the Time of Change
Developing Compassion
Social Systems and Their Relationship to the Earth Changes
The New Cycle Comes through a "Death-cadence"
The Laws of Octaves
Sound Vibration and the Mental and Emotional Bodies
Astral Projection
Individuality
"Of the One"
Destiny and Self-Awareness

Dimensional Acceleration:

This is a system of new energies that are present on the earth as outlined in the teaching, "Vibrational Shifting," which includes these processes:

1. The thinning of the barrier or sheath that exists between the Third and Fourth Dimensions.
2. Insanity is sometimes caused by small tears in the barrier skin of the dimensions and the thinning of the dimensions. This produces the phenomenon of "dimensional plane-ing," as the dimensions slip into one another.
3. *Dimensional plane-ing* affects the entire human chakra system, good and bad, depending on the ability of the individual to qualify the new energies.
4. During times of Dimensional Acceleration the I AM Presence assists the awakening of the chakras.
5. Dimensional Acceleration assists and aids the Ascension Process, known as "the Higher Law."
6. The Violet Flame calms the energy centers—chakras—during this process.
7. To begin the process of integrating new energies, take saltwater baths. Dissolve one container of table salt or one cup of Epsom Salts along with an essential oil of your choice, e.g. violet, rose, jasmine, sandalwood, and so on.
8. During Dimensional Acceleration, the reflection from the moon's emotional energy through the earth is intensified within the individual.
9. The collective psychological body of humanity is affected by this phenomenon.

Prophecies of Change:

1. Many souls will choose not to experience the upcoming changes, and will leave the planet before the Earth Changes begin. They will do so by:
   a. Insanity
   b. Involvement in addictions
   c. Disease

2. Many people are urged inwardly or currently *called* to live in areas that are prophesied to be Devastated and unlivable during and after the Earth Changes. In fact, many present-day cities will be under ocean waters in the future. It is explained that many of these souls need to live in these areas to fulfill their destinies and remain committed to the choices they have made for this lifetime. This helps them to complete a cycle of their soul's growth.

3. Only a few will have the ability to move to or live in a safe place.

4. During this time the entire planet and all of its kingdoms are completing a cycle.

The Law of Octaves (the Law of Seven):

The relationship of planets, colors, and musical notes are said to be based on the Law of Octaves—also known as the *Law of Seven*. The ancients knew and understood this concept. They saw the sun as analogous to that of white light; it contained the seeds of every tone and color potential. Since sight has a restricted cognition of range, as compared to hearing (the ear can register nine to eleven octaves, the eye registers seven fundamental color tones), certain colors are compared to musical notes, this table follows:

1. Red, the lowest color tone, equals the musical note, Do
2. Orange = Re
3. Yellow = Mi
4. Green = Fa
5. Blue = Sol
6. Indigo = La
7. Violet = Ti

The eighth color tone that completes the scale becomes a higher octave of red. It is also important to note that the three fundamental notes of the musical scale, the first, the third, and the fifth, correspond with the three primary colors—red, yellow, and blue. Interestingly, the seventh note and color—violet—is the transition to the next octave.[1]

Another way to understand the Law of Octaves is to understand vibrations and their infinite patterns of appearance: ascending and descending orders; fine and coarse; weakening and strengthening; crossing and colliding; and so on. Octaves can accelerate or retard at different moments of development. This is due to the structure of the musical seven-tone scale, including intervals and absent semitones. Because of this, the progress and the development of phenomena on all planes are not ruled by straight lines; the difficulty of thoughts and harmonious actions often come about in ways opposite to what we wanted or anticipated. Yet, what this law teaches is invaluable.

The Law of Octaves demonstrates that nothing in the world stays the same and nothing is static; everything is changing and moving along the lines of octaves. Nothing can develop by staying on one level, yet in understanding descending and ascending cycles, vibrations develop in an orderly manner, following the same direction in which they Started.

In ascending cycles, according to the Law of Octaves, the first interval occurs between *Mi* and *Fa*. A greater intensity is needed to develop between *Ti* and *Do*. In descending cycles, the greatest interval occurs at the beginning of the Octave after the first *Do*; the material that fills it is found within itself or in lateral vibrations. For this reason alone, descending cycles develop easier than ascending octaves.[2]

Earth Changes Prophecies:

Since much of Alaska and the Aleutian Islands are affected by the Ring of Fire, it is prophesied that these areas will experience many violent earthquakes and volcanoes.

Individuality:

To understand the spiritual meaning of this word, return to its Latin root "individuus," which means indivisible and whole; cannot be divided.

Unana (Unity Consciousness):

The path leading to this state or level of consciousness Starts with the simple Mastery of thoughts, feelings, and actions. The union of these three energy bodies—the mental, emotional, and physical—produces the Alchemical marriage of the masculine and feminine forces in the body. "This initiates Unity Consciousness," says Master Saint Germain. He adds, however, that individuality or the undivided state comes first. Proceeding is the next natural state, contact with the ONE. This higher form of consciousness is all-knowing, all-pervading, and all-powerful. In this state of existence, all is connected as one larger, non-physical, yet thinking and feeling body. "Unana," (pronounced ooh-nah'-na) is the name the Ascended Masters have given to this level of inter-connectedness, where the mind moves beyond individuality and into a unified field of consciousness.

APPENDIX I

[1] Manly Hall, *The Secret Teachings of All Ages, Diamond Jubilee Edition* (Los Angeles: Philosophical Research Society, Inc.), page 84.

[2] P.D. Ouspensky, *In Search of the Miraculous: Fragments of an Unknown Teaching* (New York: Harcourt Brace Jovanovich, Publishers), pages 122-132.

APPENDIX J

Topics and Terms for Closing the Circle

The Law of Attraction and Repulsion
Addictive Substances and Subjective Energy Bodies
Limitation and Addiction
The Power of Recognition
"The Dead Zone"
Closure
Opposites and Contraries
"Victims of Circumstance"
The Purpose of Ceremony
Awake or Asleep
The Book of Revelations

The Law of Attraction and Repulsion:

This physical and spiritual truth serves as the foundation of the Law of Duality—the Yin and the Yang. In simple terms, like charges repel and unlike charges attract: the Law of Polarity. Under these circumstances, everything in nature follows one of two opposite paths, each with its own essence. Life exists on a spectrum, one that offers an infinite number of possibilities between its opposite ends: darkness is less light; fear is less courage. Of course, this notion applies to the intricacies of daily life when humans are faced with innumerous viewpoints or solutions to a problem. Indeed, opposites exist within each other.

Prophecies of Change:

1. Much of society is de-structuring and eroding the fiber of life: cultures, individuals and families.

2. This societal undoing induces a need to escape reality, something mankind will face more frequently over the next two decades as the changes accelerate.

Subjective Energy Bodies:

A spurious type of energy—often encountered through drug and alcohol abuse—subjective energy bodies produce a false sense of consciousness. When triggered, it elicits a lower consciousness and a behavior-changing "thought-form." Popular belief perpetuates this notion: the idea that addictive substances increase a person's state of euphoria and relationship to a higher power. When in reality, nothing could be farther from the truth. Drugs and alcohol actually suppress lower energy fields and block the ability to create elevated states of consciousness. The experience of love without fear, the sense of pure joy without anxiety, and the ability to live on life's terms are rare. Yet, the exhilaration produced by a high compels the user to chase experiences sans the emptiness of lower vibrating energy. But, as tolerance necessitates the need for more, the addict or alcoholic futilely struggles to achieve an artificial divine connection authentically produced through sincere and careful spiritual cultivation. What's left, after the intoxication ebbs, is a more desperate need to fill that spiritual void.

Humans, however, can suppress lower vibrations through contact with a higher consciousness: meditation and other spiritual disciplines are excellent means to achieve this end.[1] But, because this growth is achieved through the Transmutation of lower level energies, subjective energy bodies are not present or created. This base force has limited range; it floats in astral planes and passes from one lifetime to the next in the form of discordant, obsessive thoughts and behaviors. Repetitious ideas, feelings, and actions carry consciousness or Karmic "energetic patterns" of which one is not responsibly aware. The Master Teachers calls this an "invisible creation."[2]

The Closure Ceremony:

Saint Germain observes this ritual to recognize and cease addictive and Karmic energy patterns. It marks the end of a person's tendency to assume oppositional, abusive, vengeful, and adversarial positions. Upon completion of the ceremony, the soul is ready and open to learn through new Laws of Attraction and Unity. But it's not for everyone. A person will achieve the best results if he or she has already developed the ability to contact spiritual helpers and guides. Components of this ceremony include:

1. Changes in energy-field magnetism
2. The removal of subjective energy bodies
3. Asking for the assistance of spiritual helpers and guides
4. Performance at full moon
5. A location near a body of water, which allows the proper attraction of magnetism. Lenz's Law—one that refers to the behavior of diamagnetic materials—forms the basis of this practice. Fin de siècle chemist Henri Louis Le Chatelier discovered the properties of chemical equilibrium: Le Chatelier's Principle.

> "Every change of one of the factors of equilibrium occasions a rearrangement of the system in such a direction that the factor in question experiences a change, in a sense opposite to the original change," he wrote. "(It is) a state of rest or balance due to the equal action of opposing forces." [3]

6. Sound Vibration: The basis of physical manifestation is sound. This knowledge is carefully taught in Vedic mantras and practiced in Native American drumming, which simulates the heartbeat of the Earth Mother.

The (One) Hundredth Monkey:

Twentieth century author Ken Keyes, Jr. based his book, *The Hundredth Monkey*, on the work of botanist Lyall Watson. Watson originally coined the term in his work, *Lifetide*. His book discussed the work of primatologists in the 1950s who observed the macaques monkeys on the Japanese island of Koshima teaching each other to wash sweet potatoes. Keyes expanded Lyall's findings to the realm of human consciousness.

> "The Japanese monkey, Macaca fuscata, had been observed in the wild for a period of over 30 years. In 1952, on the island of Koshima, scientists were providing monkeys with sweet potatoes dropped in the sand. The monkeys liked the taste of the raw sweet potatoes, but they found the dirt unpleasant. An 18-month-old female named Imo found she could solve the problem by washing the potatoes in a nearby stream. She taught this trick to her mother. Her playmates also learned this new way and they taught their mothers, too. This cultural innovation was gradually picked up by various monkeys before the eyes of the scientists. Between 1952 and 1958 all the young monkeys learned to wash the sandy sweet potatoes to make them more palatable. Only the adults who imitated their children learned this social improvement. Other adults kept eating the dirty sweet potatoes. Then something Startling took place. In the autumn of 1958, a certain number of Koshima monkeys were washing sweet potatoes—the exact number is not known. Let us suppose that when the sun rose one morning there were 99 monkeys on Koshima Island who had learned to wash their sweet potatoes. Let's further suppose that later that morning, the hundredth monkey learned to wash potatoes. Then it happened! By that evening almost everyone in the tribe was washing sweet potatoes before eating them. The added energy of this hundredth monkey somehow created an ideological breakthrough! But notice. A most surprising thing observed by these scientists was that the habit of washing sweet potatoes then jumped over the sea ... Colonies of monkeys on other islands and the mainland troop of monkeys at Takasakiyama began washing their sweet potatoes. Thus, when a certain critical number achieves an awareness, this new awareness may be communicated from mind to mind. Although the exact number may vary, this Hundredth Monkey Phenomenon means that when only a limited number

> of people know of a new way, it may remain the conscious property of these people. But there is a point at which if only one more person tunes-in to a new awareness, a field is strengthened so that this awareness is picked up by almost everyone!" [4]

[Editor's note: Since its original 1984 publication, *The Hundredth Monkey* has been criticized for lacking substantial evidence. It is included here for the reader as context to the lesson, "Closing the Circle." Saint Germain often says, "Never believe anything that I say! Take it unto the laboratory of self!"]

[1] David R. Hawkins, *Power vs. Force, The Hidden Determinants of Human Behavior: An Anatomy of Consciousness* (Sedona, AZ: Veritas Publishing), page 84-86.

[2] Lori Toye, *New World Atlas: Earth Changes for a Planet in Transition, Volume Three* (Payson, AZ: Seventh Ray Publishing), pages 67-69.

[3] *Grolier Encyclopedia of Knowledge, Volume 11, Lenz's Law* (Danbury, CT: Grolier Inc.), page 244.

[4] Ken Keyes Jr., *The Hundreth Monkey*, http://www.worldtrans.org/pos/monkey.html (2007).

APPENDIX K

Topics and Terms for Doomsday-Peace Day

The Gathering of the Prophets
I AM America Provenance
"Mission of Peace"
Prophecies of Civil Unrest and Media Deception
Cellular Acceleration
"The Spark of Freedom"
Ascension Teachings—the Divine Mission
The Terrible Vial and New Diseases
"Placing the Capstone"

Prophecy Conference:

The original Prophecy or Prophet's Conferences were sponsored by I AM America in 1995 and 1996. The first was held in Philadelphia, Pennsylvania, the second, in Phoenix, Arizona. The following Prophets participated in the conference and shared their prophecies: Lori and Lenard Toye; Robert Ghost Wolf; Dannion Brinkley; Joya Pope; Michael Schuster; Judi Zion (Sion); Tuieta; Annie and Byron Kirkwood; Dr. Chet Snow; Dr. Norma Milanovich; Elewtale Lakatschet (Priscilla Pinkham, Nez Perce Elder); Dolores Cannon; Dr. Terry Friedmann; Dr. Louis Turi; Krsanna Duran; and Penelope Greenwell.

Capstone:

The capstone is the highest point of a structure—referred to as an apex. This term is used throughout the teaching, *Dooms Day—Peace Day*, as a metaphor.

Earth Changes Prophecies and Prophecies of Change:

1. The state of California, Starting with civil unrest, will undergo profound social changes. The media perpetuate this crisis; the turmoil escalates and spreads to Phoenix, Arizona.

2. The first of seven plagues is identified: it is the corruption of the media through greed and sensationalism.

3. A small activation of the Ring of Fire, which actually happened on or about October 18, 1995, will focus our attention on this area. According to the prophecies, once the Ring of Fire becomes active, crop failures and price wars over gas, oil, and food will follow.

4. Violence will continue in Bosnia and bleed into Russia. The threat of a nuclear disaster between Russia and Japan develops.

5. Increased rainfall, including monsoons and flooding, is prophesied for Europe. This weather change is a result of global warming.

6. The prophecies say Arizona will experience a severe drought and a mega-forest fire.

7. A droplet from a deadly vial will pollute earth and create many new illnesses. According to the prophecies, western and southwesterly winds will purify this strain of the disease.

Cellular Acceleration:

This is the second step of the Cellular Awakening. It comprises a new planetary energy designed to biologically initiate the Ascension Process. The following highlights and recommendations are associated with this process:

1. Prophecies advise humans to live as close as possible—within a forty-mile radius—to the apexes (Stars) of Golden Cities.
2. As the awakening consciousness embraces the physical and light bodies, physical Ascension joins spirit and soul. This momentum of energy raises the physical body out of this dimension and into a New Dimension where it is freed of physical limitation. The soul is then individualized through the *spark of freedom*.
3. Ascension is available for those who seek to fulfill a meaningful *Divine Mission*.
4. The Law of Balance is always present in Golden Cities during physical and cellular accelerations. Don't confuse the Law of Balance or Equilibrium with the Law of Cause and Effect. The Law of Balance brings everything to a neutral, peaceful state, void of excess or extreme, including all kingdoms of creation, emotional and mental states, and any and all influences and powers. Spiritual leaders describe the phenomena of Vortices and the influence of equilibrium in numerous works:

> "If we look on our planet from above, we will observe, besides the evident volcanoes, particular Vortices of light and darkness. The human spirit can create powerful manifestations of energy. One may state that the Vortices of Light are saviors of the equilibrium of the planet. Nor is it far from the truth to state that the Vortices of Darkness contain a destructive gas, which is not only deadly to the crust of the planet but can alter the climate and even significantly effect a shifting of the poles. Thus powerful is the significance of the human spirit. Hence, we treasure the Ashrams where

purified Agni is gathered. Many teachings have pointed out the importance of pure places where psychic energy can be affirmed. References to the importance of pure places are found in the Sacred Writings, in the Bible, and in the Rig-Veda; the Tao likewise contains knowledge of these treasure-places of earth. We rejoice when we notice the rise of new Ashrams, for people so seldom think of the power of their spirits!" [1]

[For more on the "Cellular Awakening," see Appendix E]

Spiritual Prophecies:

1. Ascended Masters will help the planet avert the most cataclysmic Earth Changes. We can contribute to this effort through our positive thoughts, prayer, and meditations.

2. In the times to come, mankind may witness events and circumstances that are difficult to understand. Comfort yourself with the knowledge that many souls have chosen to experience this particular time together.

3. Many are not ready to hear this message, while others will hear it and awaken, even in the twilight hours.

[1] Agni Yoga Teachings, *A Treasury of Terms and Thoughts*, http://www.agniyoga.org (1992, 2002)

APPENDIX L

Topics and Terms for The Fountain of Life

Destroying the Death Consciousness
The Science of Decrees and the Power of the I AM
Addressing Speech Patterns
On Asking Permission
Fourth Dimensional Consciousness
Choice and Conscious Awareness of the Manifestation Process
Walking in Balance
The Sovereign Individual

Thought, Feeling, and Action:

Thought, feeling, and action, according to Ascended Master teachings and tradition, serve as the cornerstones of the co-creative process. The mental (causal) body and the Yellow Ray represent thought; the emotional (astral) body and the Pink Ray, feeling; and the physical body and the Blue Ray, actions. Imbalances in any of these processes form the foundation of disease (dis-ease).

The principles of thought, feeling, and action, however, aren't limited to esoteric doctrine. Astrological teachings also utilize these fundamentals to indicate the strengths, the weaknesses, and the influences of astral powers: the sun, causal body; the moon, astral body. Action incorporates the will, and the choices we make and act upon.

I AM or I AM Presence:

The essence of the I AM bridges the physical, the spiritual and the transmigratory activity of human existence. *I AM* represents God's infinite spirit; the *I AM Presence* embodies the individualized presence of God—the relationship between the human self and the Divine Presence within and around us. The resulting energy unites and becomes the taproot of all God powers: life, intelligence, power, and action.

During each lifetime, the light, life, and energy of the soul flow from the I AM Presence to our physical and light bodies. This twining connection of energy and light—also known as the Silver cord—follows the pull of gravity. Light streams through the crown of the head where it cascades to the heart of the Presence and circulates to the base of the brain: the medulla oblongata. Tiny threads of light radiate energy to every cell of the body. The Hindus call these healing filaments Nadis; chakras form at points of intensity. Light then surges from these tributaries of energy—Nadis and chakras—to a mighty confluence of light energy known as the Pillar of Light or the Tube of Light.

The Ascended Masters rely heavily on the power of the I AM Presence for protection. Conscious calls to the I AM Presence activate the Pillar of Light, insulating lower bodies—causal, astral, and physical—from difficult Karmas. The Pillar of Light and the addition of the Violet Flame construct a spiritual shelter much like the protective force of mantras, spiritual ceremonies, and prayers. That's why the consistent practice of these transcendental exercises raises spiritual consciousness: the summoning of greater fields of light ameliorates and eliminates seemingly insurmountable difficulties, and creates miracles.

The Christ Self—also known as the Higher Self or Guardian Angel—protects the physical body, even though it operates at a lower vibratory rate than the Presence. It also provides an intermediary power between the I AM Presence and the outer human form. Simply speaking, this intelligent body of light serves the energies of the I AM as a Step-down Transformer and a propellant of action in the physical plane. Scholars say the bodies of the I AM Presence and the Christ Self are just as tangible in their own realms of vibratory action as the body in its physical world.[1]

Decrees:

Similar to prayers and mantras, these statements of intent and power are often integrated with the use of the I AM and requests to the I AM Presence. And when it comes to activating these spiritual channels, the possibilities are endless. Some express decrees silently through prayer and meditation, while others opt for forceful pronouncements of intent. Rhythmic chanting and singing, therapeutic journaling, and write-and-burn techniques provide just a few conduits of worship.

Decrees form the foundation of Ascended Master teachings; these simple affirmations create a conscious contact with the I AM Presence, shifting consciousness, expanding awareness, and activating the co-creation process.

A classic Ascended Master decree for the Violet Flame is as follows:

"Violet Flame I AM, God I AM Violet Flame!"

APPENDIX L

Within the text of the Chapter 12 teachings, *The Fountain of Life*, Saint Germain gives a decree to command life unto your being:

I AM the effervescent life flowing through.
I AM the effervescent life transmuting.
I AM the effervescent life of life!

Spiritual Prophecies:

1. Consciousness opens our awareness and forms our experiences in the Fourth Dimension. This insight underlies of the Ascension Process; and during the times of Planetary Acceleration, the Fourth Dimension of Vibration becomes ever more apparent. [For more information on the Fourth Dimension see Appendix D.]

2. Lower spiritual states now dominate the collective consciousness; therefore, the Ascended Masters rarely, if ever, assume physical form. That's why the responsibility of seeking spiritual connections and raising consciousness falls on humans. The pursuit of the Masters' knowledge, teachings, and personal guidance rely on a person's ability to develop and increase consciousness to a Fifth Dimensional level: the realm of the Masters. Simultaneously, the Master Teachers lower their consciousness—through the *Law of Energy for Energy*—to the Fourth Dimension, a dimension of vibration, to achieve contact with aspirants, students, chelas, and initiates.

3. An increase in the vibration and the energy of the collective consciousness heralds the beginning of the Golden Age. According to prophecies, the Ascended Masters, at this time, will assume physical bodies and appear in the Third and Fourth Dimensions. The shapeshifting of the Masters occurs after the material migration of the poles, causing a great fluctuation in the spiritual consciousness of humanity.

4. The greatest gift of the Ascended Masters, the Violet Flame, has the ability to *transmute and change any situation at any time* if practiced on a widespread basis.

5. "Humanity is on the brink of Devastation; but, humanity is also upon the brink of great evolution and spiritual awakening."

6. This is the Time of the *death of the guru*—an era when humanity is released from the authoritarian restraints and testing imposed by an "Outer Guru." Mankind awakens to and learns spiritual knowledge from *within*. In Vedic tradition, this is known as Pratyaksa—direct perception.[2] This freedom promotes the process of individuality, or the undivided state of consciousness apparent in the HU-man or God-Man. [See Appendices H and I.]

The Rule of Asking Permission:

Mankind's conscious contact with the Great White Brotherhood is a matter of choice. That's why the Ascended Masters follow the cardinal rule of asking permission when it comes to human interaction. By vow and practice, the Masters never intrude: they don't demand deference from or dictate a doctrine to a chela or student. Instead, their directions are based on suggestions and affirmations. The Masters identify the presence of natural laws that may affect or alter the course of one's life. Their knowledge and teachings uplift our consciousness, vibration, and energy. The disciple is free to heed the message and act on it—or not. [For more information see Ascended Master, Appendix E.]

The Fountain of Life

The Fountain of Life is a spiritual teaching based on the transformation of common and difficult situations and circumstances. As a powerful metaphor for the *Fountain of Youth*, teachings of the Fountain of Life are based on:

1. Grace
2. Forgiveness
3. Transmutation

The application of these principles germinates the fruits of regeneration, beauty, and co-operation—the sources of the Ascension Process and immortality. The Fountain of Life then cleanses the consciousness of death, and feeds everlasting life.

Forgiveness:

The Ascended Masters never encourage Forgiveness as a matter of *turning the other cheek*. Rather, absolution is based on the metaphysical notion of the Law of Purification: the act of transmuting slower, base energies into a higher form. It's about discarding a perception of a situation or a circumstance, and seeking freedom from objectionable or undesirable elements. This involves the process of atonement, but not in the theological sense.

Esoterically speaking, At-One-Ment is the birth of the Christ Consciousness within: the realization of divinity, wholeness, unity, harmony, and clarity of consciousness; and not the reconciliation between Man and God via the blood of Jesus Christ. From this viewpoint, Forgiveness allows humanity to forever close the door on and disengage the processes of dark and deceptive energies.

The Refreshing Drink:

The Refreshing Drink is an allegory of the Universal Supply of Life. It originates from the work of Guy Ballard, who, under the pen name Godfré Ray King, authored the classic theosophical book of Ascended Master teaching, *Unveiled Mysteries.*

Ballard's work evolves from a simple meditation during a hike on Mount Shasta. On a warm day, Ballard—asking God to define his path—finds his way to a stream and fills his Cup with its water. A drink of the liquid sends an electrical current through his body. Suddenly, a young man materializes and telepathically relays this message: "My Brother, if you will hand me your Cup, I will give you a much more refreshing drink."

The young man later on reveals himself as Saint Germain; Ballard's water flows directly from the Universal Supply, "[as] pure and vivifying as Life itself; in fact it is Life—Omnipresent Life—for it exists everywhere about us." [3]

[1] A. D. K. Luk, *Law of Life, Book One* (Pueblo, CO: ADK Luk Publications), pages 19-23.

[2] Bhaktitrtha Swami Krishnapada, *About Vedic Prophecies* http:www.stephen-knapp.com, (2007).

[3] Godfre Ray King, *Unveiled Mysteries* (Schaumburg, IL: Saint Germain Press), pages 2-4.

APPENDIX M

Topics and Terms for The First Golden City

The Time of Shamballa
Gobean—the First Activated Golden City for the New Times
Significance of Golden City Apexes (Stars)
The Star of the Magi—the Christ Consciousness
Celebration of the Four Elements

Shamballa:

Shamballa, which means to *make sacred,* is the earth's first Golden City. The notion of Shamballa represents peace, happiness, and tranquility. It's a place of spiritual cleanliness and divine dominion; it's the ethereal home and sanctuary of Sanat Kumara.

To understand Shamballa's metaphysical antiquity is to grasp its complex timeline. According to modern occult literature, this mystic metropolis existed more than 60,000 years ago. Other sources suggest that Sanat Kumara's legion of volunteers descended to earth millions of years ago to build and inhabit the first incarnation of Shamballa. Over its long and calamitous history, the White City experienced a series of cataclysmic Earth Changes that destroyed it three times during sensitive alignments with the Galactic Light of the Great Central Sun. This cosmic susceptibility occurs when the progression of yugas (periods of Vedic timekeeping) move from one age of light to another. Sanat Kumara's followers rebuilt Shamballa twice; the third time the White City ascended beyond the physical realm where it now exists in etheric perpetuity. This is the thirty-sixth Golden City Vortex of Gobi, known today as the City of Balance. It is located in China over the Qilian Shan Mountains next to the Gobi Desert.

This *City of White* served a specific purpose: to save the earth and humanity from certain annihilation. Stories like this in the Bible abound. Man's faith falters; his connection with God dims; and moral, physical, and spiritual depravity prevail—as was the state of the earth before the Time of Shamballa. In a theosophical sense, universal principles demand a certain level of spiritual enlightenment for an entity to exist. The earth and its inhabitants, however, consistently fell short; so a cosmic council of divine luminaries, including Sanat Kumara, voted to destroy the unfit planet.

But the compassionate Venusian Lord wouldn't allow earth to fall into oblivion. Instead, he offered his light to balance the planet's metaphysical darkness and disharmony. As word spread of the Master's plans, devotees—144,000 of them—volunteered to accompany their guru on his Karmic Mission. One hundred of Sanat Kumara's stalwarts arrived on earth 900 years beforehand to proliferate light; propagate the Flame of Consciousness; and prepare for the coming of Shamballa.

But, Sanat Kumara's volunteers paid a heavy spiritual price: Karma. No longer would their Venusian souls enjoy the fruits of constant consciousness. Instead, as terrestrial bodies bound to the wheel of embodiment, they would follow the Laws of Earth—death, birth, and the passing of forgotten lifetimes—as their incarnating light energy lifted the consciousness of earth.

Esoteric teachings say fellow Venusian Serapis Bey served as Sanat Kumara's first volunteer. With an affinity for architecture, this Master Teacher—along with the Seraphic Hosts he served with on the planets of Mercury, Aquaria, and Uranus—offered to oversee the creation of Shamballa.[1] Serapis Bey, the exalted being of light, performed one of the greatest sacrifices in Ascended Master legend by descending—as the light of heavens dimmed—into a physical body. On earth, with his legions of seraphim, Serapis Bey oversaw the building of the White City for nine centuries. His sacrifice awarded him the honor of the Divine Architect of Shamballa.

This legend is analogous to the Hindu deity Tvashtri, later known as VishvaKarma, the celestial architect credited with the designing of the Universe and its contents.[2] VishvaKarma represents the power of regeneration and longevity. Serapis Bey later incarnated as Phidias, the great designer of the Parthenon, the classical sculptor of the Statue of Zeus, and the architect of the Temple of the Goddess Athena.

The builders of Shamballa modeled it after the opulent Venusian City of the Kumaras. On a white island in the sapphire-colored Gobi Sea (present-day Gobi Desert), workers erected the Elysian metropolis of light and consciousness. An ornate bridge of marble and Gold connected the White Island to the mainland. They adorned the city with hundreds of white, dome-and-spire-capped temples—that's where Shamballa earned its moniker, the City of White. Against this whitewashed backdrop, the luminous Temples of the Seven Rays and their corresponding hues—blue, pink, yellow, pearl-white, green, ruby, and violet—stood prominently along a landscaped avenue. At its terminus rose the Temple of the Lord of the World, Sanat Kumara's annular, Golden-domed sanctuary. Here, the Ascended Master; three other Venusian Kumaras (lords); and thirty high priests, also known as Lords of the Flame, held conscious light for earth to sustain her place in the solar system. During his time in Shamballa, Sanat Kumara provided more than a spiritual safe harbor for the earth's denizens. He also formed the Great White Brotherhood—the fellowship of the Ascended Masters.

Thus, Shamballa defined itself as the earthly seat of selflessness. Divine beings, including the unascended, flocked there to volunteer their efforts and services. To elevate their consciousness, and prepare them for upcoming lifetimes and undertakings, Sanat Kumara magnetized their energies with his Divine Love. Others seeking the Master's Heart Flame trained as messengers at Shamballa's numerous temples. Many of these servants became initiates of the Great White Brotherhood.

During Shamballa's physical existence on earth, ascended and unascended members of the Great White Brotherhood returned annually for sanctuary, retreat, rejuvenation, and instruction for the upcoming year. After the third destruction of the city, and Shamballa's subsequent Ascension to the Fifth Dimension, ascended beings continued this tradition. But, without their aid, earthbound souls could no longer enter the City of White. To gain access, ascended members escorted the unascended to the etheric temples of the City of White by accelerating their light bodies during meditation and dreamtime.

For now, Shamballa will continue to exist in the ether, but Sanat Kumara prophesies its return:

> "[It] shall remain there until it is lowered again, permanently, into the physical appearance world as the Golden Age proceeds and mankind, individually and collectively prove themselves worthy to sustain it for all eternity. It will be My Gift to the evolution that I have loved, and will remain a part of the Star of Freedom, long after I have returned to my home..." [3]

[See also: Appendix A, Golden City Vortex; Appendix B, the Unfed Flame; Appendix C, Shamballa and the Development of the Mystery Schools; Appendix E, Ascended Master; Appendix F, Shamballa Message; Appendix H, Serapis Bey.]

Mythical Names for Shamballa from other cultures:

Hindu: Aryavarsha
Buddhist: Shambhala, a hidden community of perfect and semi-perfect beings.
Chinese: Hsi Tien, western paradise of Hsi Wang Mu, the Royal Mother of the West.
Greek: Hyperborea
Russian: Belovodye and Janaidar
Jewish and Christian: Garden of Eden
Celtic: Avalon
Esoteric: Shangri-La; Agartha; Land of the Living; Forbidden Land; Land of White Waters; Land of Radiant Spirits; Land of Living Fire; Land of Living Gods; Land of Wonders.[4]

Prophecies of Change:

1. Gobean is the first activated Golden City in the New Times. This activation began in the late 1970s and continued through the early 1980s. Master Teachers from Shamballa, or the Golden City of Gobi, sponsored the creation of this city with energies from the etheric Temples of Shamballa. [See Appendix G, Golden City Activation]

2. The Stars, or apexes, of Golden Cities are critical points. They can be used to influence and change the collective consciousness of humanity.

3. The Golden City of Gobean is a place of geophysical significance for spiritual works. Prayer and meditation originating from Gobean is powerful enough to facilitate and create peace on earth, and influence humanity's collective consciousness.

4. The New or Golden Age hasn't yet been realized at its height of energies; however, it has Started and is influencing the earth.

5. Shamballa was originally created to hold perfect spiritual consciousness for the evolution of humanity. This is the purpose of the Golden Cities, and they establish a new energetic template within the spiritual hearts of all.

Critical Point:

A critical point is defined in energy systems as the location where the least amount of force will create the greatest effect.

The Celebration of the Four Elements:

Over four weeks (twenty-eight days), esoteric followers, including Ascended Masters, honor the Celebration of the Four Elements during the Shamballa festivities. It begins December 17—accompanied by lighting of the Eternal Flame Candle, or the Fireless Light—on the altar of the main temple. This etheric celebration is divided into the following four parts:

1. Week One: December 18 to December 24. Element: Earth. The celebration and thanksgiving offered to Mother Earth. Ceremonies and rituals for Earth Healing are held at Shamballa during this time. Bowls of salt, which represent earth united with spirit, are placed on all the altars in the Temples of Shamballa.
2. Week Two: December 25 to December 31. Element: Air. Celebrations of gratitude and thanksgiving to the World Teachers and the messengers of the Great White Brotherhood who have selflessly served humanity are held this week. Krishna, Jesus Christ, Buddha, and other well-known avatars and saviors are also lauded. Doves of Peace are symbolically released this week.

3. Week Three: January 1 to January 7: Element: Water. A thanksgiving for our Soul Families is held during this week. This phase of Shamballa Celebration is about revering love and friendship, and performing Cup Ceremonies. A Cup Ceremony is a water ceremony that celebrates the union of Mother Earth and Soul Families. A Cup of water is passed and infused with the prayers of the devoted. The prayer-charged water is then poured on the earth.
4. Week Four: January 8 to January 14: Element: Fire. This week is a celebration of Spiritual Fire. This time is set aside for personal purification, intentions, reflection, and meditation for the upcoming year. This is an important period for the Brotherhoods and Sisterhoods of Light to review plans for the following 365 days. Candles for each of the Seven Rays, representing the seven Hermetic Laws, are lit this week.
5. The Sealing of Divinity: January 15 and 16: Celebrations of Unity—Unana—and the ONE.
6. The Closing of Shamballa: January 17: the light of the Eternal Flame returns to Venus.

[1] Tellis Papastavro, *The Gnosis and the Law* (Tucson, AZ: Group Avatar), page 28.

[2] Hart Defouw and Robert Svoboda, *Light on Life: An Introduction to the Astrology of India* (London: Penguin Books Limited), page 232.

[3] Tellis Papastavro, *The Gnosis and the Law* (Tucson, AZ: Group Avatar), page 103.

[4] Mary Sutherland, *In Search of Shambhala*, http//www.living in the lightms.com (2003).

APPENDIX N

Topics and Terms for The Ever-Present Perfection

The Eight-Sided Cell of Perfection
All Perfection and the Absolute Perfection
The Two Types of Intuition: The Intuitive Mind and the Expressive Intuition
Twin Flame
Yin and Yang Concepts
The Directions and Corresponding Relationships to Energy Movement within (Microcosm) and Geomantically (Macrocosm)
Spiritual Disciplines Associated with Each Direction
Teachings on Balance, Vibration, and Energy
Thought Creates!

Spiritual Prophecies:

1. Those who resonate with the Prophecies of Change will become influenced by the light, the sound, and the light bodies of the Ascended Masters.

2. Those enlightened individuals will build and experience the Golden Age through the understanding of divinity and perfection.

3. Understanding and applying the spiritual teachings of the movement of energy in the Eight-Sided Cell of Perfection will assist and integrate Unity Consciousness.

Earth Changes Prophecy:

In Chapter 14, *The Ever-Present Perfection,* Saint Germain suggests that imminent Earth Changes will serve as a wake-up call for mankind, "Humanity refuses to move forward!"

Prophecies of Change:

Since spiritual light and spiritual energy enters the earth from the North Pole, esoteric science considers the North Pole yang—a positive, male energy. The South Pole is considered yin—a negative, feminine energy. Humanity's collective consciousness is affected and directed by these invisible light and energy patterns.

The Eight-Sided Cell of Perfection Energy Map

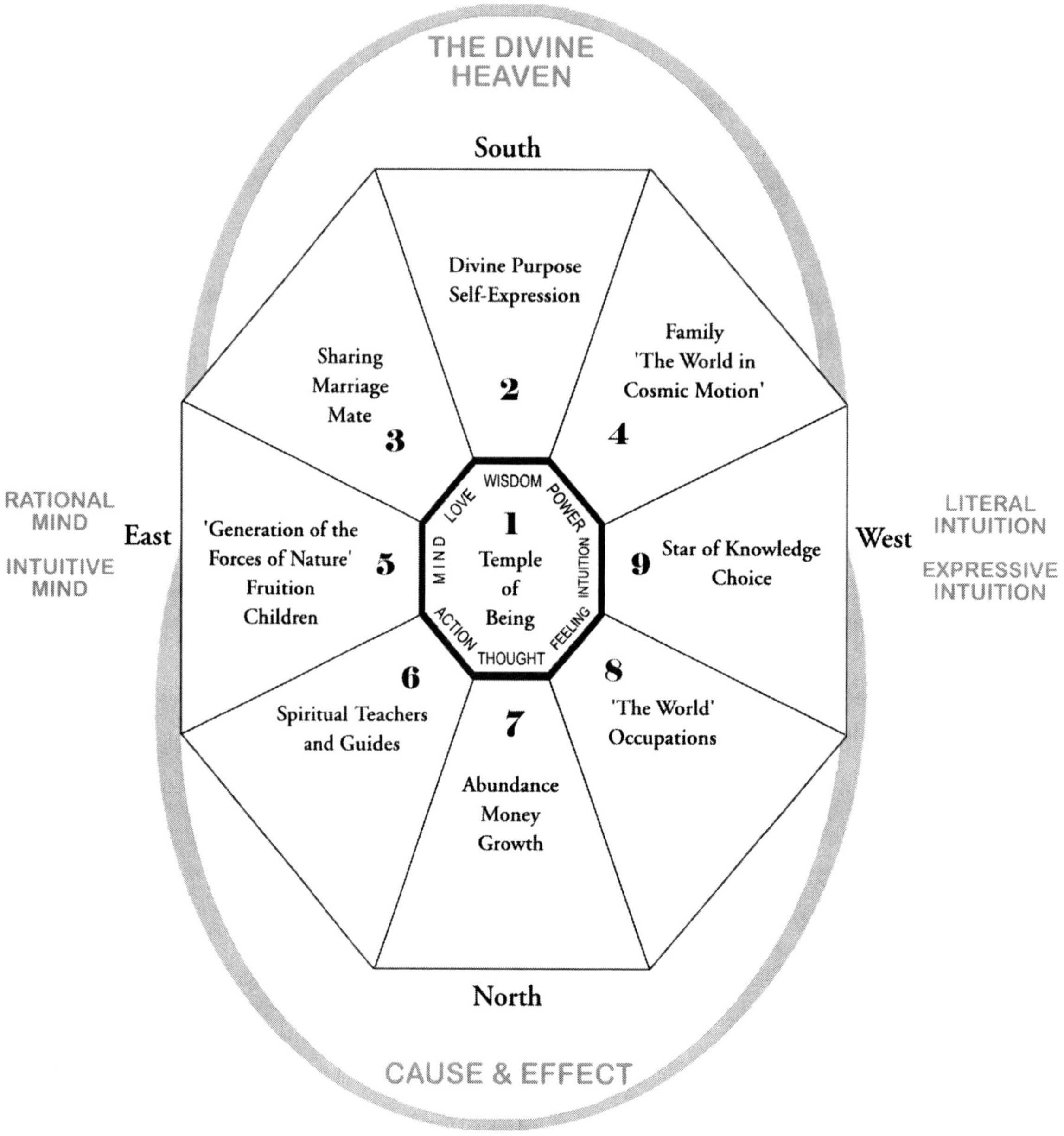

FIGURE 6-A
Eight-Sided Cell of Perfection Energy Map

1. Currently there is less light entering the North Pole, and because of this there is a "darkened perspective upon life."

2. Once we enter the New Times of the Golden Age, earth will receive more spiritual light and spiritual energy. This etheric light will enter from the South Pole.

3. Heightened spiritual energies and spiritual light entering the earth from the South Pole help to create a more enlightened humanity alongside a feminine, creative culture.

The Eight-Sided Cell of Perfection:

The *Eight-Sided Cell of Perfection* provides a direct link to the core of Cellular Awakening during the Earth Changes. According to the Ascended Masters, within each person lies one perfect cell known as the Eight-Sided Cell of Perfection. It is associated with all aspects of perfection; it contains and maintains a visceral connection to the Godhead, e.g. the God within, the God realization, and the God manifestation in all creations and perceptions. This cell is located in the *Chamber of the Heart,* surrounded by a mandala of energy: the Unfed Flame of Love, Wisdom, and Power. The vibral-core axis provides a material connection to the Eight-Sided Cell of Perfection in physical form. Located near the Solar Plexus Chakra, it serves as the central energy current that runs through the human body. Here, the aura ties to the seven chakras (energy centers); the core of the planet; and the spiritual over-soul. The over-soul is also known as the energy system that incorporates the Christ Self and the I AM Presence. As earthly energies increase in vibration and frequency, the Eight-Sided Cell of Perfection awakens, stimulating Cellular Awakening and spiritual growth. [For more information see Appendices B and E.]

The Principal of Perfection:

According to Ascended Master teachings, perfection is often seen as balance or harmony; perfection is associated with self-knowledge and Mastery. It is also understood as a state of evolution.

The Intuitive Mind:

Intuition, instinct, gut feeling, sixth sense—these definitions aptly explain the Intuitive Mind on a basic level, but according to esoteric teachings, it encompasses much more. The Intuitive Mind comprises the entire energy field, including the aura; the chakras; the energy meridians; the bonds with spirit and the Earth Mother; and the connections to higher wisdom and knowledge. With the help of the Intuitive Mind, the soul grows at its own rate and Vibration of development.[1] Albert Einstein summed it up best, "The Intuitive Mind is a sacred gift and the rational mind is a faithful servant. We have created a society that honors the servant and has forgotten the gift."

Expressive Intuition:

Expressive intuition is an innate psychic gift, but to the degree a person develops this aspect of the Intuitive Mind is their choice. Artists, psychics, and channels dip into the intuitive-driven supersenses—clairvoyance, clairaudience, clairsentience, and clairgustance—to practice their craft. The great Prophet Edgar Cayce spoke often about intuition in spiritual teachings, "The more and more one is impelled by that which is intuitive or the relying upon the soul force within; the further, the deeper, the broader, the more constructive may be the result." [2] Literal Intuition is also known as *instinct.*

Mentalism:

Mentalism is the study of mental perception and thought processes—it's the understanding that these states are to action as cause is to effect. Author James Allen said it best in his book *As a Man Thinketh*, "Every action and feeling is preceded by a thought."

Maps of Energy Movement:

Many schools of thought address energy movement—chi, orgone, or prana—in some capacity. Two doctrines, however, express these principles in a comprehensive historical perspective, Vastu Shastra and Vastu Vidya. They form the foundation of the 4,500-year-old *dwelling sciences* of Vedic philosophy and Classical Chinese Feng Shui, the Taoist art and science of living in harmony in the environment.[3]

The Yantra:

The Yantra is a sacred geometrical tradition of Vedic philosophy—a visual tool often used during meditation that helps the mind tune out mental noise. Permutations of shape and mathematics create decorative and magical patterns such as the mandala, kolam, and rangoli. The source of these structures stems from one of the oldest systems of mapping unseen energies: the Vedic Square, also known as the Paramashayika. It's based on and derives its power from the number nine, considered a sacred numeral in Vedic Astrology—Jyotish—based on nine *grahas* or planets. The Vedic Square also represents what lies beyond. This energy map contains divisions of nine equal parts, forming a diagram of eighty-one squares (9 x 9). The larger square depicts the macrocosm; the detailed squares of eighty-one segments calculate the microcosmic nuances of space.

APPENDIX N

The Vedic Square

The Nine Planets with Corresponding Directions

North

West / East

Moon Chandra	Jupiter Guru	Sun Surya
Mercury Budha		Venus Shukra
Saturn Shani	Venus Shukra	Mars Kuja

South

FIGURE 7-A
Vedic Square (yantra) Energy Map of the Nine Planets and their directions

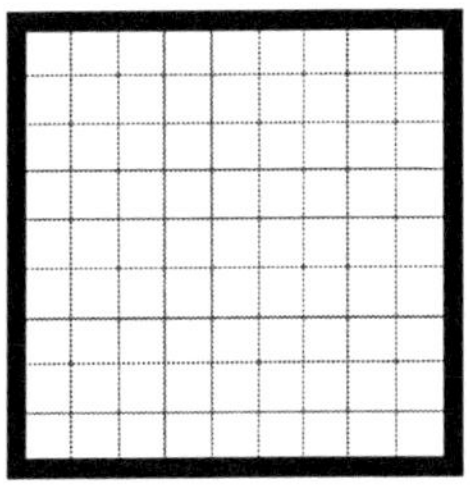

FIGURE 7-B
(Above) Vedic Square: 81 Portions

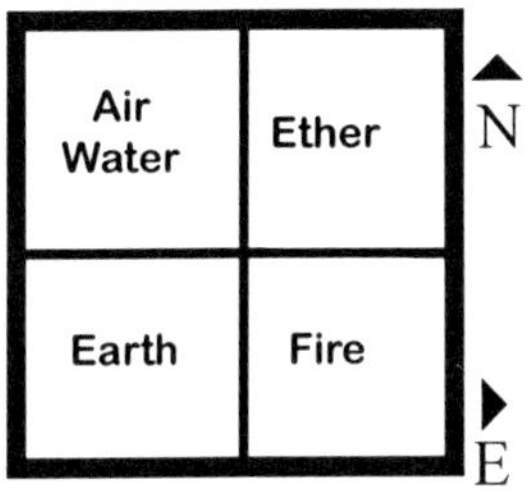

FIGURE 7-C
(Above) Vedic Square: The Five Elements The Five Elements and their respective directions. Each element is in constant flux through the three forces represented in Hinduism as the three faces of God: Brahma the Creator (rajas), Vishnu the Preserver (Sattva), and Shiva the Destroyer (tamas).

The Nine Directions and Vedic Deities

North

West / East

Vayu	Kubera	Soma
Varuna	Brahma	Indra
Niritti	Yama	Agni

South

FIGURE 7-D
(Left) Vedic Square (yantra) Energy Map of the Nine Directions and Vedic Deities

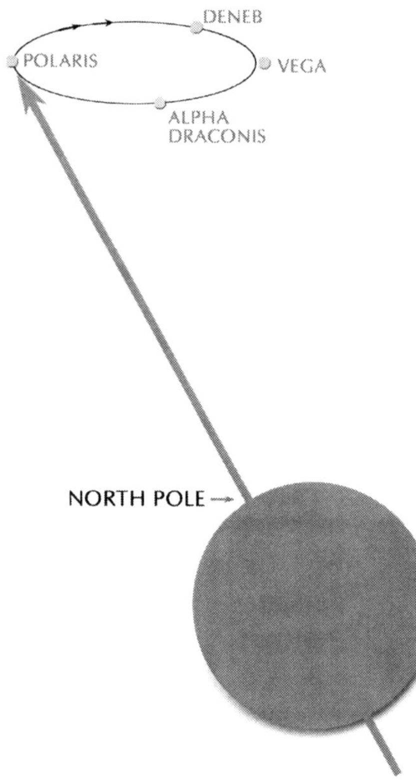

FIGURE 8-A
Earth's Wobble and Pole Stars

Earth's Wobble and Precession:

The ancient Vedic rishis—advanced spiritual teachers who lived in the previous ages of superior light and truth—gave humanity the science of Vastu, gross energies, and Vaastu, subtle energies. They recognized the earth's natural energy conduits, also known as lei-lines, which form a grid around the planet. This esoteric system of latitudinal and longitudinal striae, running from the dipolar magnetic points of north and south and from east to west, follows the path of the sun. This web of electromagnetic energy creates a subtle influence on an individual's mind and body as it transforms the causal and astral body (light bodies). This effect becomes noticeable as these changes reshape physical health in the body and overall life experiences. The earth's imperfect spin perpetually shifts to the fixed position of the Stars. The following visible results demonstrate the wobble of the earth:

1. In the fifteenth century, the pole Star Polaris was first used to navigate true north. Yet in the year 150 BC, it moved 12° 24 minutes from these coordinates. In 13,000 years the Star Vega will replace Polaris as the pole Star.[4] Not all ancient cultures followed Polaris as its focal point. The ancient Egyptians relied on Alpha Draconis (Dracaenas) as their pole Star in the construction of the pyramids.

2. The wobble of the earth also causes precession of the equinoxes. Precession is the slow backward shifting motion of the earth as it rotates.[5] This slight tilting of the pole is calculated at approximately 23.5°; it's the source of the Vedic Ayanamsha, which differentiates planetary movements against the position of Stars—sidereal astrology. In contrast, tropical or Western astrology tracks planets in reference to seasonal points according to a point of view from earth. Vedic astrology adjusts for precession; the Western system does not.

Energy Lines:

First, to understand the language buried within energy maps and concealed in their concurrent lines and formulas, one must delve into the ancient Indian knowledge of Vastu Vidya—the science of dwelling. From this esoteric perspective, the external (macro) life and the internal (micro) life are interchangeable, and the same laws and underlying energies that govern the weather are the same that control the organs of the human body. Today, this important and universal link is non-existent, and our societies and cultures have become disconnected and alienated from nature. The planet mirrors our ignorance as delicate ecosystems rapidly change through man-made threats to the environment, perilous Global Warming, and the possible extinction of numerous species of plants and animals. The ancients understood the hidden and stabilizing forces of the universe, and employed these same cosmic principles and universal laws that controlled the movement of the sun and the moon; the light and the energy of the sun, and the magnetic and the gravitational field of the earth. Application of this venerated knowledge restores balance between the cosmos and our personal environments, creating a timeless and positive vibration that results in health, wealth, and happiness. [6]

The Vedic rishis calculated the significance of lei-lines to determine the *wobble factor*. These scholars ascertained that the flow of the lines meandered primarily from northeast to southwest. At times, however, the energy currents change and run north to south and from east to west. Vastu philosophy understood the profundity of this phenomenon, and assigned deities to govern and protect these matrices.[7]

The Movement of Prana—The Vital Breath:

Prana—also defined as the *vital breath* and referred to as *chi* in Chinese Feng Shui—excludes air, wind, or exhalation in the traditional sense. Rather, it encompasses the essence of the soul: immortality. It is pure, untainted, and unattached from any manifest form. In the physical body, this spirit reflects an energy known as Asasya, and without its presence the body fades and dies. Prana, as the sages observed, wanders like lei-lines. So they studied prana to determine its movement and how to best harness it. During this process, they perceived its current streams from the northeast to the northwest and then toward the southwest; it also flows from the northeast toward the southeast, and then toward the southwest. Since benevolent energies meet in the southwest, entrances are never placed in these locations; energy flows don't affect centers, however—that's why middle ground serves as open courtyards. [8]

☉ SU	Krittika North	Uttara Phalguni East	Uttara Ashada South
☽ MO	Rohini East	Hasta South	Shravana North
♂ MA	Mrigashira South	Chitra West	Dhanistha East
☿ ME	Aslesha South	Jyestha West	Revati East
♃ JU	Punarvasu North	Visahka East	Purva Bhadrapada West
♀ VE	Bharani West	Purva Phalguni North	Purva Ashada East
♄ SA	Pushya East	Anuradha South	Uttara Bhadrapada North
☊ RA	Ardra West	Swati North	Shatabisha South
☋ KE	Ashwini South	Magha West	Mula North

FIGURE 9-A
The 27 Nakshatras (Moon Signs) are the basis of the Vedic Science of Ayadi.

The Science of Ayadi:

The professional practice of Vastu Vidya, the Vedic doctrine of space planning, employs zodiac-referenced mathematical calculations to harmonize a person's living (or work) area with his or her birth Star—this is the science of Ayadi. An individual's moon sign is used during important phases of the planning and building of a home or office. An edifice is considered a living being, influenced by the force of astrology.

Vedic Astrology uses a lunar-based system founded on twenty-seven signs, also known as *nakshatras* or lunar mansions. Each nakshatra has three specific orientations (north, south, east, and west) in relation to its ruling planet.[9] According to Hindu lore, Chandra, the moon deity, married twenty-seven wives, each residing in their own constellate homes. Thus, Chandra visits one wife a day, completing the zodiac in twenty-seven days. Ancient astrologers perceive Chandra, though male, as feminine because of his perpetual female influence.

Vastu's Child—Feng Shui:

Vastu is the parent: Feng Shui is the child. The science of Feng Shui is old; the practice of Vastu, however, predates its Chinese counterpart by thousands of years. And as the old saying goes, "The apple doesn't fall far from the tree." Feng Shui, the pattern of wind and water, relies on many of the same tools as Vastu to maximize the flow of energy in a particular living space.

The movement of chi—the vapor of life—is well documented in the history and culture of China. Practitioners of Feng Shui (pronounced fung-shway) depend on intricate, Vastu-like energy maps and a modified Paramashayika to apply these principles in practical applications.

Feng Shui evolved from two shaman Emperors, Fu Hsi of the San Huang Dynasty (twenty-ninth century BC) and Yü, the first ruler of the Xia Dynasty. Scholars credit Emperor Fu Hsi, the patron saint of the divination arts, with the discovery of Ho-t'u—the *Earlier Heaven Pa-k'ua.* (A pa-k'ua is similar to a Vedic yantra, another type of energy map). The revelation came to him after he witnessed a horse materialize from the Yellow River. On its side, he noted geometrical markings, which he later understood as the ideal structure of the universe and humanity.

Yü, the first emperor of the Xia Dynasty, ascended the throne approximately 700 years later. As a gift for saving the kingdom from a torrential flood, Shun, the reigning leader, named Yü his heir—a Prophecy fulfilled after Yü received the book *Power Over Water* from an immortal. As the floodwaters subsided, the future king observed a tortoise—its shell emblazoned with a pattern—emerge from the receding deluge. Yü recognized the ornamentation and identified it as the *Later Heaven Pa-k'ua* energy map. The interpretation of it can predict phenomena of flux and change. Today it's known as the Lo-shu.[10]

Feng Shui and the I Ching:

The I Ching, also called the *Book of Changes*, is perhaps one of the oldest examples of Chinese texts in the vast timeline of the culture's history. It's an attempt to create order out of chaos based on the enduring principles of philosophy, cosmology, and mathematics.

Over millennia, scholars studied and recalculated the trigrammatic divination formulas of the Ho-t'u and the Lo-shu. Scholars credit Zhou Dynasty ruler King Wen with devising the sixty-four sequence hexagram. His grandson, Emperor Shing of the Chou Dynasty, combined these doctrines of divination; his knowledge of the compass; and the tenets of the I Ching to form the territory of terrestrial and celestial prediction.

Niels Bohr, the 1922 Nobel Prize winner in physics, understood and appreciated the parallels of the I Ching's probabilistic concepts in relation to its Prophetic application of popular phenomena. He even incorporated the Tai Chi symbol in his coat of arms when he was knighted in 1947. Other scientists, too, have attempted to apply I Ching principles in contemporary applications. For instance, the sixty-four hexagrams of the I Ching correspond to the sixty-four DNA condons of the genetic code.

APPENDIX N

The energy maps on the following pages depict the legendary Lo-Ching. The first is the Earlier Heaven Pa-k'ua used with a compass for city planning. Practitioners apply the Later Heaven Pa-k'ua alongside landforms and the movement of the Stars to design countermeasures for adverse conditions.[11]

The Science of Feng Shui Evolves:

During the Tang Dynasty (618-960 AD) the geomancer's compass (lo-p'an)—used to identify the flow of earth's energy—grew to seventeen rings and twenty-four directions. Feng Shui practitioners depend on a similar compass in contemporary applications. Since its early inception thousands of years ago, Classical Chinese Feng Shui describes the research and the observations of the Ancients:

1. The science of landform—the dragon's vein
2. The interaction with the heavenly bodies
3. Cycle of changes in the universe
4. The science of burial sites
5. Integration of numerology and symbology
6. Classification of mountains
7. The cycle of eras and small changes
8. Analysis of an individual's Karma in evaluating the Feng Shui of a location
9. Auspicious timing

The Early Heaven Pak'ua

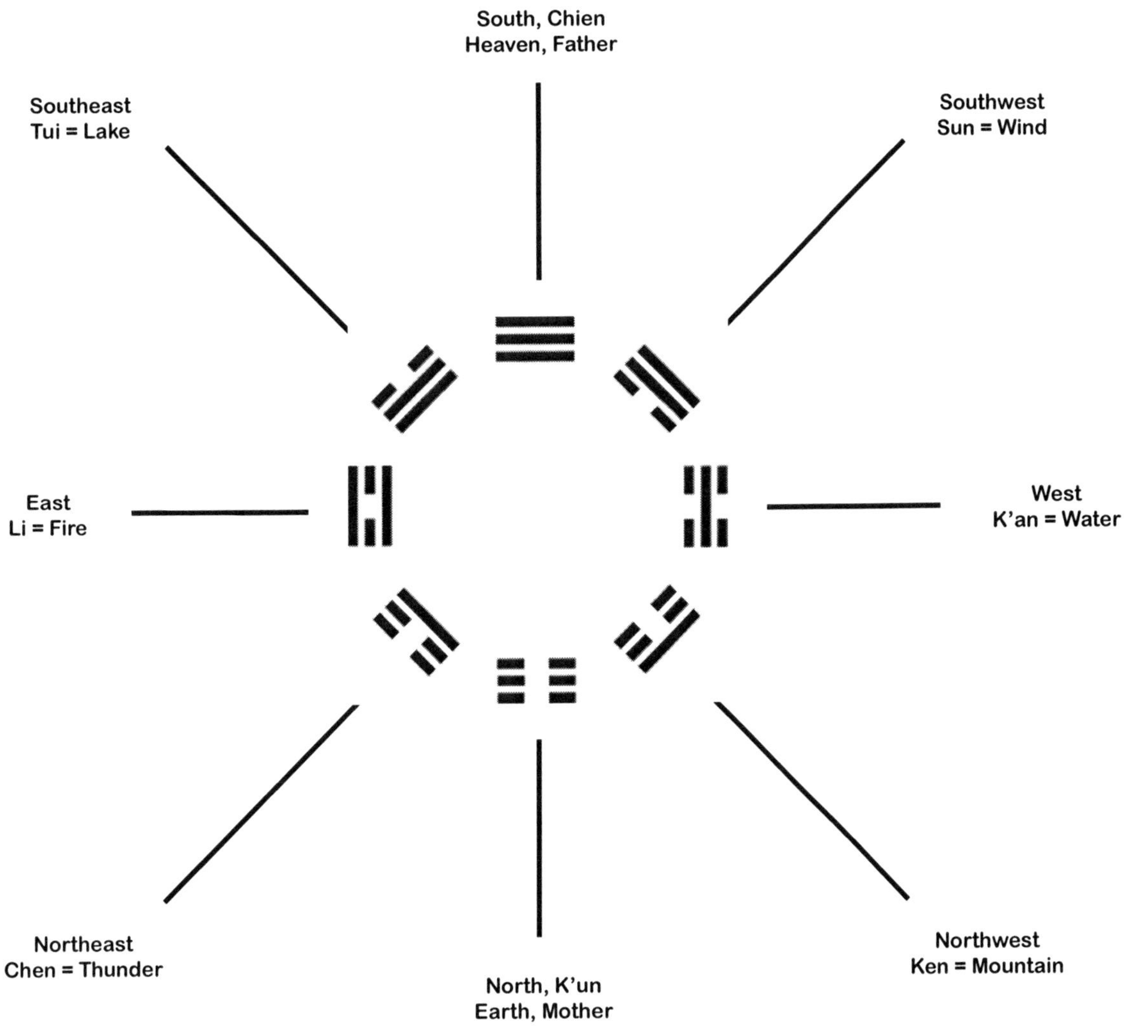

FIGURE 10-A
Chinese Pak'ua or Ba Gua Energy Map
Early Heaven devised by Fu Hsi

The Later Heaven Pak'ua

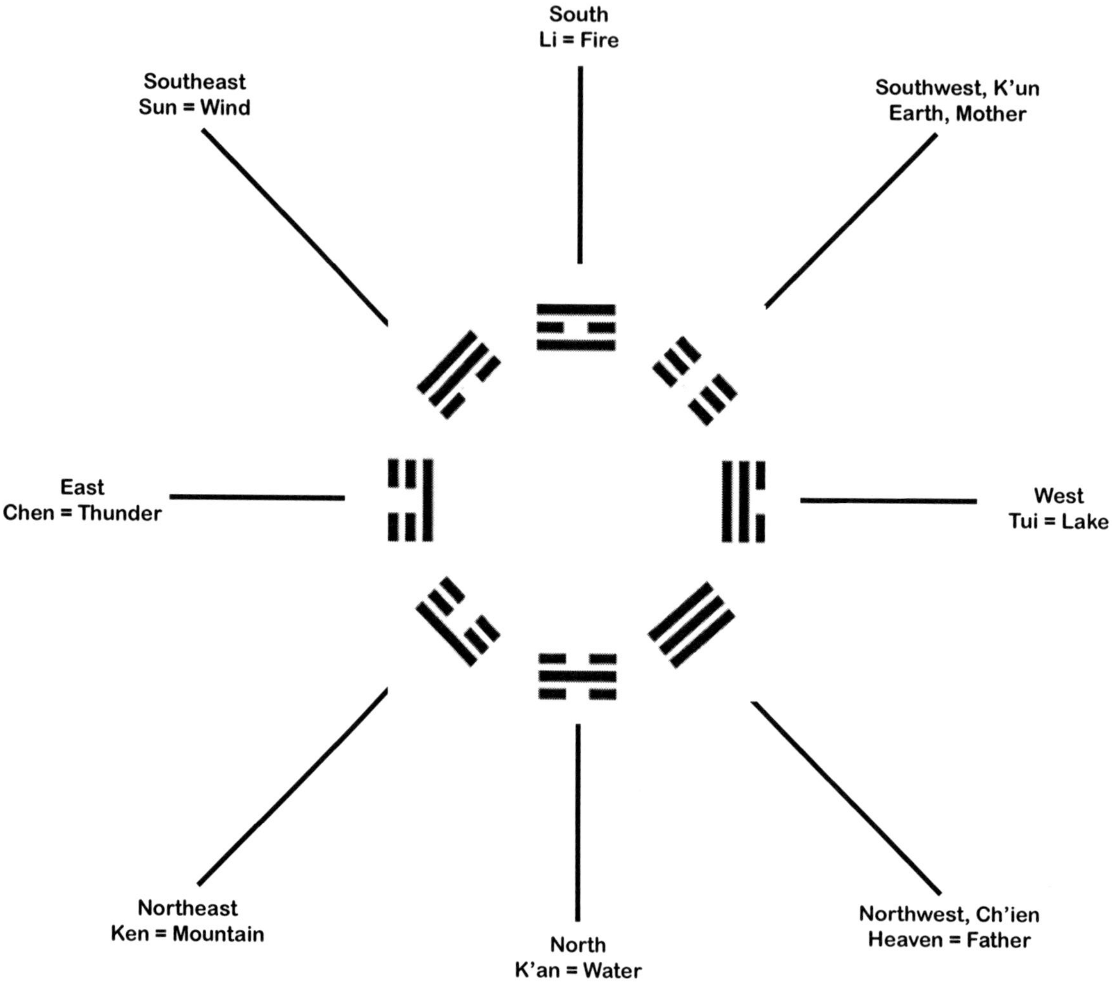

FIGURE 10-B
Chinese Pak'ua or Ba Gua Energy Map
Later Heaven devised by Yü

The following Energy Map depicts the flow of energy through the Nine Palaces of Classical Feng Shui. The Nine Palaces comprise the eight directions of the compass plus the center. The five elements—water, earth, metal, wood, fire—and their cycles of creation and destruction form the underpinnings of this movement. [12]

Path of Energy Movement through the Nine Palaces

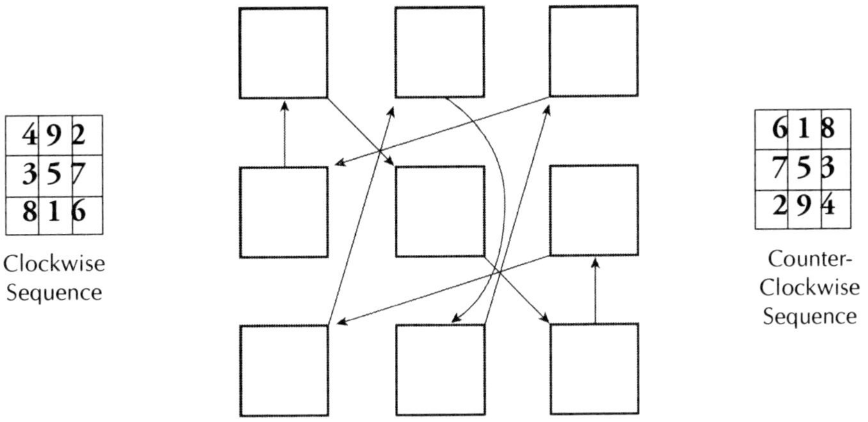

FIGURE 11-A
Energy Movement Through the Nine Palaces of Classical Chinese Feng Shui

(Below) This is the energy map that depicts the flow of energy through the Eight-Sided Cell of Perfection as taught in, "The Ever Present Perfection."

Path of Energy and Consciousness Movement in the Eight-Sided Cell of Perfection

(Resembles infinity, the Yin/Yang, and the figure 8.)

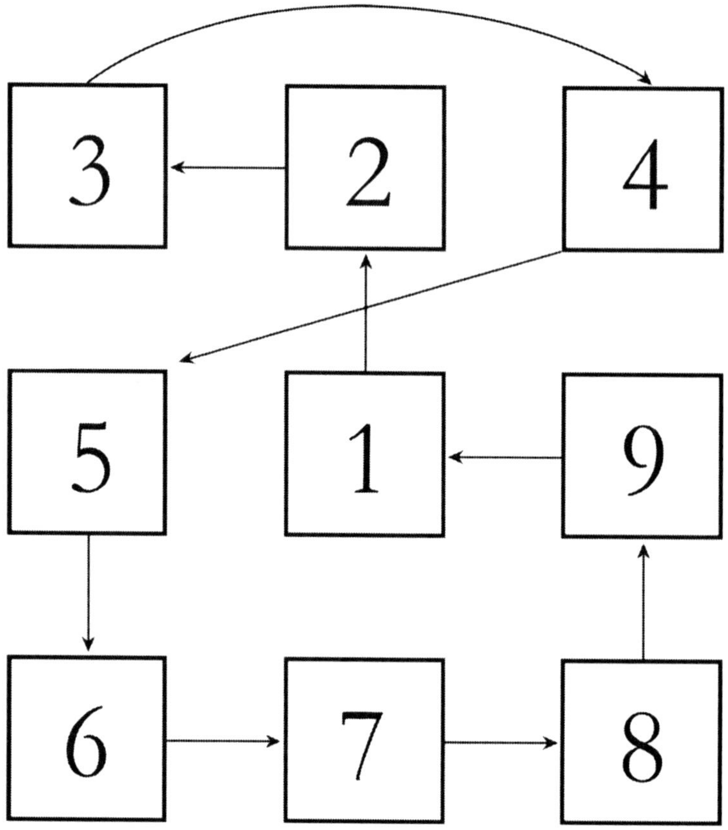

3 2 4
5 1 9
6 7 8

Clockwise
Sequence

FIGURE 11-B
The Nine Movements of Consciousness Through the Eight-Sided Cell of Perfection

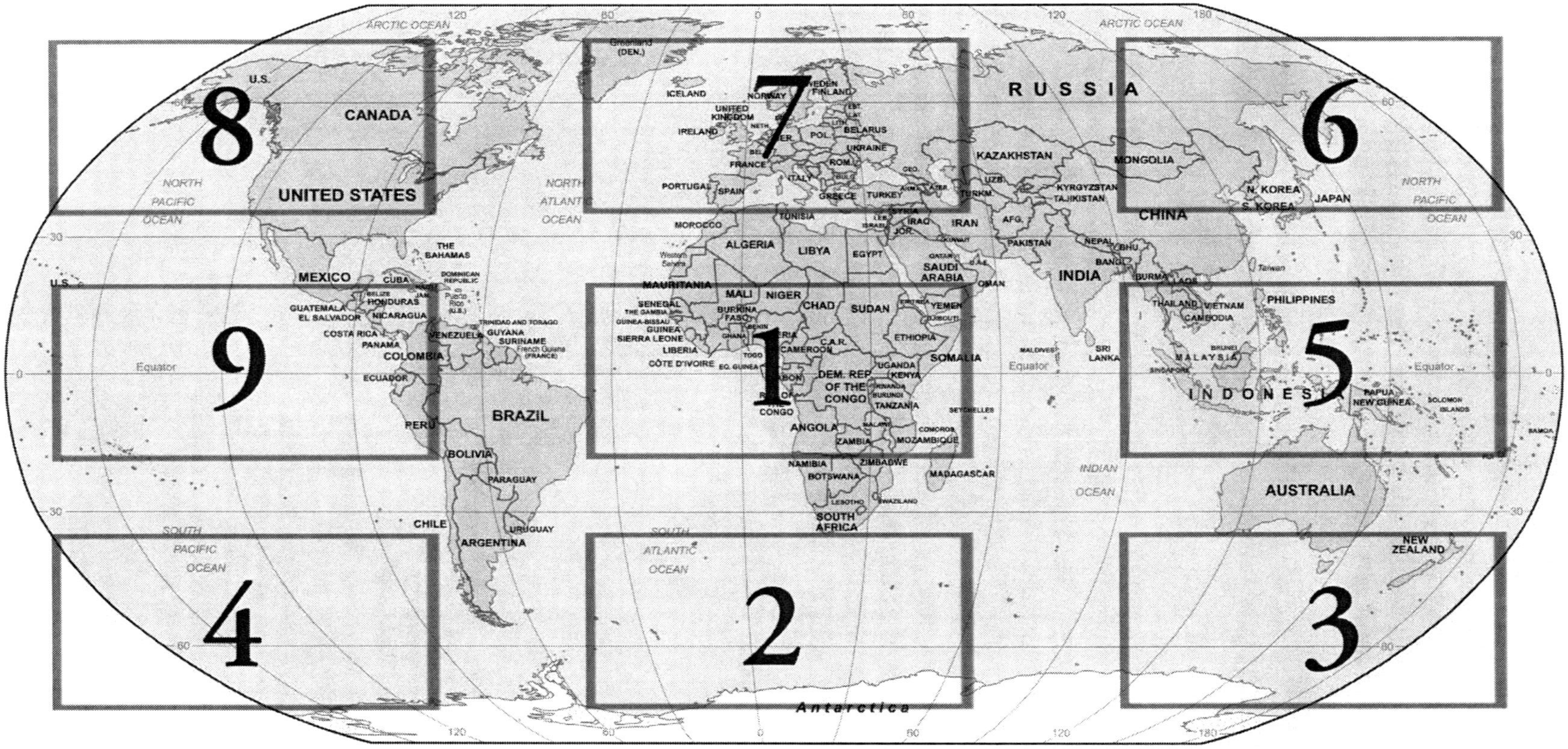

FIGURE 11-C *World Map of the Nine Perfected Movements of Consciousness:* Depicted above is the movement of energy and consciousness through the Eight-Sided Cell of Perfection overlaid on a world map. It shows the possibilities for the movement of the Collective Consciousness. Please note that any place on the earth could be referenced as the center, or the Temple of Being, and in doing so, would create entirely different Consciousness Zones on earth. From this simplistic perspective, observe the different Zones of Consciousness by centering the first movement in Africa, the birthplace of the Aryan, and the second to a southern orientation. Keep in mind, the number two, a feminine numeral, is present in the south, which also corresponds to the birth of femininity. The third movement is to the southeast. This pattern continues to follow the sequence of energy movements described by Saint Germain in The Ever-Present Perfection. Map: *Robinson Projection, not to scale.*

APPENDIX N

The Three Gifts for Kali Yuga:

Kali Yuga is one of the four stages of development the earth experiences as its consciousness evolves (or deteriorates) as the case may be. According to ancient texts, the world entered Kali Yuga, or the *Age of Quarrel,* thousands of years ago when Maharaja Yüdhisthira noticed the Vedic antagonist darkening his kingdom. The king ceded his throne to his grandson Raja Parikshit, and the court, including its wise men, retreated to the Himalayas.

Wise and benevolent souls knew the consequences of these dire times, so the Seers, the Vedic rishis, and the Master Teachers gave humanity the following three gifts: the written word, Vastu Shastra, and Jyotish.

The sages prophesied that humans would suffer from diminished recall and an inability to sustain oral tradition, thus losing historical knowledge to oblivion—that's why they bestowed the alphabet on humanity. Vastu Shastra, the ancient science of geomancy, was the world's second gift. Maharaja Yüdhisthira's exile in the mountains created a dearth of Vastu knowledge among the Hindu people.[13] So, the ancient practice, in effect, reincarnated in another culture. Legend says Vastu Shastra leaped across the Himalayas where it conceived a child—the practice of Feng Shui. Most of all, the wise men knew humanity would need spiritual liberation from the cycle of death: the gift of Jyotish, the personal and intricate science of moksha (liberation). The ancient gurus imparted this knowledge of the soul's journey on earth and its relationship with the astral and causal bodies.

[1] Nancy Rebecca and Yvonne Kilcup, *The Intuitive Mind,* http://www.intuitivemind.org (2005).

[2] Edgar Cayce, *The Edgar Cayce Readings,* http://www.edgarcayce.org, 792-2 (2007).

[3] Juliet Pegrum, *The Vastu Vidya Handbook: The Indian Feng Shui* (New York: Three Rivers Press), page 29.

[4] Jeffrey Armstrong, *God/Goddess the Astrologer: Soul Karma and Reincarnation: How We Continually Create Our Own Destiny* (Badger, CA: Torchlight Publishing), 38-39.

[5] Braha, James, *How to Predict Your Future: Secrets of Eastern and Western Astrology* (Hollywood, FL: Hermetician Press), page 241-243.

[6] Juliet Pegrum, *The Vastu Vidya Handbook: The Indian Feng Shui* (New York: Three Rivers Press), page 10-11.

[7] Ibid., page 56-57.

[8] Ibid., page 49.

[9] Dennis Harness, *The Nakshatras: The Lunar Mansions of Vedic Astrology, First Edition* (Twin Lakes, WI: Lotus Press).

[10] Eva Wong, *Feng Shui: The Ancient Wisdom of Harmonious Living for Modern Times* (Boston: Shambhala Publications, Inc.), page 15-16.

[11] Ibid., page 18.

[12] Ibid., page 59.

[13] Sri Yukteswar, *The Holy Science, Kaivalya Darsanam* (Los Angeles: Self-Realization Fellowship), page 15.

APPENDIX O

Topics and Terms for The Point of Perception

The Relationship of Prophecy to Co-creation and Choice
Collective Consciousness
The Unified Field of Thought
Time Surfing
Teachings on Consciousness and Simultaneous Experiences or Realities
Simultaneous Lifetimes
Shapeshifting
Not Less Than, Equal To
The Dream World: Projection into Conscious Creation
Conscientious Consciousness
Six Earth Changes Scenarios
Perceive—Receive
The Universe Responds without Judgment or Hesitation
Perceptions on the Ageless, Deathless Body

Inner Systems of the Soul:

The science of souls is defined through realities perceived by various systems of the soul, including:

1. *The Soul's Intention:* An overall plan or theme carried forward throughout every lifetime. This intention or destiny evolves over lifetimes.
2. *Individual Purpose:* Each lifetime fulfills a specific purpose. This may be a particular quality or aspect related to the soul's overall intention of growth.
3. *Significance of Choice:* Before a new lifetime, the soul chooses the circumstances of birth, his or her parents, and the time to re-enter the physical plane. The work of Dr. Michael Newton, a life-between-life therapist, has documented this concept extensively:

   "This depends on the nature of the upcoming life, the Karmic lessons to be addressed ... prior to some lives, only one or two body choices are offered, at other visits to the place of life selection they may be given up to five (body choices) ... souls seem to know which body would be their best choice for learning and they usually choose it." [1]

A soul, according to Newton's research, will test various potentials and possibilities in large screening rooms before each lifetime. The examination offers a snapshot of possible events and potentials. Though the certainty of future events isn't written in stone, the soul is already prepared for the opportunities, choices, and challenges in the upcoming lifetime. Newton describes this process as:

> "An indefinite number of futures connected to a present in the now Time of the spirit world. And yet, while there must be many futures, souls seem to view the most likely futures in a matrix of possibilities and probabilities. On the screens, events and opportunities of a future life may be enlarged and drawn out, or reduced in size for soul analysis. It is like looking at the large trunks and smaller branches of trees. I use this analogy because some timelines combined with certain life scenes seem more prominent than others."[2]

4. *Co-creation:* An advanced system, which addresses thought, feeling, and action, utilized by the soul. It directs the soul as a contributing Creator of reality, circumstance, and situation.
5. The application of the *Law of Harmony* (balance) in all situations. The consciousness of the soul is at all times in touch with its intention; therefore, it is aware of the situations and the circumstances of previous lifetimes, and the contexts of future lifetimes. The soul's efforts and actions are often focused on this unconscious yet prevailing knowledge and insight.

Collective Consciousness:

Saint Germain defines collective consciousness as a higher structure or a "higher-arching (hierarchy)" of "individual consciousness." Simply defined as "two or more," collective consciousness is also known as a unified field of thought or Unana among more than one being. [See Unana, Unity Consciousness, Appendix I]. Some define collective consciousness as a field of awareness and intelligence that exists in all human beings. This phenomenon allows our ability to intuitively sense and interact with the physical, emotional, mental, and spiritual energy fields of others, primarily beyond the constraints of space and time. Well-documented examples of this activity include telepathy and remote-viewing.[3] Advanced uses of collective consciousness thought-fields—through the use of focused attention or intention—can create order in physical systems and synchronization among nervous systems. This is known as remote or long-distance healing. Research shows marked reductions in crime rates, drug abuse, traffic fatalities, and unemployment in cities and areas where Transcendental Meditation programs have applied the "pervasive field of collective consciousness." These projects influence coherence and neutralize stress.[4]

Time Surfing:

The ability to adjust experiences in the past, present, or future by intentionally choosing various scenarios and re-languaging them with new perceptions and choices.

Simultaneous Reality:

In the linear world we experience a concrete past and anticipate an unknown future. Therefore, the future pulls us toward our expectations.[5] *Simultaneous reality*, however, is based on a non-linear perspective of time. It prepares us for potential possibilities in all situations—past, present, and future—and retains the capacity for multiple encounters and outcomes. Each reality exists side by side, so humans can consciously open up to these events to gain insight and self-knowledge. Author Lynda Madden Dahl discussed simultaneous reality in her book *The Wizards of Consciousness*: "The sudden answer to a current problem, the strength just when we need it, the optimism that seemed lacking yesterday, but floods today, sometimes comes from other portions of our self who are experiencing those issues." [6]

Diagram for Simultaneous Points of Perception:

(As taught by Saint Germain)

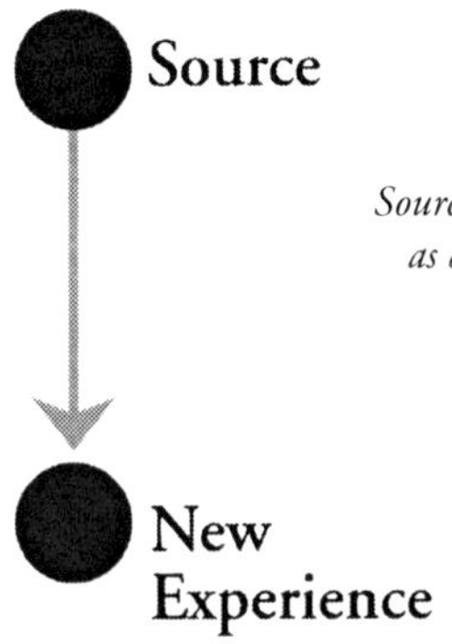

FIGURES 12-A & B
Source, New Experience, and the Web of Creation as diagramed by Saint Germain in the lesson, "The Point of Perception."

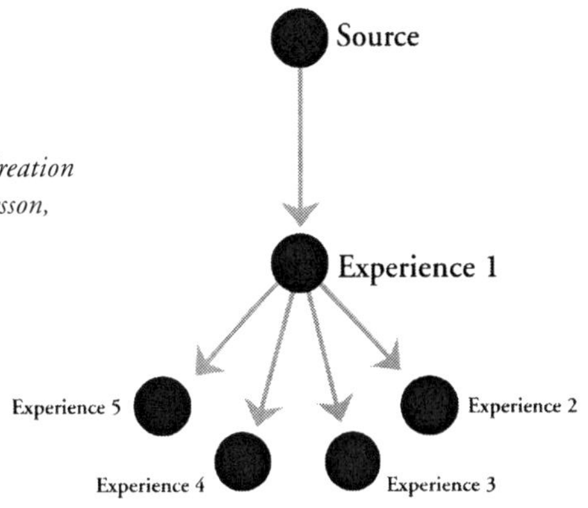

Shape Shifting:

Saint Germain teaches that shapeshifting occurs when we move from one point of perception to another, becoming "necessary to fulfill the desire of creation." John Perkins, founder of Dream Change, identifies the three levels of shapeshifting. [7]

1. *Cellular:* Indigenous people can shapeshift into a plant or an animal. In the modern Western culture, this type of occurrence is analogous to cancer that miraculously disappears. Or losing weight, toning your body through exercise, and changing your physical appearance.
2. *Personal Transformation:* Examples include overcoming an addiction, and spiritual growth, and awakening.
3. *Societal or Cultural Transformation:* Transforming the institutions that shape our lives: corporations, governments, laws, workplaces, businesses, media, schools, and churches. According to the Ascended Masters, this is one of the important purposes of the Golden Cities.

Diagram for Not Less Than, Equal To:

(As taught by Saint Germain. For more information on this technique refer to the lesson, Points of Perception.)

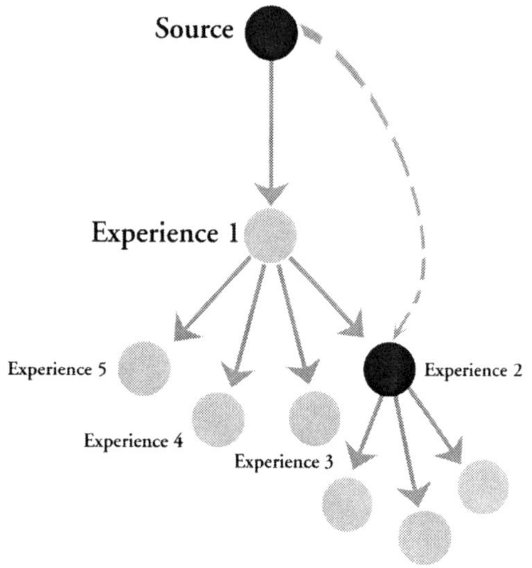

FIGURES 12-C & D
Projection of Light Bodies
"You are equal to."
Diagrams by Saint Germain from the lesson,
"The Point of Perception."

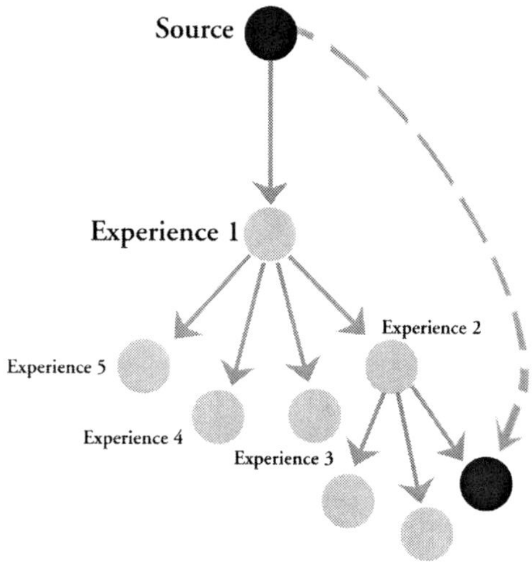

Directed Stream:

Recurring dreams and frequent visits to specific locations in the dream world expand an energy known as directed stream. When a repeated pattern of consciousness occurs, the directed stream suggests that an experience is gaining force and energy. The following examples illustrate this point:

1. Visions
2. Lucid dreaming
3. Out-picturing through meditation and visualization.

A directed stream of consciousness is the outgrowth of developed memory. This expanded use of memory is the result of tapping into the co-creation process through thought, feeling, and action.

Bi-location:

The ability to be in two or more locations simultaneously. This is first achieved through the conscious dream state and meditation techniques. As the consciousness is further trained and developed, physical bi-location is achieved at the cellular level, similar to cellular shapeshifting techniques.

[1] Michael Newton, *Life Between Lives: Hypnotherapy for Spiritual Regression* (St. Paul, MN: Llewellyn Publications), page 176.

[2] Ibid., page 177.

[3] Robert Kenny, *The Science of Collective Consciousness*, http://www.wie.org (2007).

[4] David Orme-Johnson, *Summary of Scientific Research on the Transcendental Meditation and TM-SIDHI Program*, http://www.tm.org (2001).

[5] Lynda Madden Dahl, *The Wizards of Consciousness: Making the Imponderable Practical* (Eugene, OR: The Woodbridge Group), page 119.

[6] Ibid., page 33-34.

[7] John Perkins, *Shapeshifting*, http://www.dreamchange.org (2007).

Bibliography

Agni Yoga Teachings. *A Treasury of Terms and Thoughts,* http://www.agniyoga.org, 1992, 2002.

Armstrong, Jeffrey. *God the Astrologer: Soul, Karma, and Reincarnation—How We Continually Create Our Own Destiny,* New York, NY: Three Rivers Press, 2001.

Bailey, Alice. *Unfinished Autobiography,* New York, NY: Lucis Publishing Company, 1951.

Beckman, Howard. *Vedic Cosmology: The Planets of the Material Universe,* Sedona, AZ: ACVA Journal 7.2, 2002

Braha, James. *How to Predict Your Future: Secrets of Eastern and Western Astrology,* Hollywood, FL: Hermetician Press, 1995.

Bridges, Orin. *Photographing Beings of Light: Images of Nature and Beyond,* Highland City, FL: Rainbow Press, Inc., 1993.

Cayce, Edgar. *The Edgar Cayce Readings,* http://www.edgarcayce.org, 2007.

Dahl, Lynda Madden. *The Wizards of Consciousness: Making the Imponderable Practical,* Eugene, OR: The Woodbridge Group, 1997.

Defouw, Hart. *Light on Life,* London, England: Penguin Books Ltd., 1996.

Dieterle, Richard. *Waterspirits (Wak'teexi),* http://www.hotcakencyclopedia.com/ho.Waterspirits.html, 2005.

Fox, Emmet. *The Sermon on the Mount,* New York, NY: Harper & Row Publishers, 1934.

Hall, Manly. *The Secret Teachings of All Ages,* Los Angeles, CA: Philosophical Research Society, 1989.

Hall, Marie Bauer. *Foundations Unearthed,* originally issued as *Francis Bacon's Great Virginia Vault,* Fourth Edition, Los Angeles, CA: Veritas Press, 1974.

Harness, Dennis. *The Nakshatras: The Lunar Mansions of Vedic Astrology,* First Edition, Twin Lakes, WI: Lotus Press, 1999.

Hawkins, David R. *Power vs. Force, The Hidden Determinants of Human Behavior: An Anatomy of Consciousness,* Sedona, AZ: Veritas Publishing, 1995.

Johnson, Paul K. *The Masters Revealed: Madam Blavatsky and the Myth of the Great White Lodge (Suny Series in Western Esoteric Traditions),* Albany, NY: State University of New York Press, 1994.

Kenny, Robert. *The Science of Collective Consciousness,* http://www.wie.org, 1991-2007.

Keyes, Ken. *The Hundreth Monkey,* http://www.worldtrans.org/pos/monkey.html, 2007.

Kilcup, Yvonne. *The Intuitive Mind,* http://www.intuitivemind.org, 2005.

King, Godfre Ray. *Unveiled Mysteries,* Schaumburg, IL: Saint Germain Press, Inc., 1982.

Knapp, Stephen. *About Vedic Prophecies,* http://www.stephen-knapp.com, 2007.

Luk, A.D.K. *Law of Life, Book I and II,* Pueblo, CO: A.D.K. Luk Publications, 1960.

Müller, Rosemarie. *Heinrich Hofmann Painter of Christ,* http://www.yogananda-srf.org/writings/srm_w2004_pv.html, 2007.

Newton, Michael. *Life Between Lives: Hypnotherapy for Spiritual Regression*, St. Paul, MN: Llewellyn Publications, 2004.

Orme-Johnson, David. *Summary of Scientific Research on the Transcendental Meditation and TM-SIDHI Program,* http://www.tm.org, 2001.

Ouspensky, P. D. *In Search of the Miraculous: Fragments of an Unknown Teaching,* New York, NY: Harcourt Brace Jovanovich, Publishers, 1976.

Papastavro, Tellis S. *The Gnosis and the Law,* Tucson, AZ: Group Avatar, 1972.

Pegrum, Juliet. *The Vastu Vidya Handbook: The Indian Feng Shui*, New York, NY: Three Rivers Press, 2000.

Perkins, John. *Shapeshifting,* http://www.dreamchange.org, 2003-2007.

Rebecca, Nancy. *The Intuitive Mind,* http://www.intuitivemind.org, 2005.

Sutherland, Mary. *In Search of Shambhala,* http://www.livinginthelightms.com, 2003.

True, Aumear. *EarthStar, A Treasure Map Rediscovered:* Ashland, OR: Rosetta Publishing, 1995.

Toye, Lori.

I AM America Map of Earth Changes, [I AM America Map]. Scale: From Rand McNally Cosmopolitan Series, reduction is 53%. Payson, AZ, I AM America Seventh Ray Publishing, International, 1989.

A Starseed, 1991.

Freedom Star: Prophecies That Heal Earth, Payson, AZ; I AM America Seventh Ray Publishing, International, 1995.

New World Atlas: Earth Changes for a Planet in Transition, Volume Two, Payson, AZ: I AM America Seventh Ray Publishing, International, 1993.

New World Atlas: Earth Changes for a Planet in Transition, Volume Three, Payson, AZ: I AM America Seventh Ray Publishing, International, 1996.

I AM America Six Map Scenario: Detailed Prophecies of Earth Change Progressions to the I AM America Map, [6-Map Scenario]. Scale not given. Payson, AZ: I AM America Seventh Ray Publishing, International, 1997.

I AM America: United States Golden Cities. Scale not given. Payson, AZ: I AM America Seventh Ray Publishing, International, 1998.

Wong, Eva. *Feng-shui: The Ancient Wisdom of Harmonious Living for Modern Times*, Boston, MA: Shambhala Publications, 1996.

Yukteswar, Sri. The Holy Science, Kaivalya Darsanam, Los Angeles, CA: Self-Realization Fellowship, 1984.

Discography

This list provides the recording session date and name of the original selected recordings cited in this work that provide the basis for its original transcriptions.

Toye, Lori

Earth Healing, Earth Healing - Forgiveness, I AM America Seventh Ray Publishing International Audiocassette. © ℗ No. 062294, June 22, 1994.

Love's Service, I AM America Seventh Ray Publishing International, Audiocassette. © July 11,1994.

Changing the Guard, I AM America Seventh Ray Publishing International, Audiocassette. © October 27, 1994.

The Fourth Dimension, Fourth Dimension - Teachings on the Golden Cities, I AM America Seventh Ray Publishing International, Audiocassette. © ℗ No. 071495, 1994.

The Work of a Master, I AM America Seventh Ray Publishing International, Audiocassette. © November 22, 1994.

No Need for Change?, I AM America Seventh Ray Publishing International, Audiocassette. © December 30, 1994.

Weaving the New Web, I AM America Seventh Ray Publishing International, Audiocassette. © May 29, 1995.

Golden City Classes, I AM America Seventh Ray Publishing International, Audiocassette. © July 14, 1995.

Vibrational Shifting, I AM America Seventh Ray Publishing International, Audiocassette. © August 7, 1995.

Closing the Circle, I AM America Seventh Ray Publishing International, Audiocassette. © August 17, 1995.

Dooms Day—Peace Day, I AM America Seventh Ray Publishing International, Audiocassette. © October 10, 1995.

The Fountain of Life, I AM America Seventh Ray Publishing International, Audiocassette. © September 27, 1996.

The First Golden City, Three Shamballa Messages, I AM America Seventh Ray Publishing International, Audiocassette. © ℗ No. 500, 1996.

The Ever-Present Perfection, I AM America Seventh Ray Publishing International, Audiocassette. © December 11, 1996.

The Point of Perception, The Point of Perception, I AM America Seventh Ray Publishing International, Audiocassette. © ℗ No. 102497, 1997.

Index

A

Absolute Harmony, 38
definition, 151
abundance, 55, 127
Acceleration, 26, 35, 56
dimension, 91
dimensional, 229
of energies, 19
planetary, 35
Activation, 25, 26
ceremonial, 82
"is the seed, the Start", 85
active intelligence, 36
Addiction, 91, 93, 100
patterns, 144
adept, 84
definition, 151
adjutant points, 35
Gobean Northern Door, 217
African tribal peoples, 83
Age of Aquarius, 75
Age of Cooperation, 64, 65
definition, 151
Age of Peace
definition, 151
Age of Reason, 65, 203
aggregate body of light, 77, 81
definition, 151
agreement, 18
Air, 37, 110, 122, 184
purification, 56
Akashic Records, 226
Alaska, 95
Alchemy, 38, 48
definition, 151
Fourth Dimension, 35
of the soul, 33
Aleutian
Islands, 95
time-bridge, 83
alien technologies, 60
alignment
assimilation, 27
definition, 151
A.M. Current, 196
America
destiny, 73, 206
history, 32
Animal Kingdom, 26, 80
apex
definition, 151
archetypes, 86
Arizona water supplies, 111
Aryan, 23, 36, 175, 177, 267
definition, 151
Ascended Master
consciousness linked to ours, 136
definition, 151, 192
"guard the evolution of humanity at this time", 130
"intent and our service", 60
manifestation in Stars, 72
Mission, 47
role in assisting humanity and the Earth, 194
shamans of energy movement, 130
Ascension, 44, 45, 47, 70, 73 *See also Fourth Dimension; See also Klehma: Golden City of*
"attaches to what is real", 83
definition, 151
global, 48, 77, 83
mass, 48, 206
mass rapture, 54, 195
physical, 110, 238
Ascension Valley, 195
Asking Permission, the Rule of, 116, 244
asleep, 105
asteroid, 53
Astral
body, 94
plane, 100
projection, 95
Atlantean, 23, 36, 176, 206
Atlantis, 36, 73
New, 181
At-One-Ment, 244
attention, 119
attraction, 35
attributes
hope, faith, trust, and love, 86
Aura, 25, 56, 78, 135, 138
definition, 151
auric vision, 48
Australia
crop failures, 109
avatar
definition, 152
Awaken
the greater memory, 141
"to the conditions that exist outside", 62
awakened
"many in the twilight hours", 112
Awakening, 104
critical Time of, 50
fear of, 105
Prayer, 197
Awareness, 47
open, 48
Ayadi, 260

B

Babajeran, 32
definition, 152, 169
Mother Earth, 46, 81, 128
Bacon, Sir Francis, 180
Bailey, Alice, 223
Balance, 45, 87, 111
definition, 152
perfect, 129
walking in, 117
Ballard, Guy, 245
bartering, 34, 184
beauty, 117
belief systems, 116
Belt of Golden Light, 69
definition, 152
bi-location, 35, 47, 146, 275
definition, 152

birth pains, 65
Blavatsky, H. P., 221, 223
body
dropping of, 145 *See also death: consciousness departs*
Bohr, Niels, 261
Bosnia, 109
breath, 40
Brotherhood and Sisterhood of the Light, 33
Brotherhood of Darkness, 33
business practices, 24

C

camps of orphans, 40
Canada, 32, 70
crop failures, 109
capstone, 108, 112, 237
Cascade Mountains, 18
cause and effect, 127
causeless cause, 54
causes, 44
Cayce, Edgar, 256
Celebration of the Four Elements, 250
Cellular
Acceleration, 110
definition, 238
Awakening, 56, 92, 110
definition, 152, 195
memory, 31, 33
Central America, 32
Ceremony, 73, 123
Cup, 124, 251
definition, 152
for Closure, 101, 234
gathering in, 57
Star of Gobean, 111
symbols, 103
Chains
"broken through the initiation of experience", 109
Chakra
definition, 152
Chakras, 27, 37
system, 91
Chamber of the Heart, 255
Change, 36, 62, 69, 103, 117
political and social systems
United States, 92
psychological body of humanity, 92
changes within the heart, 24, 32
"change your mind
change your existence", 49
channeled information, 84
Charity
acts of, 88
chela
definition, 152
chi, 110, 261 *See also prana*
definition, 152
children, 60, 127
flame within their hearts, 55
spiritual guidance, 191
Chohan
definition, 152
Choice, 26, 32, 34, 41, 45, 54, 66, 73, 79, 95, 97, 102, 105, 128, 271
and addictions, 100
and circumstances of birth, 133
"Men have the choice to create truth or ignorance.", 143
time-surfing, 135
Christ, 23, 119
"breaks all barriers", 65
consciousness, 87, 219
definition, 152
nine movements of energy, 126
servants of the devoted, 55
the energy of, 19
Unana, 69
Christian biblical Prophecy, 88
Christ Self, 242, 255
churches, 105
cinnamon, 25
Circle of Known
definition, 152
citrus, 56
City of White, 247
civil unrest, 108
youth, 109
Classical Chinese Feng Shui, 260, 262, 268
Nine Palaces
flow of energy, 265
closure, 101
Closure Ceremony, 234
Co-creation
definition, 152, 272
rhythm, 137
six possible realities, 141
Co-Creator *See HU-man*
"What you see, you have created.", 134
Collective
choice, 92
consciousness, 32, 46, 53, 79, 82, 131
and Prophecy, 134
definition, 152, 272
fallen to lower states, 116
illustration, 267
leap in, 19
healing, 27
mind, 104
thought, 20
will, 54
color
aquamarine, 71
Gold, 56, 71
green, 27, 56
violet, 27
commitment, 26
common sense, 37, 65, 112
compassion, 38, 39, 92
competition, 61, 67
conflict
spiritual guidance, 192
conscience
definition, 152
conscience and consciousness, 102

Consciousness, 19, 36, 38, 41, 72, 82, 87, 105, 116, 134
conscientious, 140
definition, 152, 177
focal point, 79, 142
mass, 26
movement, 126
of choice, 33
of death, 115
projecting, 136
training and ingraining, 144
"Consciousness can change all things.", 41
control, 27
cooperation, 61, 80
natural, 83
Cosmic Teachers
definition, 152
Cosmic Teachers for Earth, 126
Cosmic Wave Motion, 71, 217 *See also Time Compaction*
definition, 152
Council of the Great Violet Flame, 33
courage, act of backing away, 54
creation
"is held in thought", 75
crime, 34, 61
critical point, 250
Cup, 28, 42
definition, 153
of conscious light, 73
of Life, 42
Cycle, 219
ending, 95
"the sequence of birth, growth, maturity, decay", 87
"we cannot alter the cycle" we can alter the outcome of cycles..., 87

D

Dahl,Lynda, 273
dark
Brotherhood, 37
force, 41
and the media, 108
government, 37, 41
definition, 153
Dead Zone, 101, 104
definition, 153
Death
and illusion, 118
cadence
"breakdown is inevitable", 93
consciousness
departs, 145
erase, 40
programs, 116
Decision of 1952, 35
decree, 38, 242
power of sound, 115
descent and ascent of spirit, 45
desire
definition, 153
despair, 109
Destiny, 33, 97, 111, 112
fulfilling, 95
"in the heart of divinity", 62
Devas, 80
defined, 200
definition, 153
Dharma
definition, 153
dietary changes, 25, 172
difference, 64
Dimensional
Acceleration, 229
leaping, 71, 138
Shift, 31, 32
dimensions, 36, 43, 47
Directed Stream
defintion, 275
discipline, 65, 70
"necessary for the survival", 66
disease, 112
definition, 153
western and southwestern winds, 238
disembodied spirits, 100
definition, 153
disharmony, 24
dissolution of patterns, 28
Divine
Cloak
definition, 153
Conception, 19
human, 118
inheritor, 33
Mission, 238
Mother, 64
definition, 153
Spark
definition, 153
divinity
definition, 153
DNA, 31, 36, 105
changes in, 184
sound and language, 61
doubt, 117, 143
dove, 25
definition, 153
"down with death", 40, 115
dream
lucid, 139
of the mind, 41
state, 95
world, 138
dreaming, 94
lucid, 275
Druid cultures, 81, 83
duality, 39, 99, 127
definition, 153

E

Eabra
Golden City of, 70, 82
definition, 153
ear, 43
Earlier Heaven Pa-k'ua, 263

earth
element, 103
energy movement magnetic poles, 125
leaps in consciousness, 71
Earth Changes, 35, 40, 53, 73, 92
Alaska, 95
and perception, 145
aquifers, 37
Arizona fires, 111, 238
Ascended Master intervention, 239
ash, 37
averting, 111
California, 108, 237
Cascade Mountains, 32, 166
crop failures, 109
definition, 153
Europe, 110, 238
Gulf of Mexico, 32
Indonesia, 32
Mount Rainier, 32
Mount St. Helen, 32
Nevada, 41
new diseases, 112
New Mexico, 41
North America coastline, 32
nuclear explosion, 109
Pacific Rim, 32
Polar and Dimensional Shifts, 184
price wars, 109
rains, 110
Ring of Fire, 32, 37, 109, 183, 238
rivers and streams, 37
Sea of Okhotsk, 109
Seventh Moon, 183
six possibilities, 141
social and political change, 112
violence, 109
Earth Changes Prophecies, 220, 231, 253
Earth Healing
technique, 56
Earth Plane
definition, 153
Earth's
Wobble and Precession, 258
Earth's
Core, 125
Grid, 208
definition, 153
East, 126
Eastern Door, 74
definition, 153
economy
balanced, 60
invest in natural resources, 34
"effervescent life
I AM", 116
ego, 26
Egypt, 78, 258
Egyptian mystics, 80
eight
earth in duality, 125
Eighth light body, 71, 205
defined, 216
definition, 154
Eighth Ray, 195
Eight-Sided Cell of Perfection, 125
abundance, 127
and healing, 127
and the Unfed Flame, 126
and Unity Consciousness, 253
children, 127
choice, 128
consciousness movement, 126
defined, 255
definition, 153
Divine Heavens, 127
Divine Path-Dharma, 126
"each of these directions
is a spiritual discipline", 128
eight perfect mirrors, 125
energy map, 266
family, 127
flow of energy, 266
four directions, 126
macrocosm, 127
Map, 254
marriage, 127
microcosm
the remaining five directions, 127
occupation, 128
perfect focus, 130
Star of Knowledge, 128
Temple of Being, 126
the Christ, 126
"two become as one", 127
World Energy Map, 267
elections misconduct, 34
electrical field of the body, 25
electromagnetic shocking, 25
Elementals, 20, 80
defined, 200
definition, 154
El Morya, 26, 80, 117, 122, 131, 221
definition, 154
Gobean, 78
Elohim, 20
definition, 154
Emergent Evolution, 35
emotion, 94
Emotional body, 135
definition, 154
higher, 94
Energy
alignment, 28
Field Balancing, 194
definition, 154
forms
injurious words, 67
"moves through light, sound", 129
shifting
Dimensional Plane-ing, 93
stagnant and dead, 129
unstable, 37
Vortices
chakras of the planet, 35
Energy Fields
definition, 154
Energy Lines, 259
Energy Maps, 262–268

environment, 62
pollution, 56
Europe, 33
Evolution *See Laws of Attraction and Repulsion*
and spiritual teachers, 127
of humanity, 20
expanding consciousness, 46
experience, 135
adjusting, 134
of many embodiments, 45
Expressive Intuition, 256

F

family, 19, 26, 60
fear, 26, 55, 66, 87, 89, 99, 101, 108, 109, 110, 220
and churches, 105
feeling, 94, 129
feminine
definition, 154, 255
feminine energy, 33, 38, 65, 130
Fifth Dimension, 18
definition, 154
finances
spiritual guidance, 191
fire element, 103
fireless light, 124
Fires of Initiation, 39
fish
in the diet, 28
Flame
of desire, 41
of Freedom, 33
flesh, 28
meat eating and vibration, 26
Flower Kingdom, 80
focus, 26, 142
food
elements of light, 25
requiring less, 37
Forgiveness, 23, 24, 26, 115
defined, 244
"is not turning the other cheek", 118
"spend time in silence", 55
Fountain of Life, 116, 244 *See also Ascension*
Fountain of Youth, 116, 117
Four Directions, 126
Fourth Dimension, 18, 19, 32, 35, 36, 39, 44, 45, 116, 187, 243 *See also Ascension; See also Golden City Vortices*
definition, 154
Klehma *See Ascension*
Fourth Dimensional Consciousness, 35
fragrances
violets, jasmine, cinnamon, 25
Freedom, 34, 81 *See also Wahanee: Golden City of*
Flame, 73
definition, 154
Star, 249
definition, 154
the new Earth, 71, 206
"truth is pathless", 88
Freedom Star Map
definition, 154
Free Energy, 37
definition, 154
Free Will, 33, 72, 87, 96
qualification of energy, 125
Fu Hsi, 261

G

Galactic
Beam, 195
Web, 75, 110, 124, 168
definition, 155
Garden of Eden, 249
gardens, 81
genetic code, 33
geometric languages, 33
definition, 155
geo-sensitive
definition, 155
ghosts, 100
Giza, 226
Glastonbury, 81, 226
Global Warming, 110
Gobean
Golden City of, 24, 26, 36, 69, 72, 121, 250
ceremonial work, 111
definition, 155
geology, 168
Shamballa, Egypt, 78
harmony and cooperation, 79
purpose, 80
Gobi, 121, 247
Desert, 248
God
"true son of", 119
Gold, 130
light, 25
Golden Age, 206, 250, 253, 255
Pole Shift, 130
"the time beyond the changes", 131
Golden Belt, 194
Golden City Vortex, 167, 171, 206
definition, 155
Perspective Diagram, 216
Plan View Diagram, 216
Ray Force diagram, 227
Golden City Vortices, 36, 46, 69, 219 *See also Ascension*
activation, 69, 124, 174
Ascended Master, 207
ceremonial, 207
geophysical, 207
Great Central Sun, 208
ancient cultures, 226
apex, 71, 110
ceremonial activations, 70
classes, 79
connect with a Master Teacher, 113
consciousness of neutrality, 48
doorways
Black Door, 211
Blue Door, 211
Red Door, 213
Yellow Door, 214
Earth Healing, 57
electromagnetism, 78

lighted stance, 71
living in, 113
moving to, 50
preparation, 71
Roles During the Prophecies of Change, 220
Spiritual Migration, 113
The Star, 71, 111, 215, 238, 250
Golden Flame
definition, 155
Government
alien, 60
"based upon the laws of harmony", 61
games, 34
inner circle, 53
money and greed, 53
Wahanee's role, 81
grace
definition, 155
"grace after siege", 43
Great Central Sun, 194
definition, 194
Great Purification
by fire, 53
Great Reason, 77, 221
Great White Brotherhood, 46, 62, 192, 249, 250
definition, 155
Great White Lodge, 108, 119
An Invitation, 193
Greed, 33
thirst for
"when these two ignorances are wiped", 63
Grey Man, 40
definition, 155
"grow your own food", 37
Guardian Angel, 242
guilt, 28, 119
guru
death of, 119, 243
definition, 155

H

Harmony, 38, 80, 100
definition, 155
First Jurisdiction, 134
of the spheres, 18
perfect, 125
predestiny, 97
"two or more", 134
with Nature Kingdom, 81
hate, 119
Hatha Yoga, 36, 176
headache
Cellular Awakening, 56
healing *See Eight-Sided Cell of Perfection*
planetary, 67
health care involvement, 57
health systems, 61
Heart
awakening, 77
blood of the, 41
Nine Movements, 126
of Humanity, 23
of Intent, 23
of Love, 25, 26
open, 77
Heart's Desire, 54
Helios and Vesta, 20
definition, 155
Hermetic Law, 124, 127, 137
definition, 155, 188
hierarchy, 138
higher frequencies, 20
Higher Self, 242
high-pitched ringing
Cellular Awakening, 56
Hilarion, 41
definition, 155
hitaka
definition, 155
holograms
of perfection, 126
holographic
body
used by Ascended Masters, 47
patterns
dissolving, 28
holo-leaping, 169
honeysuckle, 56
HU-man, 26, 79, 119, 221
definition, 155
humanity
"on the brink of Devastation", 117

I

I AM, 26
defined, 155, 241
Forgiveness
the calming effect, 49
land, 33
Presence, 255
definition, 156
Race, 33, 182
definition, 156, 176
the word, 115
I AM America, 57
Mission of Peace, 108
I AM America Map, 107
definition, 156
Iamblicus, 67, 203
I-Ching, 261
illusion, 41
and death, 118
immaculate concept, 73
incarnation process, 40
India, 83
indigenous people
North and South America, 83
individuality, 96
definition, 231
sovereign, 119
individualized, 54, 81, 110
definition, 156
Indus River, 83
Infinity, 128
Ninth Direction, 128
initiation, 41

injustice, 118
Inner-self
  cleansing, 80
Inner Spark, 20
insanity, 34, 94, 184
  symptom of vibrational shifting, 91
integrity, 61
intention, 38, 111
Intuitive Mind, 255
Involution of Consciousness, 20

J

jasmine, 25, 56
Jiva, 21, 23, 74
  definition, 156
joy
  "is lived each day as chosen", 82
judgment, 26, 119
Jyotish, 268

K

Kali-Yuga, 268
Karma, 20, 32, 41, 179
  definition, 156
  past, 173
Keyes, Ken, 235
Klehma
  Golden City of, 19, 25, 70, 73, 82
    definition, 156
Kuan Yin, 18, 23, 34, 38, 43, 64, 149
  definition, 156
  "perfect harmony with a perfect path", 131
Kuthumi, 32, 80, 81, 222
  definition, 156
  K. H., 119
Kybalion
  Hermetic Philosophy, 188

L

labor, 70
land, 34
Later Heaven Pa-k'ua, 264
laws
  micro and macro, 104
Law(s) of
  Alchemy, 49, 118
  Attraction, 102
  Attraction and Repulsion, 99, 233
    definition, 156
  Balance, 39, 110, 238
  Cause and Effect, 20, 32, 39, 44, 45, 49, 238
    definition, 156, 189
  Ceremonial Order and Alchemy, 43
  Change, 49
  Cooperation, 19
  Correspondence, 43, 45, 188
    As above, so below., 39, 104
    definition, 156
    lower and higher dimensions are both present, 47
  Death and Rebirth, 99
    definition, 156
  Divine Inheritor, 38
  Energy for Energy, 243
  Forgiveness, 23, 34
  Gender, 189
  Grace, 17
  Harmony, 17, 166, 272
  Love, 38, 80, 89, 220
    definition, 156
  Mentalism, 188
  Momentum, 104
  Octaves, 93
    definition, 156
    the Law of Seven, 230
  Opposites, 73, 218
    definition, 156
  Perfection, 67
  Polarity, 49
    definition, 156, 189
  Purification
    Forgiveness, 118
  Repulsion
    the contrary, 102
  Rhythm, 43, 45, 48, 93, 99, 137, 189
    "all things change", 49
    definition, 156
  Synchronicity
    "all things are effect of causes", 46
    definition, 156
  Transmutation
    Forgiveness, 118
  Truth, 34
  Vibration, 39, 189
  Violet Flame, 48
leadership, 60
lei-lines, 35, 219
  definition, 157
  wobble factor, 259
Lemuria
  definition, 157
Lemurian, 23, 36, 176
Lenz's Law, 234
Liberty, 41
Liberty and Freedom
  versus monarchy, 34
life, 40
Light, 49
  bodies
    adding, 138
    create physical bodies, 146
  body, 48, 135
    activation, 78
    definition, 157
  definition, 157
  government, 41
  "love in action", 81
Lighted Stance
  definition, 157
Literal Intuition, 256
Lords of the Flame, 248
Lords of Venus, 20, 23, 24, 39, 170, 173, 179
  definition, 157

lotus
definition, 157
Love, 23, 25, 38, 50, 61, 110
definition, 157
Love, Wisdom, and Power, 129
luminaries
sun and moon, 81
lungs, 37
lymphatic system, 25

M

Magadha, 226
magnetism
ceremony, 102
male domination
consciousness, 130
Maltese Cross, 74
definition, 157
Malton *See Glastonbury*
Golden City of, 25, 70, 73, 80, 220
definition, 157
Mantle of Consciousness
definition, 157
Map(s) of
Rings, 221
Creation Grid, 78
Marriage, 60, 126
Inner, 38, 65, 96, 169 *See also Thought, Feeling, and Action*
masculine energy, 65
definition, 157
Master K.H., 40
Masters, 41
Master Teacher
definition, 157
Mastery, 39, 54, 57, 110
definition, 157
"over their created world", 130
through the eight paths of perfection, 131
"through the spiral of evolution comes increased duty", 130
your web of creation, 139
materiality
"realize the paradise revealed within", 109
maturation process through light
fruits and vegetables, 25
media, 108
meditation, 26, 27
memory, 45
conscientious, 141
developing, 139
full, 140
Mental
block, 143
Body, 135
definition, 157
overwhelmed, 94
Mental Equivalent, 189
mentalism, 129, 188, 256
Mercy, 26
Micah
Great Angel of Unity, 225
mind
creates the body, 104
definition, 158
Mineral Kingdom, 26, 27, 80
mirroring
definition, 158
Mission, Divine, 110
Missions, 85
Monad, 18, 20, 23, 24, 26, 33, 36, 42, 74, 138, 139
definition, 158
moon, 92
Mother Earth
"time's servant of change", 112
Mother Mary, 19, 64, 66
definition, 158
Mount Meru, 177
music
energy and vibration, 129
mystery schools
development of, 179

N

nadis, 242
nakshatra, 260
Native Americans, 83, 219, 226 *See also Klehma: Golden City of*
natural resources, 34
Nature
humanity's lessons, 35
negative energy, 41
neutrality, 45
Nevada, 41, 95
New Age, 63
definition, 158
New Dimensions, 35, 116, 184
New Mexico, 41
new species, 205
Newton, Dr. Michael, 271
north
"direction humanity is facing", 126
Northern Door, 70
definition, 158
North Pole, 253
nuclear war, 53, 238

O

octaves, 99
Omni-essence, 40, 50, 59
omnipresence, 40
definition, 158
omniscience
definition, 158
ONE, 24, 33, 37, 45, 50, 61, 64, 79, 96, 131, 134, 137, 140, 171
Cellular Awakening, 56
definition, 158
servants of, 55
"the One truth, which is within", 105
One-hundredth monkey, 104, 235
Oneship, 18, 23, 26, 34, 55, 59
definition, 158
One World Government, 60
Open Ears, Open Eyes
definition, 158

open heart
definition, 158
opening the heart, 46, 50
Open Society, 61, 200
opposites
attracting, 99
orange blossom, 56
out-picturing, 79, 130, 139, 143, 275
definition, 158
Over-soul, 255

P

pakua, 261
paper money, 34
parenting, 60
past
and future, 43
past life, 45
Path of Adeptship, 42
Path of Unities, 102
Peace, 25, 36, 63, 108
"is ready to burst from every heart", 109
"peace out of turmoil", 43
perceive
definition, 158
Perceive-Receive, 142
Perception, 88, 135
creates reality, 136
Point of, 136, 142
bi-location, 146
creating bodies, 145
points of
diagram, 273
shifting, 137
Perfection *See Violet Flame*
"perfection mirrors more perfection", 125
the principle of, 255
perfect thought, 19
perfect world, 59
Perkins, John, 274
Permission
The Rule of Asking, 244
perseverance, 139
pesticides and chemicals
in food, 37
petrochemicals, 60
physical immortality, 35
physical life, 40
physiology
changes, 25
Pillar of Forgiveness, 28
Pillar of Light
definition, 158, 242
pineal gland, 36, 116
Plane of Cause, 44
Plane of Neutrality, 48
Point of Perception
definition, 158
polarity, 33, 45
poles
magnetic, 125
Pole shift, 35, 184
and Consciousness Shift, 116
south orientation, 130
westerly directions, 130
Pole Star, 258
Political and Social systems
changes, 92
outcomes of Earth Changes, 92
Portia, 70, 82, 131
definition, 159
"practice makes permanent", 66
prana, 37, 110, 259
definition, 159
prayer, 26, 27, 88
precession, 259
predestination, 97
prediction
definition, 159
presidential elections
prophecies, 92
price wars
gas and food, 109
projection
into dream-world, 139
Prophecies of Change, 32, 131, 184, 190, 205, 230, 233, 237, 250, 253
Prophecies of Peace, 17, 24, 25, 26, 32, 108, 165, 171
Cellular Awakening, 56
"constantly hold the vision for a new world", 109
Paradise, 26
Prophecy, 33, 87, 133
definition, 159
given for the present moment, 88
purpose of, 59
"strives to unite love and hate", 86
"The Time is Now!", 134
"you create your Prophecy each day of your life", 88
Prophecy Conference, 107, 237
Prophet, 60
the work of, 55
psychic prediction, 87
purification, 41, 118
purpose, 271

Q

Quickening, 195

R

Racial unrest, 108
Phoenix, 108
Ray
definition, 159
Golden Cities, 79
reality
altering, 140
Reappearance of the Masters, 243
recognition, 101
patterns, 103
re-embodiment
definition, 159
Refreshing Drink
definition, 159, 245
remote healing, 272
republic, 200
response
to vibration, 47
retreats, 46
Revelations, Book of, 105, 177

rights taken, 35
right to vote, 34
Ring of Fire
  definition, 159
rite of passage, 101
Rooms of Consciousness, 47
rose
  definition, 159
  hips, 26
  "lotus of the west", 75
  quartz, 27
rosemary, 28
Rosicrucians, 33, 180
  definition, 159
Russia, 109, 238

S

Sacred planet, 67
  definition, 203
sacrifice, 70, 110
Sahara Desert
  Ancient Civilizations, 226
Saint Germain
  adjusting the energy, 32
  and the Violet Flame, 149
  definition, 159
  Holy Brother, 33, 180
  Kajaeshra, 181
  Map of Political Changes, 181
  Sanctus Germanus, 33
Salamanders, 201
salt-water
  baths, 28, 92
Sananda, 34, 41, 54, 63, 70, 100
  biography and picture, 225
  definition, 159
  "I fear not, for the I AM is with me.", 109
  "in order to pour new wine", 142
  outpicturing of the Christ, 82
  "the difference is the experience", 136
  "two or more", 79
Sanat Kumara, 172, 247
  definition, 159
sandalwood, 28, 56
Sattva, 43, 55
  definition, 159
  harmonious response to vibration, 44
saturn, 173
Seal of Solomon, 123
Seamless Garment, 77, 221
  definition, 159
  light bodies, 145
self-awareness
  "the right way is always coming forward", 97
"Send this message to the earth with love.", 41, 54
Serapis Bey, 70, 82, 83, 223, 248
  definition, 160
service, 24, 28, 40, 50, 72, 84, 97
Servile Planet, 67
  definition, 203
seven plagues
  "the first of", 108
Seventh
  dimension
    consciousness, 35
  Manu, 20, 21, 169
    definition, 160
  Moon, 32
    definition, 160
  Ray, 43
Shalahah
  Golden City of, 25, 26, 70, 82, 220
    definition, 160
    geology, 168
    role during the times of most tumultuous change, 82
shaman
  definition, 160
Shamballa, 59, 121, 172, 179, 247
  Celebration of the Four Elements, 250
  definition, 160
  Eternal Flame, 250
  Message, 199
Shape-Shifting, 137, 274
sheeple, 41
Sierra Madres, 18
Simultaneous
  embodiment, 135
  experience, 135, 141
    definition, 160
  reality, 141
    definition, 273
Sir Francis Bacon, 33
Sisterhood of the Light, 46
Sister Thedra, 225
Six-Map Scenario
  definition, 160
Soleteta
  definition, 160, 202
  the divine feminine, 65
Solomon's Temple, 181
Soul
  choices, 111
  completing lessons, 103
  cycles, 45
  definition, 160
  families, 251
  group, 123
  Inner Systems of, 271
  lessons, 99
  Mates, 86, 226
    definition, 160
soul's intention, 271
Sound
  higher frequency, 43
  music, 129
  vibration, 102
  voice, 129
Source and Destination, 72
  definition, 160
south, 126
South America, 32
Southern Door, 74
  definition, 161
South Pole, 253
Spark of Freedom, 60, 110
speech patterns, 115

Spiritual
Awakening, 39, 56, 104
definition, 161
fire, 123, 251
Hierarchy, 46
definition, 161
intervention, 53
Kingdom
words from, 50
Migration
definition, 161 *See also Golden City Vortices*
preparedness, 36
Prophecies, 219, 239, 243, 253
teachers, 127
spoken word, 38, 67
sponsorship
definition, 161
Star, 206
definition, 161
Star of Knowledge, 128
Star of the Magi, 122, 209
Star seed consciousness, 70 *See also Golden City Vortices*
defined, 161, 209
Step-down Transformer, 242
definition, 196
"stewards of a greater plan", 47
storage of water, 37
stress, 25
Subjective Energy Bodies, 28, 100, 144
definition, 161, 234
suffering, 39, 63
sunlight
carries energy, 129
sunrise, sunset, 27
Symbols
repeat the new law, 103
Shamballa, 123
universal language, 103

T

taxation, 61
temple, 126
Temple of Mercy, 149
Temples of the Seven Rays, 248
Terra
definition, 161
Mother Earth
intergalactic destiny, 66
Thinning of the Veil, 40
Third and Fourth dimension, 35, 91
Third Dimension, 19
third eye
definition, 161
opening, 56
Thought, 67, 73
moves light, 129
"perfect union with sound is known as feeling", 129
the seed of all creation, 49
unifed field of, 134
use to contain emotion, 94
Thought, Feeling, and Action, 96, 104, 115, 241
definition, 161
movers of light and sound, 129
the Mighty Three, 70
Time, 93, 134 *See also dimensional plane-ing*
and the co-creation process, 134
Compaction, 71, 206, 217
definition, 161
"is a web", 147
"marches on and changes all things", 112
of Awakening, 21
of Changes, 35, 37, 41
definition, 161
of Peace, 21
of Transition, 20, 24, 35, 45, 53, 78
"a time when choice awakens the will", 104
definition, 162, 187
timekeeping systems
changes in, 71
toxicity
food substances, 25
Transfiguration, 71 *See also Eighth light body*
definition, 162
Transformation, 244
Transmitters
of energy, 27
of light, 25
Transmutation, 38, 43, 115, 118
definition, 162
True State Economy, 60
definition, 162, 199
truths, 83
Tube of Light, 242
Twelve Jurisdictions, 55, 191
definition, 162
twin flame, 127

U

Unana, 71, 78, 79, 95, 119, 134, 206, 272
definition, 162, 231
the activated Christ, 69
underground explosions, 41
Unfed Flame, 129, 172, 255
definition, 162
of Love, Wisdom and Power, 126
United
American Sisterhood, 33
European Brotherhood, 33
States, 33
Civil War, 33
Declaration of Independence, 182
will go through these geophysical changes first, 92
States of Europe, 33
Unity, 38, 61, 92
Consciousness, 231
Unana, 96
Universal Laws
definition, 162
Universal Mind, 24

universe
"responds without judgment", 145
Utopia, 63, 66
New Age of, 202

V

Vaastu
subtle energies, 258
Vastu
gross energies, 258
Shastra, 256, 268
Vastu Vidya
science of dwelling, 259
Vedic
Square, 256
Vedic Square, 257
Vegetable Kingdom, 26, 28, 80
venus, 124
Vibration, 32, 35, 44, 46
initiation in, 50
key to understanding Ascension, 44
of those around you, 94
"those who read these words", 50
Vibrational
frequency
rise in, 28
shifting, 91
Toning, 25, 171
definition, 162
victim
"each day you are choosing your destiny", 103
Violet Flame, 23, 24, 25, 26, 28, 38, 40, 67, 92, 116, 117, 118, 195, 242, 243 *See also Law of Perfection*
attunement to the Galactic Beam, 195
Decrees
purpose of, 143
definition, 162, 173
financial abundance, 107
for nuclear threats, 109
invocation at sunrise, sunset, 149
of Forgiveness, 28
Spiritual Lineage, 149
use for violence, 109
use in planning, 111
Violet Ray
definition, 162
violets, 25
VishvaKarma, 248
visions, 275
voice
"a pleasant voice is the benevolence of the Gods", 129
volcanoes, 37
Vortex, 166
definition, 162
Vortices
influence of equilibrium, 238
older, 19
voting
the power of, 34

W

Wahanee
Golden City of, 25, 70, 73, 81
definition, 163
wars
Middle East, 116
water, 37, 110, 111, 122, 184
purification, 56
Watson, Lyall, 235
wealth, 127
west, 126
Western Door, 74
definition, 163
will, 79
alignment, 78
choice, 102
conscious, 105
definition, 163
greater than the individual, 134
wind element, 103
Wisdom, 44
World War II, 41

Y

yantra, 256
Yin and Yang, 127
youth, 44, 109
ageless body, 145
Yu, 261

Z

Zadkiel
Order of, 173

About Lori Toye

Lori Toye is not a Prophet of doom and gloom. The fact that she became a Prophet at all is highly unlikely. Reared in a small Idaho farming community as a member of the conservative Missouri Synod Lutheran church, Lori had never heard of meditation, spiritual development, reincarnation, channeling or clairvoyant sight.

Her unusual spiritual journey began in Washington State, when, as advertising manager of a weekly newspaper, she answered a request to pick up an ad for a local health food store. Upon entering, a woman at the counter pointed a finger at her and said, "You have work to do for Master Saint Germain!"

The next several years were filled with spiritual enlightenment that introduced Lori, then only twenty-two years old, to the most exceptional and inspirational information she had ever encountered. Lori became a student of Ascended Master teachings.

Awakened one night by the luminous figure of Saint Germain at the foot of her bed, her work had begun. Later in the same year, an image of a map appeared in her dream. Four teachers clad in white robes were present, pointing out earth changes that would shape the future United States.

Five years later, faced with the stress of a painful divorce and rebuilding her life as a single mother, Lori attended spiritual meditation classes. While there she shared her experience, and encouraged by friends she began to explore the dream through daily meditation. The four Beings appeared again, and expressed a willingness to share the information. Over a six-month period, they gave over 80 sessions of material, including detailed information that would later become the I AM America Map.

Clearly she had to produce the map. The only means to finance it was to sell her house. She put her home up for sale, and in a depressed market, it sold the first day at full asking price.

She produced the map in 1989, rolled them on her kitchen table, and sold them through word-of-mouth. She then launched a lecture tour of the Northwest and California. Hers was the first Earth Changes Map published, and many others have followed, but the rest is history.

From the tabloids to the New York Times, The Washington Post, television interviews in the U.S., London, and Europe, Lori's Mission was to honor the material she had received. The material is not hers, she stresses. It belongs to the Masters, and their loving, healing approach is disseminated through the I AM America Publishing Company operated by her husband and spiritual partner, Lenard Toye. Working together they organized free classes of the teachings and their instructional pursuits led them to form the School of the Four Pillars which included holistic and energy healing techniques. In 1995 and 1996 they sponsored the first Prophecy Conferences in Philadelphia and Phoenix, Arizona.

Other publications include three additional Prophecy maps, four books, a video, and more than 60 audio tapes based on sessions with Master Teacher Saint Germain and other Ascended Masters.

Spiritual in nature, I AM America is not a church, religion, sect, or cult. There is no interest or intent in amassing followers or engaging in any activity other than what Lori and Lenard can do on their own to publicize the materials they have been entrusted with.

They have also been directed to build the first Golden City community. A very positive aspect of the vision is that all the maps include areas called, "Golden Cities." These places hold a high spiritual energy, and are where sustainable communities are to be built using solar energy alongside Classical Feng Shui engineering and infrastructure. The first community, Wenima Village, is currently being planned for development.

Concerned that some might misinterpret the Maps' messages as doom and gloom and miss the metaphor for personal change, or not consider the spiritual teachings attached to the maps, Lori emphasizes the Masters stressed that this was a Prophecy of choice. Prophecy allows for choice in making informed decisions and promotes the opportunity for cooperation and harmony. Lenard and Lori's vision for I AM America is to share the Ascended Masters' prophecies as spiritual warnings to heal and renew our lives.

About I AM America

I AM America is an educational and publishing foundation dedicated to disseminating the Ascended Masters' message of Earth Changes Prophecy and Spiritual Teachings for self-development. Our office is run by the husband and wife team of Lenard and Lori Toye who hand-roll maps, package and mail information and products with a small staff. Our first publication was the I AM America Map, which was published in September, 1989. Since then we have published three more Prophecy maps, five books, and numerous audios/CDs based on the channeled sessions with the Spiritual Teachers.

We are not a church, a religion, a sect or cult, and are not interested in amassing followers or members. Nor do we have any affiliation with a church, religion, political group, or government of any kind. We are not a college or university, research facility, or a mystery school. El Morya told us that the best way to see ourselves is as, "Cosmic Beings, having a human experience."

In 1994, we asked Saint Germain, "How do you see our work at I AM America?" and he answered, "I AM America is to be a clearinghouse for the new humanity." Grabbing a dictionary, we quickly learned that the term "clearinghouse" refers to "an organization or unit within an organization that functions as a central agency for collecting, organizing, storing and disseminating documents, usually within a specific academic discipline or field." So inarguably, we are this too. But in uncomplicated terms, we publish and share spiritually transformational information because at I AM America there is no doubt that, "A Change of Heart can Change the World."

With Violet Flame Blessings,
Lori & Lenard Toye

For more information or visit our online bookstore, go to:
www.iamamerica.com

To receive a catalog by mail, please write to:
I AM America
P.O. Box 2511
Payson, AZ 85547

Navigating the New Earth
I AM AMERICA
I AM America Map
US Earth Changes
Order #001
I AM AMERICA
FREEDOM STAR
Freedom Star Map
World Earth Changes
Order #004
Since 1989, I AM America has been publishing thought-provoking information on Earth Changes. All of our Maps feature the compelling cartography of the New Times illustrated with careful details and unique graphics. Professionally presented in full color. Explore the prophetic possibilities!
Retail and Wholesale prices available.
Purchase Maps at:
www.IAMAMERICA.com
I AM AMERICA
6-Map Scenario
US Earth Changes Progression
Order #022
I AM AMERICA
Golden Cities Map
United States
Order #110
I AM AMERICA
P.O. Box 2511
Payson, Arizona
(800) 930-1341

Direction for the New Times
New World Atlas
Earth Changes Prophecies For Europe & Africa
New World Atlas Series
ISBN: 978-1-880050-01-9
978-1-880050-07-1
978-1-880050-05-7
Points of Perception
Prophecies and Teachings of Saint Germain
LORI ADAILE TOYE
Golden City Series: Points of Perception
ISBN: 978-1-880050-18-7
FREEDOM STAR
LORI ADAILE TOYE
Freedom Star Book
ISBN: 978-1-880050-04-0
Divine Destiny
Prophecies and Teachings of Saint Germain
LORI TOYE
I AM America
Coming Soon!
Golden City Series: Divine Destiny
I AM AMERICA
P.O. Box 2511
Payson, Arizona
(800) 930-1341
www.IAMAMERICA.com

CPSIA information can be obtained at www.ICGtesting.com
Printed in the USA
BVOW050525220413

318753BV00002B/14/P

9 781880 050187